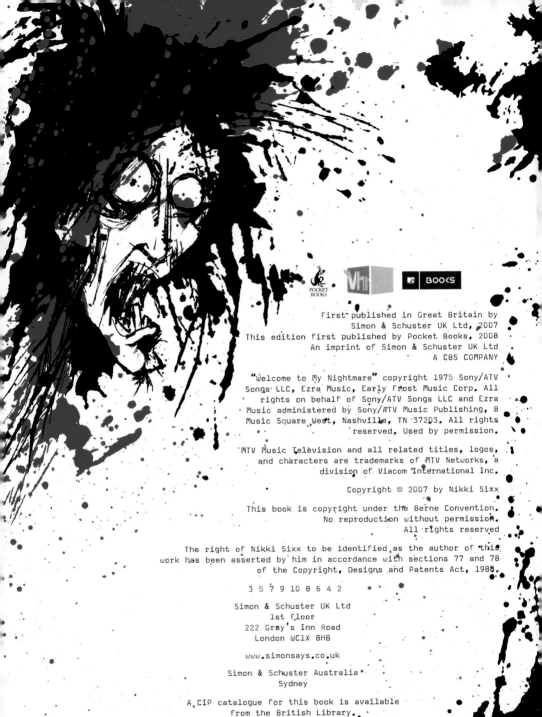

First published in Great Britain by
Simon & Schuster UK Ltd, 2007
This edition first published by Pocket Books, 2008
An imprint of Simon & Schuster UK Ltd
A CBS COMPANY

3 5 7 9 10 8 6 4 2

Simon & Schuster UK Ltd
1st Floor
222 Gray's Inn Road
London WC1X 8HB

www.simonsays.co.uk

Simon & Schuster Australia
Sydney

A CIP catalogue for this book is available
from the British Library.

ISBN: 978-1-84739-206-0

Printed and bound in Italy

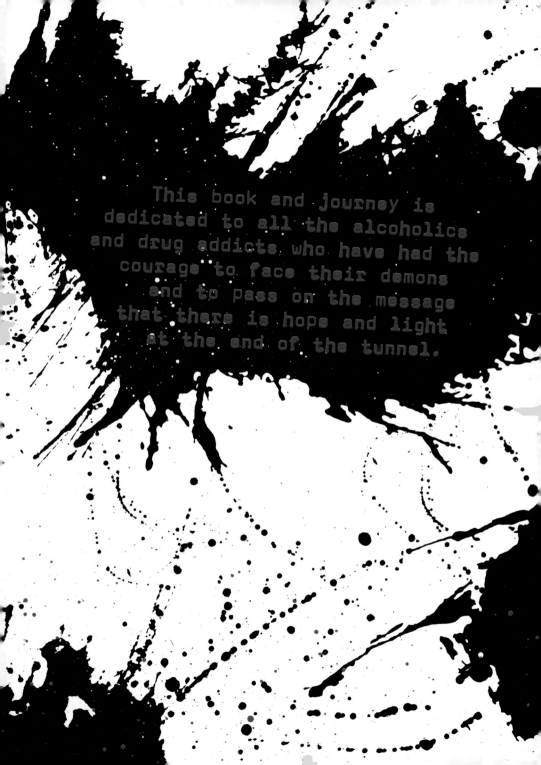

This book and journey is
dedicated to all the alcoholics
and drug addicts who have had the
courage to face their demons
and to pass on the message
that there is hope and light
at the end of the tunnel.

I never thought Nikki Sixx would live beyond the third Mötley Crüe album. People like me, Bowie and Elton John were professional abusers but Nikki went further than us—he used needles, which we never dared to do. I knew Jim Morrison well and Nikki reminded me a lot of him. When Jim died at twenty-seven, we weren't shocked because he had died; we were shocked that he had got that far in the first place.

—Alice Cooper

Acknowledgments

I would like to extend a huge French kiss and a super-sized thank you to the players who had the moxie to tell their side of this dark and sometimes tasteless story. In not knowing whether the outcome would be spectacular or disastrous, you still rose to the challenge without fear. Your insight and truth helped create this book, which I hope paints a fuller picture of addiction.

To Ian, who hounded, pushed and coaxed me to stay on the path of truth and discovery, and who did thankless hours of research and interviews to fill in the gaps in my scribblings. Thank you, Ian. Your talent and passion speak volumes in this book.

And to those of you who didn't have the balls or courage to return calls or emails, or out and out just lied and said "OK" but then went underground thinking being in this book might "tarnish your image." It's clearer to me now more than ever why you are who you are in life–and that is simply spineless.

N.S.

JUST
UCKING
KILL
ME

A Short Medical Dictionary

Definitions from wikipedia.org

addiction (ə-dĭk'shən) *n.*

A compulsion to repeat a behavior regardless of its consequences. A person who is addicted is sometimes called an addict.

The term addiction describes a chronic pattern of behavior that continues despite the direct or indirect adverse consequences that result from engaging in the behavior. It is quite common for an addict to express the desire to stop the behavior, but find himself unable to cease. Addiction is often characterized by a craving for more of the drug or behavior, increased physiological tolerance to exposure and withdrawal symptoms in the absence of the stimulus. Many drugs and behaviors that provide either pleasure or relief from pain pose a risk of addiction or dependency.

alcoholism (ăl'kə-hô-lĭz'əm, -hŏ-) *n.*

A term that describes the excessive, and often chronic, consumption of alcohol. Among the characteristics of alcoholism are compulsion and addiction. It can also be characterized as an illness or allergy, and many believe it to be a biological disease.

cocaine (kō-kān', kō'kān') *n.*

Cocaine is a crystalline tropane alkaloid that is obtained from the leaves of the coca plant. It is a stimulant of the central nervous system and an appetite suppressant, creating what has been described as a euphoric sense of happiness and increased energy. Cocaine is highly addictive, and its possession, cultivation and distribution is illegal for non-medicinal/non-government-sanctioned purposes in virtually all parts of the world.

depression (dĭ-prĕsh'ən) *n.*

Clinical depression is a state of sadness or melancholia that has advanced to the point of being disruptive to an individual's social functioning and/or activities of daily living. Although a mood characterized by sadness is often colloquially referred to as depression, clinical depression is something more than just a temporary state of sadness. Symptoms lasting two weeks or longer, and of a severity that begins to interfere with typical social functioning and/or activities of daily living, are considered to constitute clinical depression.

Clinical depression affects about 16 percent of the population on at least one occasion in their lives. The mean age of onset, from a number of studies, is in the late twenties. Clinical depression is currently the leading cause of disability in the United States as well as in other countries, and is expected to become the second leading cause of disability worldwide (after heart disease) by the year 2020.

heroin (hĕr'ō-ĭn) *n.*

A semi-synthetic opioid. It is the 3.6-diacetyl derivative of morphine (hence *diacetylmorphine*) and is synthesized from it by acetylation. The white crystalline form is commonly the hydrochloride salt, diacetylmorphine hydrochloride. It is highly addictive when compared to other substances. A few of the popular street names for heroin include dope, diesel, smack, scag and H.

psychosis (sī-kō'sĭs) *n.*

A generic psychiatric term for a mental state in which thought and perception are severely impaired. Persons experiencing a psychotic episode may experience hallucinations, hold delusional beliefs (e.g., paranoid delusions), demonstrate personality changes and exhibit disorganized thinking. This is often accompanied by lack of insight into the unusual or bizarre nature of such behavior, difficulties with social interaction and impairments in carrying out the activities of daily living. A psychotic episode is often described as involving a "loss of contact with reality."

A SHORT ALTERNATIVE MEDICAL DICTIONARY

DEFINITIONS COURTESY OF DR. LEMUEL PILLMEISTER

(also known as Lemmy)

ADDICTION

when you can give up something any time, as long as it's next Tuesday.

ALCOHOLISM

A habit that helps you to see the iguanas in your eyeballs.

COCAINE

Peruvian Marching Powder—a stimulant that has the extraordinary effect that the more you do, the more you laugh out of context.

DEPRESSION

When everything you laugh at is miserable and you can't seem to stop.

HEROIN
A drug that helps you to escape reality, while making it much harder to cope when you are recaptured.

PSYCHOSIS

When everybody turns into tiny dolls and they have needles in their mouths and they hate you and you don't care because you have THE KNIFE! AHAHAHAHAHAHA!!!

NIKKI SIXX

"The dying could be easy…it was the living that I didn't know if I could do…"

Founder, chief songwriter and bassist for Mötley Crüe, assiduous diary keeper and the antihero of this tale. A man who was so hooked on heroin and cocaine that he had to die twice before he began to contemplate a more positive lifestyle.

TOMMY LEE

"We all went to that dark fucking place at various times—but Nikki seemed to like it there more than any of us."

A.K.A. T-Bone. Mötley Crüe's drummer and Nikki's Toxic Twin, a fellow narcotics adventurer who shared all of Nikki's '80s addictions—except heroin.

VINCE NEIL

"Nikki was spending a lot of time shooting up in the bathroom during the *Girls* sessions, and that suited me fine—it was the perfect time for me to record my vocals."

The singer of Nikki's lyrics in Mötley Crüe, and a man who spent most of the '80s hating the guts of his band's songwriter and bassist. The feeling was mutual.

MICK MARS

"When I heard Nikki was dead, my first reaction was, 'I knew that fucking prick was going to do something like that!'"

Unassuming and reclusive Mötley Crüe guitarist who was forced to accept that his role in life was to be bullied, persecuted and abused by his vindictive band mates.

DEANA RICHARDS

"You never imagine your own family will plot against you to steal your son."

Nikki's mother who endured an agonizingly long estrangement from her son after his troubled and turbulent childhood.

CECI COMER

"Nikki was rude, full of himself, he just crushed me so many times… he was an asshole."

Once adoring little sister of Nikki who accepts that their particular in-family dynamic was "maybe not your average sibling relationship."

TOM REESE

"I went to stay with Nikki once or twice, and the way of life he had was not to my liking."

Nikki's maternal grandfather who, together with his late wife, Nona, looked after Nikki in Idaho for long periods of his youth.

DOC McGHEE

"As a parting joke I'd said to Nikki, 'Don't send us any girls in Nazi helmets and Gestapo boots,' and he must have thought I meant it because they turned up in helmets but not the boots."

Former Mötley Crüe co-manager who described the physical violence he sometimes meted out to his troublesome charges as "Full Contact Management."

DOUG THALER

"Nikki showed me some gummy black substance he had that he claimed was some kind of exotic cocaine that he was going to snort. I thought, Good luck snorting a gummy substance!"

Partner to Doc McGhee, and a man resigned to receiving early-hour phone calls from Nikki informing him that there were "Mexicans and midgets" in the bassist's garden.

EVANGELIST DENISE MATTHEWS

"I don't answer to Vanity. I would much rather be a fish stuck in a pond with a starving shark than take on such a foul name of nothingness."

The Artist Formerly Known As Vanity. Former Prince pop protégée and girlfriend who turned her affections to her on-again, off-again fiancé Nikki and to freebase cocaine before finding God and becoming a born-again preacher.

TOM ZUTAUT

"Nikki told her he wasn't scared by a little bit of blood and proceeded to have intercourse with her right there."

Elektra Records A&R man who signed Mötley Crüe to the label and suffered the indignity of watching Nikki have sex with his girlfriend three minutes after he formally introduced them.

FRED SAUNDERS

"I hit Mötley a lot. I once broke Tommy's nose in Indiana, I broke Nikki's ribs and I beat the shit out of Vince many times, because...well, because he's an asshole."

Former Hells Angel, supplier of Ace in the Hole and the head of security on numerous Mötley Crüe world tours.

BOB TIMMONS

"Cocaine gave Nikki acute paranoia and hallucinations. One night he called me and asked me to get the police over to his house right away because there were little men with helmets and guns in the trees surrounding his house."

Former junkie turned drugs counsellor to the stars who fought countless valiant but losing battles to have Nikki admitted to rehab.

SLASH

"I hung out with Nikki and I found a sickening allure in his lifestyle. My junkie years were dirty and sordid, but Nikki seemed to me to have found a cool, glamorous way to be a junkie."

Guns N' Roses guitarist and the "little brother that Nikki never had" during G N' R's infamous 1987 tour of the Deep South with Mötley Crüe.

SALLY McLAUGHLAN

"Slash was paralytic and Nikki was turning blue."

Former girlfriend of Slash who moved from Scotland to Los Angeles in 1987 and spent her first day in the city saving Nikki's life.

KAREN DUMONT

"When I moved to Los Angeles I was told not to even *talk* to Mötley Crüe because they were trouble."

Record company employee who took her work responsibilities so seriously that she moved into Nikki's house to try to keep him alive.

BOB MICHAELS

"Once or twice I left my pipe out on the counter and, when I wasn't looking, Nikki sprinkled heroin in it."

Friend, neighbor and occasional companion in Nikki's rock 'n' roll misadventures.

ROSS HALFIN

"I always said that Tommy should have married Nikki because if they were gay they would be the ideal gay couple—made in Heaven."

British photographer who has photographed Mötley Crüe for nearly twenty years and still thinks Nikki is a "likable, selfish, paranoid control freak."

JASON BRYCE

"Nikki phoned down to reception and said, 'Look, I'm Nikki Sixx, I need a bottle of JD now and I will give you a thousand bucks for it.' They just told him, 'Sir, go to bed. You've had enough.'"

Callow British teenager who went on the road with Mötley Crüe as a boy and returned as a man.

BRYN BRIDENTHAL

"One of the early things Nikki used to do was set himself on fire during interviews."

Mötley Crüe publicist who knew nothing about heroin in the '80s but today, having worked with Nirvana and Courtney Love, is much better informed.

TIM LUZZI

"On my first day, Nikki came into the studio with a black eye, having spent the night in a police cell. That pretty much set the tone for what was to follow."

Nikki's bass tech for ten years, an occupation that occasionally involved enforced Jack Daniel's drinking while garbed in the robes of a priest.

JOEY SCOLERI

"Tommy pulled his cock out and started banging it against the desk."

Canadian record company executive who, as a young DJ named Joey Vendetta, hosted one of the most outrageous radio interviews in rock 'n' roll history.

WAYNE ISHAM

"Nikki always had the Devil's wiseass smile in his eyes. I guess that's why he always wore sunglasses."

Director of scores of award-winning music videos by the likes of Mötley Crüe, Ozzy Osbourne, Metallica, Britney Spears and Nikki's personal favorite, Bon fucking Jovi.

ALLEN KOVAC

"Nikki Sixx may never win a Grammy because the industry does not always judge on talent, but he deserves many."

Head of Los Angeles–based Tenth Street Management and current manager of Mötley Crüe who helped to negotiate their escape from Elektra Records.

SYLVIA RHONE

"Do I want to take part in this book? I really don't feel that would be appropriate."

Former CEO of Elektra Records who figured Mötley Crüe was spent in the late '90s and sold them the master tapes to their albums.

RICK NIELSEN

"Nikki Sixx was a big teddy bear with a nice smile. He could barely play the bass, mind you, but that never stopped Gene Simmons."

Cheap Trick guitarist and Nikki's boyhood hero, friend and occasional touring and drinking companion.

BOB ROCK

"Nikki and Tommy decided to dress as Canadian lumberjacks.…They put on lumberjack shirts and false mustaches…"

A-list rock producer of Mötley's *Dr. Feelgood* and *Mötley Crüe* albums, plus records by Aerosmith, Metallica, Bryan Adams and Bon Jovi.

JAMES MICHAEL

"Nikki is a very creative and talented guy, and he thinks in a very dark and twisted way."

Nikki's erstwhile songwriting partner, with whom he has co-written hits for Meat Loaf and Saliva.

INTRODUCTION

When I was fifteen years old, I remember Iggy and the Stooges' song "Search and Destroy" reaching out from my speakers to me like my own personal anthem. It was a theme I would carry for decades as my own hell-bent mantra. The song might as well have been tattooed across my knuckles 'cause there could be no truer words for a young, alienated teenager:

I'm a street walking cheetah
with a heart full of napalm
I'm a runaway son of the nuclear A-bomb
I'm a world's forgotten boy
The one who searches and destroys

Alice Cooper was another musical hero. Like Nostradamus, Alice must have seen the future when he sang "Welcome to My Nightmare"...or, at least, my future:

Welcome to my nightmare
Welcome to my breakdown
I hope I didn't scare you.

Yet Alice's nightmare was show business. This book is something else entirely. This is me welcoming you to a genuine living nightmare that I endured nearly twenty years ago; a nightmare that was so bad that it ended up killing me. But now I know it wasn't only the drugs—it was also my past unknowingly haunting me, and even a lethal combination of narcotics couldn't seem to kill the pain.

I guess if we could mix these two songs together you'd have the theme song of my adolescence. On Christmas Day 1986, I was a member of one of the biggest rock 'n' roll bands in the world. I was also an alcoholic, a coke addict and a heroin addict heading into a pill-popping downward spiral of depression.

Welcome to my nightmare

Musically, I always thought Mötley Crüe was a nasty combination of rock, punk, glam and pop sprinkled together with lots of sarcasm, anger and humor, love and hate, happiness and sadness. Of course, depending on the recipe, there were always larger or smaller amounts of sex in there too. I mean, what is rock 'n' roll if it's not sexy? Sleazy? Usually. Chauvinist? Always. We'd crammed all this into a blender and out came a very toxic cocktail.

Palatable for the masses like Jim Jones' Kool-Aid
Sweet to the lips and deadly to ourselves
We were the drug scouts of America
And we were louder than hell.

These diaries start on Christmas Day 1986, but that day wasn't even that special. I was an addict well before then, and stayed one for a while afterwards. Perhaps that day just brought my condition home to me. There is something about spending Christmas alone, naked, sitting by the Christmas tree gripping a shotgun, that lets you know your life is spinning dangerously outta control.

I'm a street walking cheetah with a heart full of napalm

People over the years have tried to soften the blow by saying maybe being in Mötley Crüe turned me into an addict...but I don't think it did. That stroke of genius was all my own work. Even as a kid I was never inclined to dodge a bullet. I was always the first one to take it right between the eyes. I was stubborn, strong-willed and always willing to put myself in harm's way for the betterment of chaos, confusion and rebellion—all the traits that made me famous and later infamous. The ingredients for success and failure all wrapped up in a nice package with the emotional stability of a Molotov cocktail. Then when I moved to LA in the late '70s and discovered cocaine, it only amplified these charming characteristics.

I'm a runaway son of the nuclear A-bomb

But alcohol, acid, cocaine...they were just affairs. When I met heroin, it was true love.

After we made it big, Mötley Crüe gave me more money than I knew what to do with. So naturally I spent it on the only thing I wanted to do: drugs. Before the band, I lived only for music: after it started, I lived only for drugs. OK, so maybe Mötley gave me the resources to be an addict, but...you know what? If it hadn't, I'd have found some other way to do it.

I guess we all get to live out our destiny, even those of us who have to choose the worst one imaginable. So why did I take this strange, dark trip? Well, I have a little 1-2-3 theory on this.

1. My childhood was shitty. My dad left when I was three years old and never came back.

2. My mom tried to love me, but every time a new guy came on the scene, I'd be in the way and she'd shuttle me off to live with my grandparents.

3. I was born an addict. It's no surprise that I grew up feeling angry, unloved and somehow needing...revenge.

Revenge on whom? On the world? On myself?

Welcome to my breakdown...

I was always driven, even when I didn't know where I was going. Way before I met Tommy Lee, Vince Neil and Mick Mars, I knew I would be in Mötley Crüe. I knew how we would look, what we would sound like, how we would behave (fucking badly, obviously!).

Mötley Crüe was always about music and girls... music and drugs...and music and violence. We wanted to be the biggest, dirtiest, loudest rock band on the planet. We knew we were on our way in '83 when we helicoptered in to play in front of 300,000 metal fans at a festival in LA; our only gripe was that we should have been headlining. It was only a matter of time. We were on the highway to hell and had every bad intention of destroying anything and everything in our path. You could find us by the trail of sex, drugs and rock 'n' roll we left behind us...

But two major things happened to me in '83. *Shout at the Devil* went platinum and moved Mötley even further up the ladder. And I crashed my Porsche drunk, dislocated my shoulder and started smoking heroin to numb the pain. The problem was, I carried on smoking —and then started injecting—long after the pain was gone.

Fuck, there were clues I was becoming a junkie. You'd need to be pretty self-obsessed to miss them, but if I was one thing back then, it was self-obsessed. When Vince Neil went to jail for twenty days, I didn't visit or phone our singer once. It never even occurred to me: it would've been a waste of valuable drug time.

By the end of the *Theatre of Pain* tour in '86, I was on my way to becoming a full-blown junkie. I had OD'd after a show in London and been left for dead in a garbage Dumpster. I had turned up strung out to be Tommy's best man at his wedding, with syringes hidden in my cowboy boots. And I had stayed home freebasing rather than attend my own grandmother's funeral—the woman who had loved and raised me.

And things were about to get worse. Much worse.

The strangest thing is that during the darkest, most lost time of my life...I kept diaries. At home as I was cracking up, or on tour, I scribbled down my thoughts in battered journals or on scraps of paper. Sometimes I wrote in them completely sober and sane. At other times, they were like the diary of a madman. I think that in my drug-addled comatose mind I felt my diary was the only person who really understood me. Maybe my only friend, someone to confide in...they don't say it's lonely at the top for nothing.

I had forgotten these diaries existed, or maybe I was in denial about them, until I pulled them out of a storage locker last year, buried under my musty tour programs, magazine covers and multi-platinum awards. They were genuinely shocking for me to read, a window back into a dark time in my life that I left behind a long while ago...hopefully never to return.

As I write this, Mötley Crüe is back and playing all around the world again. I fucking love it, and in some ways life in the Crüe is as insane as ever. The amps are still too loud and so is our attitude. I still love playing rock 'n' roll. In fact, I can safely say it gets me high. I feel privileged to still be around to do what I love so much, and the fact that we still do it on our own terms is extremely fucking gratifying. The difference is that I no longer come off stage from that adrenaline rush and launch a kamikaze narcotics campaign to get even higher.

Now the music and the fans are enough. Just like it should be.

I'm the same person, but I'm also a different one. You see there's Sikki and then there's Nikki, many years sober, in control rather than outta control and crazed. Occasionally it even occurs to me that I may be the kind of person that the Sikki of '86 would have hated. That's OK 'cause I don't think I'd like to know Sikki in 2006, so we're even.

I was listening to the Velvet Underground again today, and "Heroin" sounds as good as ever, especially when Lou Reed sings about heroin being his death, his life, and his wife.

Who would have thought, when I was growing up in Idaho, that one of the most inspirational songs of my life would also end up being my theme song?

I could burn these insane diaries, or put them back where I found them, and nobody would ever be the wiser. So why have I decided to publish them and show the world just what a fucked-up, strung-out madman I was at the height of my success?

Well, it's simple. If one person reads this book and doesn't have to go down the same road as me, it was worth sharing my personal hell with them. I'm also donating profits from this book to help runaway kids at a charity I set up called Running Wild in the Night through Covenant House (www.covenanthouse.org and www.nikkisixx.net).

They say to keep what you have, you have to give it away. I believe that. I also believe that you can be cool as fuck, not give a fuck and fucking kick ass in life, and not be fucked up. I'm still the first person to say "Fuck you" but I'm faster to say "I love you." If life is what you make it, I've made mine great. It took a lot of hard work and if you need to, you can do it too.

Last but not least, the lines I wrote in "Home Sweet Home" in 1985 are as true today as they were back then:

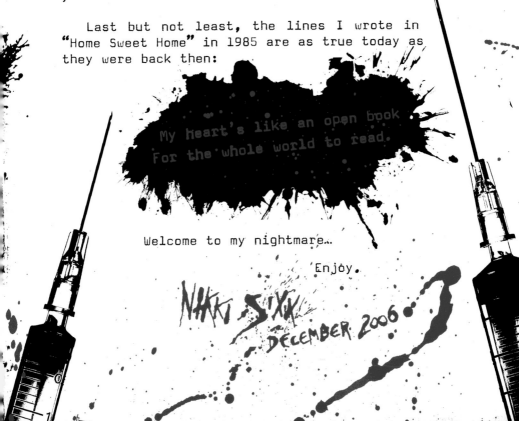

My heart's like an open book
For the whole world to read.

Welcome to my nightmare...

Enjoy.

NIKKI SIXX

DECEMBER 2006

1

INTRODUCTION II

   I first met Nikki Sixx on Valentine's
Day 1986. Mötley Crüe flew into London on
the *Theatre of Pain* tour, I was writing
for now-defunct British music magazine
Melody Maker and we exchanged a few
sweet nothings in an interview. Nikki
wasn't making too much sense: I went
away thinking, That guy is wasted. By
the end of the night, he had OD'd and
been dumped in a rubbish bin. And that was
when he really started going downhill...

   Nearly twenty years later, Nikki
asked me to work with him on *The
Heroin Diaries* and I got greater
insight into the abject mess that
he called his life back then. When
Nikki first showed me his remaining
journal scribblings and scraps of
paper from back then, I was horrified—
and could not believe he is still
alive. Some pages of Nikki's diary
were intact, many were not, but
by scouring his memory and re-
searching old notes and docu-
ments, we were able to fill
in the black holes—and piece
together the story of a man who,
at the beating heart of an over-
the-top rock band, was pro-
foundly falling apart at the
seams.

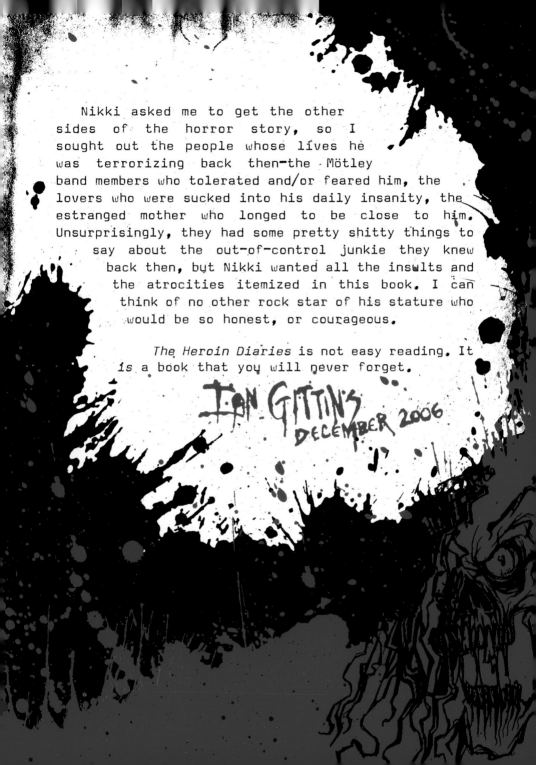

Nikki asked me to get the other
sides of the horror story, so I
sought out the people whose lives he
was terrorizing back then—the Mötley
band members who tolerated and/or feared him, the
lovers who were sucked into his daily insanity, the
estranged mother who longed to be close to him.
Unsurprisingly, they had some pretty shitty things to
say about the out-of-control junkie they knew
back then, but Nikki wanted all the insults and
the atrocities itemized in this book. I can
think of no other rock star of his stature who
would be so honest, or courageous.

The *Heroin Diaries* is not easy reading. It
is a book that you will never forget.

IAN GITTINS
DECEMBER 2006

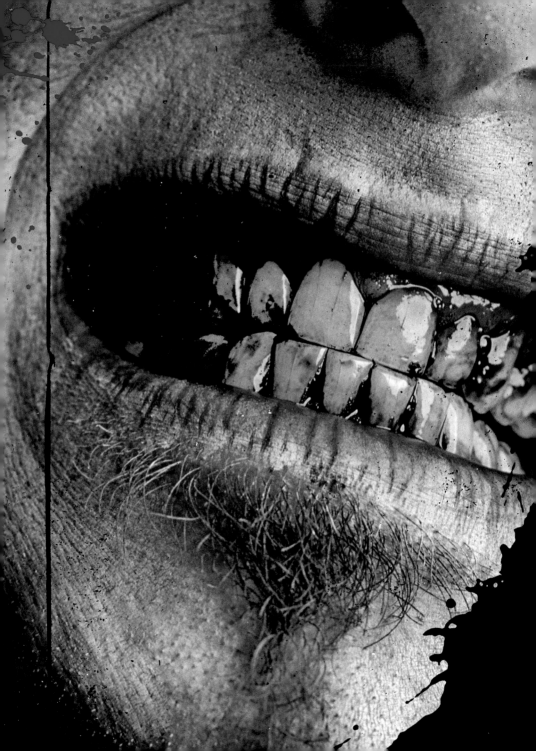

DECEMBER 1986

MERRY CHRISTMAS. WELL, THAT'S WHAT PEOPLE SAY AT CHRISTMAS, RIGHT?

DECEMBER 25TH 1986

Van Nuys, 7:30 p.m.

Merry Christmas.

Well, that's what people say at Christmas, right? Except normally they have somebody to say it to. They have their friends and family all around them. They haven't been crouched naked under a Christmas tree with a needle in their arm like an insane person in a mansion in Van Nuys.

They're not out of their minds and writing in a diary and they're not watching their holiday spirit coagulating in a spoon. I didn't speak to a single person today...I thought of calling Bob Timmons, but why should I ruin his Christmas?

I guess I've decided to start another diary this time for a few different reasons...

1. I have no friends left.
2. So I can read back and remember what I did the day before.
3. So if I die, at least I leave a paper trail of my life (nice lil suicide note).

Merry Christmas...it's just you and me, diary. Welcome to my life.

BOB TIMMONS: By Christmas 1986, Nikki had been addicted to heroin and cocaine for at least a year, possibly longer. As a drug counselor, I first met Nikki when Mötley Crüe's manager, Doc McGhee, called me in to work with the band's singer, Vince Neil. Nikki was initially very hostile to me; he tried to get me barred from going backstage or being around them.

Nikki and I slowly formed a relationship, and early in 1986 he asked me for help with his own addictions. I advised him to go into a rehab center but he refused and said he didn't need to. He was very stubborn on that issue.

Over the years I have worked with platinum-selling artists from the Rolling Stones to the Red Hot Chili Peppers and all points in between, and let me make one thing clear from the start–Mötley Crüe, more than anybody, wrote the book for decadence and partying. In that area they were the most extreme people I ever met, and Nikki was the most extreme of all. For many years, Nikki had one motto: I'm going to do exactly what I want to do, and fuck everybody else.

DECEMBER 26TH, 1986
Van Nuys, 2:10 a.m.

Jason came over again today. I was touched...so there is a Santa Claus, after all. He came mooching in, with his greasy James Dean hair and his junkie eyes that are sunk so deep in his elongated face that he looks like he's wearing makeup, and he stood by the tree and asked me how my Christmas had been. Like he cares...like he doesn't know already that it was exactly the same as his. Sometimes Jason pisses me off when he tries to make small talk. He asked me how much gear I wanted, and I asked, how much have you got? And he gave me this contemptuous, sneering look and said, that must be nice...

His Betty Page-wannabe Goth girlfriend Anastasia isn't much better. Oh, she's nice enuff, but I know on the inside I'm just her meal ticket to an easier, softer life. I know she tells Jason to jump when I call because she, more than he, wants the money. Not just for the junk, they make enuff off me to maintain their

cheap little habits, but she likes to decorate their
little one-room rat's nest with the extra money they
have left over. That's the real reason she demands he
comes at my beck and call...she likes that extra cash
for thrift shops and secondhand stores.

I see her as a sorta Suzie Homemaker from Hell, but
it's all just a fantasy-she's stuck with a habit too...

NIKKI: My dealer Jason and I had a real love-hate
relationship. I loved him because I could pick up the
phone and he'd be over in twenty minutes with everything
I needed. I hated him because it was killing me. He loved
me because I gave him hundreds (sometimes thousands)
of dollars on a daily basis. He hated me because I was a
spoiled millionaire rock star who could have anything I
wanted whenever I wanted it, and usually did.

I used to ride a Honda Shadow motorcycle around the
Valleys with my shirt off, totally out of my mind. One
time Jason started talking about Harleys and how much
he loved them. Tommy had one, so the next day I just
went out and bought one and rode it to Jason's house to
score. He was furious: it was his dream bike, he'd shown
me a picture of it and I'd bought it. He thought I was such
a spoiled brat.

Jason was as fucked on heroin as me. He was a tall, skinny guy who in another life could have been a model, or something, but he really just came off looking like a corpse. That
was the real reason he hated me: we were both living for
drugs, but I could afford as many as I wanted.

DECEMBER 27TH 1986
Van Nuys, 4:15 a.m.

The best part of freebase is before the first hit.
I love that moment, right before I put the glass pipe

to my lips...that moment when everything is sane, and the craving, the salivating, the excitement all feel fresh and innocent. It's like foreplay...the ache that's always better than the orgasm.

Yet as soon as I hit the pipe, within 30 seconds all hell breaks lose in my brain...and I keep on doing it and doing it and doing it and doing it, and I can't stop. Every day that I sit here and write, it's always the same. So-why? Why do I do this? I hate it...I hate it so much, but I love it even more.

The worst part of freebase is running out. But I have a new jones-speedballs of any kind. The junk just isn't enough anymore...I feel like I'm only halfway there...

> TOMMY LEE: Back around *Girls Girls Girls,* we were starting to make shitloads of money. With money came success, power, overindulgence and experimentation. Sixx and I, in particular, took a lot of narcotics, and he would always want to push things: "Hey, how about taking *these* two drugs together? How about heroin and cocaine at the same time?" That period led us to this really dark fucking place. We all went to that place at various times–but Nikki seemed to like it there more than any of us.

DECEMBER 28TH, 1986
Van Nuys, 9:40 p.m.

After I binged last night-or was it tonight-I was convinced yet again that there were people coming to get me. It was more than just shadows and voices, more than just fantasies...it was real, and I was scared to my core.

My bones were shaking...my heart was pounding...I thought I was going to explode. I'm glad I have you to talk to, to write this down...I tried to keep it all together, but then I gave in to the madness and became one with my insanity...

I always end up in the closet in my bedroom. Let me tell you about that place, my closet. It's more than a closet-it's a haven for me. It's where I keep my dope and where I keep my gun. I know when I'm in there I'm safe, at least until I get too high. I can't be out in the house—there are too many windows and I know I'm being watched. Right now it seems impossible that cops are peering in from the trees outside or people are looking at me thru the peephole at the front door. But when the drugs kick in I can't control my mind...

Today, last night feels like a lifetime ago. But the sick thing is I could do it again tonight.

NIKKI: This was the crazy routine I had at the time. I would start out freebasing or mainlining anywhere in the house: the front room, the kitchen, the bathroom. But as soon as the coke-induced psychosis kicked in, as soon as the insanity began, I would make a beeline for my bedroom closet. That was my refuge. I would huddle in there, surrounded by my drug paraphernalia and guns, convinced that people were in the house trying to get me, or a SWAT team was outside preparing to bust me. I would be too scared to move until I came down. The only way to bring myself down quicker was heroin. Heroin would make the madness go away: it was the easy solution. It seemed to make sense at the time.

DECEMBER 29TH 1906
Van Nuys, 4:30 p.m.

I've been thinking about last Christmas Eve when I picked up that girl in a strip club, brought her back here on my bike, took her home the next day, then had Christmas dinner all by myself in McDonald's. I haven't made much progress I see.

Today I'm listening to Exile on Main Street, reading, laying around...tanning in the backyard, naked...today I feel like my old self. Sometimes I feel like I have two personalities. One is Nikki and one is...Sikki.

ROSS HALFIN: As a photographer I've shot Mötley Crüe many times over the years for magazines and got particularly close to Nikki. I remember the first time I ever met him in LA we got on pretty well and decided to go for a drink that night. We sat talking in a booth. Vince Neil was in another booth with a girl, arguing, and Vince suddenly stood up and punched her in the face. I asked Nikki, "Should we sort it out?" And Nikki just laughed and said, "Let them sort it out themselves."

JANUARY 1st ~~1986~~ 1987
Van Nuys, 6 a.m.

Vanity showed up
yesterday with a moun-
tain of coke...it kind
of altered the day.
I'd been doing good
until that point.
I'd got a good
night's sleep for
the first time in
days. I even managed
to take a shower and
pick up my guitar.

But since this
is a new diary, let
me tell you about
Vanity...she used to
be a backup singer
with Prince, or
so she says. We
meet for all the
wrong reasons
and have only
one real thing
in common—drugs.
I mean, she's a
sweet girl, as
much as I'm a
sweet guy. She
has flowing
brown hair and
chocolate brown
eyes and has an
ability to look
very pretty, but
usually, like me,

looks like hell. As they say, misfits attract misfits...
truer words could not be said.

Mötley is back in the studio next week and I told
the guys I had some new songs. The truth is I haven't
written much of anything. I just can't seem to focus on
anything these days except...the usual.

So we did a few lines while Vanity cooked up the
base. She was talking, talking, talking about us going
out tonight for New Year's Eve, but both of us knew that
we were going nowhere. The more she talked, the more
all I could hear was my head talking...the craving, a
wet palate, for a hit on that glass pipe...it was
beautiful and it was ugly all at the same time.

Then everything went wrong, just
like it always does. The base fucked
up Vanity's head and she started
speaking in riddles, ranting on about
Jesus and spirituality like she was
still with fucking Prince, or something...She was making no sense and I
couldn't take it, so I started
yelling at her to go fuck herself and
fuck Jesus and get the fuck out of my
house. Then she was gone and I was back in my closet
with my grandfather's gun pointed at the door, needles
and dirty spoons on the floor...terrified because people had slid under my front door like vapor and were in
the house and were coming to get me.

I fucking hate that shit. I'm OK now but nobody would
believe what happens inside my head...it's haunted. Now
that I've come down it seems like a sick play I saw in
a theater. Thirty minutes ago I could have killed
somebody, or better myself. Now I'm OK...I need a padded
cell, I'm telling you.

Oh ya...Happy New Year...

11:30 a.m.

Here comes the New Year…same as the old year?

Pete said I really must open those Christmas presents soon…

NIKKI: Vanity came and went during different periods of my addiction. She was a wild black chick who had sung with Prince: she'd also been his lover for a while. At the time I thought of Vanity as a disposable human being, like a used needle. Once its purpose was fulfilled it was ready for the trash, only to be dug up if you were really desperate.

Maybe the manner in which I'd met Vanity should have told me this was to be no normal relationship. Back in '86 I used to hang out with a guy named Pete: in fact, he was semi-living in my house. Pete was a six-foot-six cross between Keith Richards and Herman Munster and looked like the coolest rock star around, except that he couldn't play shit. We used to sit in my house watching TV and snorting coke and pointing out girls that we'd like to fuck. Then I'd phone the Mötley office and they'd get us the girls' numbers so we could call them. It was a sick lil game we played…never really realizing we were playing with people's lives.

We saw Vanity on MTV, and when Pete said, "Dude, that's Prince's old girl," I said, "Excellent–he's got a tiny dick." The office rang Vanity and arranged for us to meet. She opened the door naked, with her eyes going around in her head. Somehow I had a feeling that we might just hit it off.

We became drug buddies: sometimes, you could even just about call us boyfriend and girlfriend. Vanity also taught me how to really freebase: the first time I based was with Tommy when Mötley just started and only a few times after that. So up until then, I'd been mostly snorting or injecting. But as soon as she showed me the real ins and outs of cooking up a good rock...it was love.

Not her. The drug.

EVANGELIST DENISE MATTHEWS: *Webster's Dictionary* assassinates the word Vanity, describing its meaning as worthless. What a bold mistake that was. God forgave me for that ugly name. You might say I was a collector: I collected a long list of vile addictions throughout my journey of paranoia, boldly going where most have not gone before, hiding behind the face that launched a thousand nothings.

Most don't call me Vanity any longer. My friends call me Denise; the Saints call me Evangelist. It doesn't really matter; I don't answer to Vanity. I would much rather be a fish stuck in a pond with a starving shark than take on such a foul name of nothingness. I am this new creature in Christ and I persevere to keep changing for the better.

JANUARY 3rd 1987
Van Nuys, 5:20 p.m.

Dear diary, here is a typical holiday day in my rock star paradise.

Wake up around noon...if I've been to bed. See if I'm alone. If I'm with somebody else, try to remember what her name is-but that hasn't been happening too much lately. Girls have kinda stopped coming around...

Crawl out of bed, feel hungover or dope sick. Wipe last night out of my eyes. Wonder if I need to shower. Decide that I don't...I'll only get dirty again.

On a good day, pick up my guitar. On a bad day, flop in front of MTV. Most days, do both. Do a little bump to wake me up. Some people use coffee for that...we all have our little rituals. Then it starts...

The itch starts. The coke makes me edgy, so I have a little sniff of my breakfast blend and a valium or two to calm me down. But I need Jason. If his answering machine is on, I sit here twitching until he phones back. When the phone rings—if it's Jason—it's the best thing in the world. If it's not, I want the person at the other end to die. Sometimes I wonder if they know that I am strung out, and they are calling just to torment me.

And when Jason doesn't call at all? That's when the fucking joneses start. Being dope sick is the worst feeling in the world. I hope it never happens to you. Unless you have it coming...I could name a few. When you're junk sick, you'll do just about anything for a fix. It's all you think about...it haunts you.

Eventually I go to my cottons, squeeze some lemon juice on them, and try and wring out a few cc's. I've done it all. Once I even shot up some weird stuff I found stuck in the bushes outside a drug dealer's house—then I found out it wasn't some lucky find on my part, it was fucking crystallized brown sugar. Man, I thought I'd hit the mother lode when I found that baggy.

But when Jason finally shows up, he makes everything better. It's like he's got the power to heal...and that prick shows his power every chance he gets.

VINCE NEIL: You know the problem with Nikki Sixx? He can't do anything just a little bit. He can't do a little bit of coke—he's got to do all the coke. He can't take a little bit of heroin—he's got to take all the heroin. He can't just have one sip of wine—he's got to drink the bar out. There's no middle speed for that dude—it's zero or ten.

JANUARY 4th 1987
Van Nuys, midnight

Bob Michaels came over tonight. We drank a few beers, had a couple lines...Bob is a good guy. He gets fucked up with me but he's not like me...he's normal.

BOB MICHAELS: Nikki Sixx and I had been friends ever since the day in 1983 that he moved in next door to me. I remember seeing this real tall guy in six-inch heels with lots of black hair and makeup, and thinking, Who the fuck is *that*? But we became friends real quick. That building was Party Central: I think everyone who lived there was involved in either supplying or consuming narcotics. Robbin Crosby from Ratt lived downstairs from Nikki, and Tommy was around all the time.

I stayed friends with Nikki when he moved into his next house, on Valley Vista Boulevard in Van Nuys, but by then he was struggling with all kinds of addiction–heroin, alcoholism. Nikki would put anything into his arm that he could–heroin, coke, and loads of other things that should never be put into an arm. Personally, I pinpoint his problems from Vince Neil going to jail in 1985. That made Nikki think for the first time: What would happen if the band stopped? Maybe it scared him, because that's when his drug habit started to get out of control.

JANUARY 5th 1987
Van Nuys, 9:30 p.m.

Listening to the Dolls and the Stooges. Wow. Amazing. Then mix in some John Lee Hooker or Buddy Miles. Then the first Aerosmith album...I love music...This is life, like Burroughs, or Kerouac, or Ginsberg...the flames who burn bright.

Other people hide away from life. People like me, or Keith Richards, or Johnny Thunders—we live it. We're right here, feeling everything, in the moment...the only way to be truly alive is to confront your mortality...

> NIKKI: I really used to think this way. Keith and Johnny lived like this, so why shouldn't I? I know it looks crazy now, but at the time, it seemed the only way to live. I was just another wasted, confused, unraveling millionaire rock star.

> MICK MARS: Nikki was always trying to rebel. He had enough money to act like Sid Vicious, and he always loved him, so that's exactly what he did: he role-played the part of Sid. Of course, it never seemed to occur to him that Sid ended up killing himself. Did Nikki take so many drugs back then because he was unhappy? Well, I'm pretty unhappy now, and I'm not taking them!

JANUARY 6ᵗʰ 1987

Van Nuys, 11:30 p.m.

There's this funny thing about heroin...the first time you do it, you throw up, you feel sick and you can't move. You lay on your back and your head spins and your body flips...you say to yourself, this is the stupidest drug ever. Only the dumb of the dumb would ever do it again.

So why did I do it again? Because my heroes did it...because I idolize my heroes because they didn't care; and I really don't care about anything.

Heroin, once it became my friend, became like a warm blanket on a cold night. Now I can't imagine living without it. I can't imagine not having it. I don't get sick from it now—I get sick if I don't do it.

Isn't it funny how that works?

NIKKI: Cocaine made me high until I went too far and became wild and psychotic: heroin balanced that out and made me calm. I would self-medicate in my house for days with the obsessive addiction of a research scientist. Maybe I saw it as a yin and yang thing? It all made sense in my junkie wonderland.

TOMMY LEE: The first time I took heroin was at Nikki's place at Valley Vista Boulevard. He was taking it and I thought, Fuck, I want to try this shit. I shot up on his couch, pulled the needle out and immediately had the biggest rush on the planet. I was just lying there, then within a minute I had to rush to his bathroom, spraying throw-up through my fingers. Then I came out really high, walked back to his couch and just passed out. Later I thought, I'm not sure that I like this. The needle hurt on the way in, there was a very short really high point, then I threw up and passed out. What the fuck is this?

I asked Nikki, "Are you sure about this shit?" But unlike me, Sixx seemed to be pretty fucking sure.

JANUARY 8, 1987
Van Nuys, 3:25 a.m.

Sometimes, if I didn't know better...
I'd think that my dealer is
trying to kill me.

31

```
          Little mean faces
       Here I sit in the dark
    Letting my insanity run away
 Little mean faces stare back at me
    Chanting rhythms of my fate
      I know they're not real
 And I'm sure I'm really quite sane
       Because if I was crazy
  I would have given them all
         little names
```

10 a.m.

Pete won't admit it, but he's
got a habit too.

Noon

TO-DO LIST:

Buy guitar strings
Buy food
Call management back
Return decorator's call
Get more locks for the doors
Replace busted back window

> NIKKI: My house was a site of constant misadventure.
> All sorts of mayhem would unfold. One day I would get
> a strippers' pole put in my bedroom because I thought
> it was classy. A few days later I would tear it down
> because I'd decided it was crass. There were constant
> spontaneous décor rethinks. It was very confusing
> even for such a confused time. It tends to be that way
> when you're going insane.

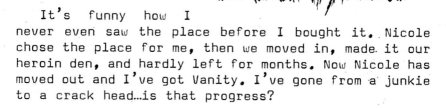

JANUARY 9ᵀᴴ, 1987

Van Nuys, midnight

I love this house...the times that I don't hate it.

It's funny how I never even saw the place before I bought it. Nicole chose the place for me, then we moved in, made it our heroin den, and hardly left for months. Now Nicole has moved out and I've got Vanity. I've gone from a junkie to a crack head...is that progress?

But I love prowling around this house from room to room. I love that it's so dark: a house that can keep secrets. I don't want to ever leave here but I have to...'cause rehearsals start next week.

NIKKI: The house was on Valley Vista Boulevard in Van Nuys, LA. My former girlfriend Nicole had chosen it for me. I was touring *Theatre of Pain* with Mötley, and she would view properties in LA, video them and bring the videos out on the road to show me. It took me about a minute to say yes. What was the big deal? I had so much money then, I could have bought anywhere.

I hired an interior decorator who would turn up for meetings with her fabrics and samples, and find me strung out of my head. She'd step over the needles, and the empty coke bindles, and the comatose naked girls on my $25,000 Persian rugs with cigarette burns on them, and she'd never even bat an eyelid. I must hand it to her—she was very professional.

My house was full of red velvet hangings, gothic furniture, antiques and gargoyles that loomed at you out of the darkness. It was a house to lose yourself in–and to lose your mind in.

JANUARY 10th 1987
Van Nuys, 9:40 p.m.

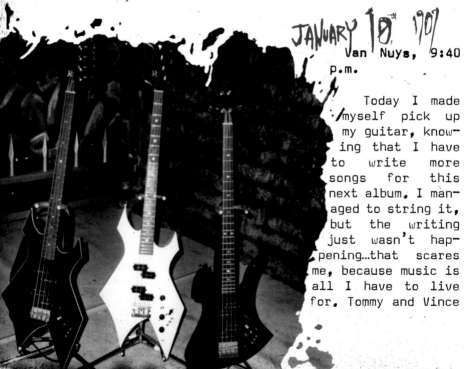

Today I made myself pick up my guitar, knowing that I have to write more songs for this next album. I managed to string it, but the writing just wasn't happening...that scares me, because music is all I have to live for. Tommy and Vince and even Mick have their families to go home to at the end of the day. Music has always been my family, and now I'm losing that too...every corner of my mind is filled with spiderwebs and fear...

JANUARY 11TH 1987
Van Nuys, 11 p.m.

Me and Pete spent the day shooting the breeze. Pete talks like he has loads of things going on, but he never really gets his shit together. He still owes me the $9,000 bail I posted for him after he got busted on probation with track marks on his arm. He says I'll get it back one day...whatever...

I've realized something about Pete. His hair always looks so cool, with all weird pieces and extensions woven into it, but I've never seen him without a hat, or without a towel over his head when he gets outta the shower. It's too perfect...is it even his own hair? I think it's a fucking wig!

NIKKI: I never did get my money back from Pete. After he vanished, I heard many stories of his adventures from people over the years. The last one I heard was that he'd been sent to jail after trying to rob a bank—on a bicycle. I have no idea if it is true, but it would be a very Pete thing to do.

JANUARY 12TH, 1987
Van Nuys, 4 p.m.

I've enrolled in a methadone program and I think it's gonna go well. Davey told me he kicked a bad Persian habit this way, so I'm hopeful...so every morning at nine I'm down there, the rock star junkie in his blacked-out Corvette, lining up in my ski cap and sunglasses with all the others for my daily dose.

I'm gonna kick this shit…I know I am. This has to work…I don't know how I'm gonna tour like this if it doesn't. I can do it…as long as I don't chip too much.

NIKKI: Most methadone programs last thirty days and are intended to wean addicts off heroin while keeping them away from dirty needles, HIV, dealers and the general paraphernalia of the drug world. I used to get my methadone dose then call on Jason for dope. Did it work? I was so strung out that I think I may have simply added methadone to my already impressive list of existing addictions.

"Davey"–whose real name cannot be disclosed–is one of the biggest rock stars in the world. I can't tell you his name…but I sure loved his music growing up…

JANUARY 13th, 1987

Van Nuys, 9 p.m.

Today I phoned my sister. I have no idea why. We have nothing to say to each other…

CECI COMER: My brother, Nikki, is seven years older than me and he is imprinted on my heart like my faith–which is strange but true, because he hasn't always deserved to be. I've never understood it, but the feeling has never left me. But there have been plenty of times I've despised him too.

When we were kids we would play together in El Paso. We made mudslides (he ripped his foot open), caught horny toads and snakes and shot Roman candles at each other on July 4 inside a cement mixer. One time Grandpa pulled a huge cactus thorn from his kneecap, another time Nikki sliced his finger on the pigpen so bad that it was hardly attached. It was just wobbling and shooting torrential downpours of blood. He even got struck by lightning in our doorway one day.

Nikki became my hero when he saved me from a big rattlesnake—I thought I could pet it, but he ran and picked me up as it was about to strike. He used to keep snakes as pets. Once one of them killed and ate my quarter turtle—I wanted to kill that snake! Nikki still owes me for that.

Then Mom and I moved to Washington and Nikki went to live with our grandparents. I think in Mom's mind it was only ever temporary and Nikki would come to join us when the dust had settled, but he never did come to stay with us. I think maybe Nikki figured Mom loved me more than him but it wasn't that—I was just younger and in her possession. And Mom tried to always have a room for Nikki in whatever house we lived in.

After Nikki got famous we really drifted apart. He'd never contact us, apart from occasionally when he was coming to town. And the times that I *did* hear from him, he was such an ass. He'd ask me how things were, then when I'd tell him he would cut the conversation short or change the subject. He was rude, full of himself, he just crushed me so many times…he was an asshole.

JANUARY 14ᵀᴴ 1987
Van Nuys, 11:30 a.m.

Last night, after Jason left, was madness…I'm not having him bring smack very often but my coke intake is up 1,000%. I was creeping around the house, listening to the voices, when I noticed all the platinum disks hanging on the walls, and suddenly I hated them. Why were they there? Mötley is about music and passion, not awards from a dumb industry that hates us and skims millions of dollars off us. So I went from room to room wrenching the disks off the walls and dumping them in the garage. Then I suddenly felt stupid...we earned those disks, we should be proud of them. So I put them all on the floor below where they used to hang.

We're back in the studio tomorrow.

BOB MICHAELS: Nikki is a very driven individual. Sometimes he'd put drugs on the back burner for a while for cars, or seventeen-foot trucks, but it got to the point where nothing else mattered but getting high. He went from being fun to never being happy unless he was totally wasted. He used to check his mailbox seven times a day, but it wasn't the mail he was after...it was the drugs that the dealers used to leave there for him. He'd go to the mailbox, then to the bathroom and come out a much more comfortable person.

Insanity runs deep in the company that I keep
Insanity runs deep in everyone but me
My padded walls you call my eyes
My dreams that you call my lies
Around my wrists my shackles lay
Razor blades and cocaine to pass the time away

JANUARY 15TH, 1987

Van Nuys, 8:30 p.m.

Today we were back in the studio, writing for the new album. I rode in on my Harley feeling all jittery and decided to stop for a small fix...went in Denny's on Gower and Sunset (always the classy guy!). I didn't have a spoon, so I bought a bottle of Pepsi, threw the bottle away, kept the cap and went in their bathroom to shoot up. The shitter was disgusting—black rings and shit stains around the bowl and the unclever graffiti all over the walls...

I sat on my motorcycle helmet on the floor and filled the cap with water from the toilet. I dunno why I didn't fill it from the sink, like any sane person would. I put the bottle cap on the toilet seat in the piss and stains, and poured coke in it. I drew it up in the syringe, washed it out in the shit water, put a little china white in the cap and cooked it, burning my fingers. I had no cottons, so I just drew it up and shot up.

The studio was fine after that...I just felt dead.

DOUG THALER: I co-managed Mötley Crüe together with Doc McGhee for many years, and when I first started Nikki was a pain in the ass. He just had a knee-jerk reaction against us as authority figures and never understood we were trying to help him. I used to go to band meetings with my stomach tied in knots.

One day I just snapped and said to him, "You can't be an ass-hole all your life." I offered that in the future I'd present ideas and strategies to him before the rest of the band, and he liked that. After that we got along a lot better: I'd like to think he saw me as some sort of elder brother, or even a mentor.

One side effect of Nikki's control-freak nature was that, whenever Mötley was in the studio, he wanted to be there every single minute of the night and day. On Girls Girls Girls, *he was a lot more* removed *from the process. He often wasn't there at all, and when he did come in, he was in no shape to do anything—he would just be making no sense. That's when I started to realize how ill he was.*

JANUARY 16ᵗʰ 1987
Van Nuys, 10:10 p.m.

Last night was a bad one. When I rode into the stu-dio this afternoon I knew I was still high, and the others seemed shocked at the state I was in. I started showing them a new song but Tommy interrupted and asked me, Dude, what's on your hand?

He'd seen my track marks, so I told him that I'd met a chick a few days ago and pulled an all-nighter, done a little shooting up...coke...Tommy just looked at me as if to say, That was no party. He could see my hands were one big scab. I'm looking at them now, as I write...all my veins have collapsed.

But Tommy never said anything. Nobody ever does. The guys aren't exactly angels themselves so it would just be the pot calling the kettle black...Mötley doesn't like confrontation and they don't like to cross me. So I taught them the new song and everything was OK.

TOMMY LEE: Nikki was turning up to the studio for the *Girls Girls Girls* sessions in a bit of a fucking mess. I guess we were all a bit of a mess, but Nikki definitely went that one step further than the rest of us. He'd show up really late, he and I would chase the dragon in the bathroom, then we'd go back into the studio to try to work. I think it's fair to say our focus was on the drugs and not on the music.

VINCE NEIL: I knew Nikki had a drug problem right back when we were doing *Shout at the Devil*. We all had drug problems, at our own levels, but Nikki's just seemed more amplified than anybody else's. But he never got in trouble for it–if anything happened, it was taken care of right away. Our management always just smoothed everything over because Nikki was writing songs and making money for everybody. Why would they want to throw a stone in the wheel and stop the money machine from turning?

TIM LUZZI: I was Nikki's bass technician for many years, including during the recording of the *Girls Girls Girls* album. I first started working for him when they made *Too Fast for Love* and remember that on my first day, Nikki came into the studio with a black eye, having spent the night in a police cell. That pretty much set the tone for what was to follow.

JANUARY 17TH 1987
Van Nuys, midnight

Today I went into the studio and everyone was staring at me and asking what happened to me yesterday. Apparently I just vanished...went to the bathroom and never came back. Between me and you, I guess I was in a bit of a blackout.

So I started teaching them a new song. I gave Vince the lyrics and showed Mick the guitar riff. They said nothing and started playing...they were good...they got it right away. Then halfway through the song I realized they knew it already. I'd already shown them the song... yesterday.

41

I didn't say anything. Of course, neither did they...what could they say? It was a very uncomfortable feeling...I think we all realized right there that this isn't what it used to be. The drugs are running the show and we're all scared to death. I'm sure they called Doug and Doc after I left. I expect a call any day. They must know I am going insane.

MICK MARS: When we were making *Girls Girls Girls*, Nikki would ride down to the studio on his motorcycle, come in, look at the place, say "OK, we're done" and then everybody would go home. That was pretty much the way it was. I don't think he even knew what he was doing: it was pretty horrible. The only good thing, from my point of view, was that it made him much less of a control freak than usual.

DOC McGHEE: As a manager I used to be very close to Nikki, but while Mötley was doing *Girls Girls Girls* he was just Out There. We saw he had a problem and I realized he was coming apart, unraveling, but it was a crazy period. We didn't talk as much as before because he was just never there...when you're a heroin addict, you just gravitate towards the few people that you do the drug with. Everybody else just stays away. I knew what the problem was and I hoped it was just something that Nikki was going through, but heroin isn't something that you just go through. It's the worst drug in the world.

JANUARY 18th, 1987

· Van Nuys, 11:40 p.m.

I don't know if this album we're making is any good. I don't know if I even like it...and if I don't like it, who will?

I have to pull it together. I don't know how to stop. I don't want to go to rehab again...but I'm at a loss for how to get off...

NIKKI: It amazes me now that nobody from Mötley said anything to me about the state I was in. I was writing some pretty lame songs, and nobody dared tell me they sucked. Were they scared to challenge me? Looking back, I don't blame them.

ROSS HALFIN: I don't think people were scared of Nikki—they just didn't care. He was their paycheck and they didn't give a shit if he was falling to bits as long as he got up there onstage. Back then was an anything goes sort of time. Doc was doing drugs, so was Doug, everyone was. The only person as bad as Nikki was Tommy, and even he wasn't doing heroin—he was just snorting coke and drinking. Without Nikki, Doc wouldn't have been making money, nor would Doug, Vince, the road crew, the record company, anybody…so they all ignored Nikki's condition and said he was fine. He was the Emperor and it was the Emperor's new clothes.

JANUARY 19ᵗʰ 1987, Van Nuys, 8:30 p.m.

Some days I'm King Kong with a bass guitar. Today Mick wanted to modulate a guitar line, and I just yelled at him, Fuck you, that's lame! Mick looked at me like I'd crapped in his amp but he never said anything…he never does. He's too kind, unlike me. I make myself sick. I can be such a pompous asshole sometimes.

I feel shitty when I do stuff like that but I know I'm overcompensating because right now I'm the weak link in the studio. But I shouldn't take it out on the band.

MICK MARS: Nikki and I have had a love-hate relationship ever since we met in a liquor store before we even formed Mötley Crüe. I went to buy some tequila and he asked me who I liked and I said, "Jeff Beck and Be Bop Deluxe," and he said, "Fuck you, I like Aerosmith and Kiss." So we hated each other from the start. But when he started taking heroin, it really pissed me off. The first time I ever saw him take it was when we were rehearsing the *Theatre of Pain* tour, and I was that angry that I called our management and told them. I told Nikki way back then not to mess with heroin, but he never listened to me. He never did.

JANUARY 21ST, 1981
Van Nuys, 11 a.m.

Vanity called last night and asked me to come over and play. I had nothing else to do so I figured, Why not? As soon as she opened the door, I could see from her eyes she hadn't slept for days...she looked at me like a scared little cartoon character.

She started showing me some of her "art" as we freebased, then I noticed a huge bouquet of flowers in the corner of the room. There must have been 24 dozen roses. I asked her who they were from and she wouldn't say, so I read the card...

Vanity~ Drop him.
Take me back.
~Prince

I am so pissed. She may be fucking insane, but she's my girl! If I see that dwarf, I'll kick his ass!

NIKKI: Vanity's "art" was crazy shit. She would get these huge boards and spray-paint them white, then stick nuts and bolts all over them. There would be a little Santa Claus she called a "gift from God" and there was always a devil in there somewhere. She'd be telling me to talk to Jesus, but I didn't feel we had much to say to each other.

As for the flowers, I found out from her sister that they weren't from Prince! She'd sent them to herself to fuck with my head. Let's give her credit: she always found plenty of ways to do that.

EVANGELIST DENISE MATTHEWS: I had more addictions than just cocaine. I have been sober now for thirteen years but the root of my problems went much deeper. There was the bitterness, envy, strife, hatred, emulations, judgmental thoughts, selfishness and the enslavement of fornication. There was the money, the fame, the fortune, the drugs and paraphernalia which naturally brought upon the demonic, the psychic and all of the witchcraft…not to mention the foul, perverted tongue and the bondage of idolatries. My iniquity was as a catastrophic snowball rolling down a ski slope collecting ugly. I definitely needed some saving.

DOC McGHEE: Nikki was into Vanity, but I think a lot of that was because she had come out of the whole thing of dating Prince. Rock stars are star-fuckers–Nikki might just as easily have grabbed Granny from *The Beverly Hillbillies*! Frankly, Vanity was not very attractive around that time. She was out of it an awful lot and she looked a real mess. Let's just say that when you are strung out, personal hygiene is one of the first things to go.

JANUARY 24TH 1987
Van Nuys, Midnight

We had a day off from the studio so Tommy came around. Heather is away, filming on location. So we chilled out and watched MTV, and I made myself wait 30 minutes before I told Tommy I had some dope. It's not cool to look too eager.

Tommy asked me to shoot him up in the same place he always does...the rose tattoo in the crook of his arm, the spot that nobody can see. If Heather knew he was around here shooting smack with me, she would be gone. She'd be history.

I love Tommy—he's the brother I never had. He loves me enough to come here and take a holiday in my hell...but then he goes. And I'm still here.

NIKKI: Tommy, my partner in crime and fellow Toxic Twin, would visit me on Valley Vista Boulevard every now and then. Sometimes we'd shoot up heroin, but Tommy was smarter than me: he never got hooked. He always said that heroin scared him because it was "just too good." He had his little packages of syringes over at his and Heather Locklear's mansion, but it was cocaine only.

TOMMY LEE: As soon as I took smack with Nikki, I realized how easily I could get addicted. I knew if I fucked with it big-time, it would either kill me or send me into a huge downward spiral of chasing some fucking fantasy. If I had taken it to a dark place, I just wouldn't have got out: I knew how much I loved it, and how careful I had to be. I always did heroin with a little bit of fear, and I guess you don't enjoy it as much if you're fearful of it. Whenever I visited Nikki, I would hang with him and get fucked up for a day or two, then I'd tell myself, "OK, let's get back to Heather–this is dark as fuck."

2:55 a.m.

One could say that I've been having a 10cc love affair...my mistress is so seductive. She sneaks, she lies—in fact, she will lie dormant, if that's what's needed to seduce me from my lifetime commitment (my music). Some could say I'm married to my music. Others...fuck them...

Is this a crisis or a needed creative outlet?

There she goes again, whispering in my ear. Sometimes I think I hear her say I'm going to die.

January 26, 1987
Van Nuys, 4:10 a.m.

Bob Michaels just left. We hung out and got high but he really pisses me off. Bob will do coke and drink all night but gets all lame whenever I try to give him some junk. I suppose I understand why but it's not like he's clean living. Maybe I should just give him some china white to snort and tell him it's coke. Fuck, he's my friend, and I know how much he'd enjoy it!

BOB MICHAELS: I used to do loads of pot and coke with Nikki, but I'd never do heroin. I was terrified of needles. Most junkies don't give a fuck what other people are doing as long as they can get their own drugs, but Nikki was different. He was always trying to get me to do a shot because it would be "awesome." Once or twice I left my pipe out on the counter and, when I wasn't looking, Nikki sprinkled heroin in it. I'd get a lot higher than I expected, and when I looked over at him he'd be laughing at me.

10:20 p.m.

I'm very impressed with myself, if I say so myself.
I'm maintaining OK in the studio. It helps if I do a
couple of lines of coke before I go in, then maybe a
snort of dope so that I don't feel too jumpy...the
methadone of course...then a few trips to the bathroom
while we're rehearsing.

It's hard, but I'm keeping an even keel until I get
home in the evenings and all hell breaks loose. It's
when I come home that it's hard...my secret room keeps
talking to me. I'm not listening. I'm really trying.

**TOMMY LEE: Nikki was coming to the studio nicely
sedated. He can be quite the control freak, but when he
was on heroin he was absolutely out of control so he
couldn't *be* in control. I just found him very lax, which
isn't his personality–Sixx is Sagittarius but he's got the
personality of a Taurus, a bull.**

JANUARY 28TH, 1987
Van Nuys, 4 a.m.

Tonight, Diary, I'm going to try something different.
Instead of writing to you after an evening of psychosis,
I'm going to write to you while it's happening. Maybe
someday somebody can read this and understand what
Hell is.

So here I sit. The curtains are drawn, the candles
are lit, and it's just me and you. My guitar's on my
lap, my diary's on the table, and I'm ready. Let's see
what happens.

I just did it.

My head is exploding. I...

I feel like throwing up.

Now I know, what I hear isn't there.
There is someone...
it's....

4:40 a.m.

I need to get on paper what just happened. I was
convinced 30 minutes ago that there were people outside
my house. There is NOBODY outside the house...what the
fuck is wrong with me?

I can't stop, but I want to still do it. I NEED
THIS. I can't stop. I don't know how to stop thinking
about it. I want to get high and I don't want to go
insane.

I know it's fake, I know it's fake. I know it's not
real. It's just the drugs...

Sometimes when I sit here alone surrounded by only
candles, the shadows dancing on the walls feel like my
only friends. I'm listening to Tommy Bolin, trying to
think of a reason to pick up my guitar...I wonder if this
is how he felt, right before he died? This isn't how
I thought life would turn out.

I can't seem to read anything lately...music seems
abrasive. The scabs on my arms are festering with
infection. I can't breathe from all the blow and I
can't seem to get drunk anymore. I'm at the edge. I
feel like I'm standing at death's door and no one will
let me in.

Why can't I do the drugs like everybody else?
Everybody else does the drugs and they're OK. I do the
drugs and things happen to me that I can't explain.

I'm trying to put it on paper, but I can't…I can only describe it and you must think I'm insane but I'm not. I'm sitting here right now sane, as sane as the next guy…it's just the drugs. It's not me.

I remember back in Idaho, going fishing and hunting as a kid. I remember discovering Deep Purple on my cheap lil AM/FM radio, my first crushes and those warm summer nights in the park. I wanna go back to those times of innocence. I've forgotten who I was.

Please, God, make it stop.

BOB TIMMONS: Cocaine gave Nikki acute paranoia and hallucinations. One night he called me and asked me to get the police over to his house right away because there were little men with helmets and guns in the trees surrounding his house. It took me quite a while to talk him down from that one.

SO GOOD, SO BAD
Chinese highs, pearly white down the mainline
So sad Susie has the blues up in Soho
Says it's cold as ice deep down in her arm
White horse screams unpleasant dreams and
pain
Blind lead the blind like the German faith
Riding high thru the graveyard of the night

JANUARY 29TH 1987
Van Nuys, 7:30 p.m.

I've been up to no good again, diary, but it's given me a killer idea for a song.

Becky came around again yesterday, during her school lunch break. As she was getting dressed again afterwards, putting that Catholic school uniform back on, I asked her about the Lord's Prayer...is it important? She looked at me wide-eyed and said, Sure, it's real important...so I got her to recite it for me, and I scribbled a few notes down. Then I dropped her back at school on my Harley.

The nuns all looked horrified when they saw me, like they were going to have a heart attack. They will too if they hear the song I'm writing.

NIKKI: Becky was a local schoolgirl who used to get *very* friendly with me on her lunch breaks. She had a real famous mom who would freak if she knew what her daughter was doing back then—so you know what? I'm not gonna tell you who she was…

JANUARY 30TH, 1987

Van Nuys, midnight

Today has turned to night. I've laid around all day, naked, playing guitar-writing, writing-this lovely lil love song called Wild Side. I think it's an ode to Lou.

Kneel down ye sinners to
Streetwise religion
Greed's been crowned the new King
Hollywood dream teens
Yesterday's trash queens
Save the blessings for the final ring
AMEN

Wild side

I carry my crucifix
Under my death list
Forward my mail to me in hell
Liars and the martyrs
Lost faith in the Father
Long lost in the wishing well

Wild side

'Fallen Angels
So fast to kill
Thy kingdom come on the wild side
Our Father
Who ain't in heaven
Be thy name on the wild side Holy Mary
Mother may I
Pray for us on the wild side
Wild side
Wild side

Name dropping no-names
Glamorize cocaine
Puppets with strings of gold
East LA at midnight
Papa won't be home tonight
Found dead with his best friend's wife

Wild side

Fatal strikes
We lie on the wild side
No escape
Murder rape
Doing time on the wild side
A baby cries
A cop dies
A day's pay on the wild side
Wild side
Wild side
Tragic life on the wild side
Wild side
Wild side
Kickin' ass on the wild side

Ah, lyrics to kill your career by...chew on that, MTV!

JANUARY 31ST 1987
Van Nuys, 11:30 p.m.

I weigh 164 lbs...40 lbs less than a year ago.

Last night I went to Vanity's and when I left this morning I stole one of her leather jackets. I'm so fuckin' thin I can wear her clothes...and some are actually baggy...

Doc came around today while Jason was here and kicked him out of the house. Fucking asshole—he may be our manager but he can't tell me what to do in my house. Even if what I want to do is kill myself.

DOC McGHEE: Nikki looked fucking awful when he became a junkie. He sank into himself, lost all his weight, and just hung around his heroin den house looking horrible. I went around there once when his dealer was there, and I told the pasty piece of shit, "If you ever see Nikki Sixx again, or I hear you've brought him even one bit of heroin, I will have you killed." I would have done it too. Nikki was all junked out and the dealer guy was just fucking vermin.

FEBRUARY 2nd, 1987
Van Nuys, 1 a.m.

When I'm losing my mind, the only thing that can save me is heroin.

I love the ritual of heroin. I love the smell, and the way it looks when it goes into the needle. I love the way the needle feels when it goes into my skin. I love watching the blood register and mix in with the beautiful yellowish-brown liquid. I love that moment just before I push...

Then I'm under that warm blanket once again, and I'm perfectly content to live there for the rest of my life. Thank God for heroin...it never lets me down.

I'm off the methadone. It didn't work.

9:30 p.m.

Daytime in the studio for a rock band is torture. When you're a creature of the night, daytime is not your best creative time, but that's when our producer wants to work. Tom Werman can be such a whiny lil fucker. I have no idea why he's producing our album. We're doing all the work...he's just on the phone most of the time or sending out for food. He hasn't come up with one idea to better our music.

I used to like this guy, but now I realize he's just a money-grubbing cheese-ball. This is his last album with us—he can go produce Poison, or some such bullshit.

I have to do all the work with Vince on the vocals and it's hard being a mess and trying to organize vocals. I always do since I write the lyrics, but Werman could at least help. Vince is just always trying to hurry through the vocals and it drives me nuts. I know I drive him crazy but he would do a half-assed job if it wasn't for me bird-dogging him. So I'm sure he hates me...that makes two of us...

VINCE NEIL: When Nikki was coming into the studio fucked up, I could only tell he was strung out because he wasn't saying anything. Nikki likes to talk. If he wasn't talking, it meant he was fucked up, and can I tell you something? I liked him like that! I was happy when he was quiet at the *Girls* sessions!

I've never had any interest in sitting around a studio watching Nikki play bass or Mick play guitar, but Nikki has always liked to be there when I record my vocals. He's always had to give his opinion or criticize me, and I've always told him, "Dude, shut the fuck up!" I listen to the album producer, not to Nikki Sixx. We've got in a few fights over that. Nikki was spending a lot of time shooting up in the bathroom during the *Girls* sessions, and that suited me fine—it was the perfect time for me to record my vocals.

TOM ZUTAUT: I was Mötley Crüe's A&R man at Elektra Records, and Nikki Sixx used to go on and on about how he was the guy who was going to set rock 'n' roll on fire and take over first Sunset Strip and then the rest of the world. I thought to myself, yeah, he's absolutely right, the kids are bored with new wave, and this glam rock Kiss meets the New York Dolls vision of Nikki Sixx's is going to change popular music.

The second time I ever met Nikki he described to me the almost cartoon-like character attributes of each member of Mötley Crüe, why they were there, the part each of them had to play within the Crüe, and how with his songs they would revive rock 'n' roll and kill new wave. At that point, I was convinced that Nikki was one of the smartest guys I ever met. The remarkable thing is that he had his vision of Mötley Crüe laid out in his head from Day One.

FEBRUARY 4TH 1987
Van Nuys, 10 p.m.

There are some good songs coming through for this album. I'm really proud of Wild Side, but other times I'm just recycling old Aerosmith riffs or repeating myself. I know I should be try-ing harder but I can't be bothered.

I never thought I would say those words.

DOUG THALER:
Nikki was normally a talented and prolific songwriter, but he just couldn't write enough good songs for *Girls Girls Girls.* You want the truth? Tom Werman made that record. We even had to include a live track, "Jailhouse Rock," on the album. Nikki wrote one song in a key that Vince couldn't even sing, and some of his lyrics were absolute dreck. One day he came in wasted, and he'd written a song called "Hollywood Nights" that was just *so* bad: really, really horrible.

LOST LYRIC

Candy coated holocaust buried in the past
Swallowed all these lies and shit it out your ass
Babies born with switchblades
Dumping bodies in the Everglades
California high tide, needles on a fishing line
Backwashed and belly up, dancin' on a land mine

FEBRUARY 6TH 1787

Van Nuys, 3:15 a.m.

It's pouring rain outside. I'm alone again, sitting here with this one candle…my pen in my hand, trying to not reach for my dope. I can't stop. I'm so strung out and I can't get off…I don't think I will ever be off drugs. I think this is my purpose in life. I'm gonna be the guy who had it all and lost it all 'cause he couldn't stop—or just another dead rock star.

The rain is making a beautiful rhythm on the roof. It's hypnotizing. Sitting here reminds me of when I was a kid, laying in bed, listening to the rain, wondering where my mom was, or if she was even coming home. I feel the sorrow still, it stings…

Everybody thinks I'm so tough as nails. If only they knew.

DOC McGHEE: Nikki Sixx was a pretty fucking angry guy in 1987. He was very nice and polite and intelligent, but he had a really dark side to him. I think it all came down to the way his family life was before he came to LA and a lot of the things that had happened to him as a child. Let's just say that he had a pretty disturbing start to his life…there are some things that I'm just not able to tell you about.

61

FEBRUARY 7TH 1987
Van Nuys, 4:40 a.m.

I can't feel my soul. This darkness has become my only friend. My new addiction is drinking tons of water right before I shoot coke, then puking it all up in the Jacuzzi as my head explodes into the strato-sphere. Why? Why not? I'm engaged in a dance of death in this house...

RANDOM LYRIC:

HOOLIGAN'S HOLIDAY

Drop dead beauties
Stompin' up a storm
Lines of hell on our face
Bruised bad apples
Crawling through the
night
Busted loose and
runaway

FEBRUARY 8TH 1987
Van Nuys, 2 a.m.

Bob Timmons came to rehearsal today. I've no idea who sent him down. He asked me straight out if I was using. Of course, I denied it, said I'd just been partying hard, doing too much blow and drinking, but I could easily stop if I wanted to.

I don't know if Bob believed me, he didn't look‧ like he did. But I'm not gonna let him put me in, rehab again—I'd kill him first...or kill myself...

NIKKI: Bob Timmons and Doc McGhee put me and Nicole in rehab in the summer of '86. I hated it and it was a disaster. The counselors kept talking about God, and in those days I agreed with my grandfather—who needs God when you've got a Chevy pickup truck and a 12-gauge shotgun?

I lasted three days. One nurse kept talking to me about God, until I stood up and yelled, "Fuck God and fuck you!" The nurse told me to sit back down, so I spat in her face, jumped out of the window and took off walking home—it was only a few blocks from my house. Bob followed me in his car until we agreed he wouldn't take me back to rehab. He took me to my house and I showed Bob my ritual room—my bedroom closet. It was covered in dirty black marks from all the spoons, and Bob and I spent hours cleaning the room. We went through it finding all the bindles of coke, pills, booze and syringes, and disposed of the lot. The only thing I didn't get rid of was my guns. I promised Bob, I can do this on my own; I don't need rehab.

The second Bob left, I picked up the phone. Jason delivered the cocaine and junk an hour later.

Then Bob came back and I wouldn't let him in. I was lying on the floor in the hall, talking to him through the crack under the front door, with my .357 cocked and loaded. He was asking me to go back to rehab and I was saying I'd rather die than go back there. I said I'd shoot myself if he tried to come in.

Except that when I came down from the cocaine, Bob had never come back at all. It had just been me and my demons, yet again.

Nicole stayed in rehab for a few weeks and got clean. She and I were inseparable drug buddies, never leaving each other's side, but as soon as she came out clean, we didn't have a thing to say to each other. We didn't even know each other. We had met via a shared love of narcotics, and as soon as that had gone, we had nothing. So that was the end of that. For now...

BOB TIMMONS: When Nikki walked out of rehab in '86, the rehab center phoned me. I happened to be in the area, and saw Nikki walking down the street. I pulled my car over and asked him what was up: he just said, "Fuck you!" So I drove real slow alongside him as he walked along and glared at me. Eventually, when I promised I wouldn't take him back to the center, he got in my car and I drove him home. When we got there we cleared out his closet of all his drug paraphernalia. It was like an exorcism–getting rid of all the bad memories that were in his living space.

Did I know that Nikki called a dealer as soon as I'd left? No. Does it surprise me? No.

TIM LUZZI: I remember once cleaning Nikki's house out of booze, bent spoons and all the needles that were lying in every closet and on every cabinet shelf. I thought I had found all of his drugs and paraphernalia, but it turned out later that he had hidden a stash in the brass balls on top of the bedposts. He came home, unscrewed one of them and shot up. There I was busting my balls cleaning his house out, and I didn't check the balls.

FEBRUARY 10TH, 1987
Van Nuys, 4 a.m.

    Today was mostly a wasted day in the sense that I didn't achieve anything other than lying around on the sofa talking on the phone all day. But today felt good. I felt like my skin wasn't crawling, my insides weren't on the outside, but I also felt sorta flat...non-committed to life.

I wish I knew what this hole in my soul is all about. Cause let's be honest, this isn't about now, it's about then...no father, no mother, no memories of a childhood other than being shuffled around the country. Nona and Tom loved me and I loved them, but something is blazingly apparent...my mother and father had other things to do than raise me, other things that interested them more...

Maybe that's why I've turned out the way I have, where my rage comes from. But I don't know how to make it go away...

NIKKI: My father left when I was very young. His name was Frank Feranna, and so was mine until I changed it in my teens because I wanted that bastard totally out of my life. My mother is named Deana and I believed she loved me when I fit into her plans, but when I was a kid she was usually nowhere to be found. When I was young, I felt every time she met a new man, she'd ship me off to live with her parents, Tom and Nona, in Idaho because I was in the way. This was an introduction to abandonment that could only lead to bad things. The whole thing left me feeling unlovable and festered into the sores of anger, rebellion and discontent. It caused a lot of the angst that I took into Mötley Crüe and my life.

DEANA RICHARDS: Nikki's father was a very selfish person. The world revolved around him and nothing else. I left him when Nikki was ten months old, and Nikki and I went to live with my mother, Nona, and her second husband, Tom. I didn't know what else to do—I was nineteen when I had Nikki, I had no parenting skills, and Frank was binging on drinking, drugging and going with other women. He never had any time for Nikki at all.

We never heard from Frank for five years until one day he turned up out of the blue at Lake Tahoe, where Nikki and I were living, and said he wanted to see Nikki. I asked him why, and he said, "I'm planning on getting married again and the woman I'm marrying can't have kids, so I want to see what kind of kid he is." He had decided to check out his son after five years to see if he was worth taking.

Nikki and I were so close when he was a little child. It was so wonderful. When he was about two or three, every time I walked in a room he would throw his arms up and shout "Darling!" and run to me. I can still remember holding him up against my chest and feeling his heartbeat, and just how precious it was to hold him.

My relationship with my own mother, Nona, was difficult. She was a very cold woman. The first time she ever put her arms around me, I was thirty-seven years old. As a child I could do nothing right and she just always asked why I couldn't be more like my older sisters. Later, she was just horribly judgmental. I was a little wild and I might sleep with a man without being married to him, and oh my God–that was the worst thing in the world to my mother! I was just a tramp to her.

Nona had married Tom when I was sixteen and I was really angry at her for doing it. I felt that she had never shown me any love and yet she had all the time in the world to give to Tom. I thought it was really unfair.

Nona and Tom were always telling me how to raise Nikki, what to say to him, what I should be doing. They were always asking me to send Nikki to stay with them for a week or a weekend at a time, and I used to do so. But I would never have imagined that they would do what they did to me. You never imagine your own family will plot against you to steal your son.

TOM REESE: Nikki's dad, Frank, was just a typical Californian hustler. I liked the guy, but then he went off the deep end into the drug thing.

When he was a boy, Nikki would stay with me and Nona in Idaho a lot. It might be for a few days, or sometimes it was as long as a year at a time. Nikki was real close to Nona: he was the son she never had, and she doted on him.

Nikki's mother, Deana, was wild. She was always going off with guys. She'd meet some guy and just go off with him and leave Nikki. She'd go off with Italian guys, truck drivers...you name it. Nikki would come to stay with us for a while, then Deana would come back and take him. Then we'd have to go get him again, then she would talk him into coming to her, then she'd throw him out and we'd fetch him again–that was just the way it went.

Deana was crazy as a kid. Even when she was eight years old, she would go to a show and her sisters wouldn't sit with her because she would end up necking with some kid. Everything came easy to her. Her sisters had to work hard to do well at school but Deana was so smart, better than everybody else. She would pick up a musical instrument and in no time she would be playing it. Deana was the smartest of the girls...but she didn't have a brain in her head.

Nona would bend over backwards for her. What she did for the other girls, she did for Deana, but you couldn't do anything for her. You would say, "Good morning, Deana" and she would fly off the handle at you. She'd sneak and steal and lie—we had a little restaurant and she used to wait tables for a while, but we had to stop her because she was stealing too much. We sent her to a psychiatrist, but she was cleverer than him.

You had to let Deana do what Deana was going to do—because you couldn't do nothing else.

FEBRUARY 11TH, 1987
Van Nuys, 6 p.m.

Some guy just came to the door preaching about the Lord so I told him that I worship the Devil to get rid of him. I've got to give it to the guy, he didn't skip a beat, just kept on trying to save my soul. Then the phone rang and I told him I'd be right back, but I forgot he was there. I guess the dude finally took the hint and split. But he did leave me this nice little pamphlet. I think I'll save it and give it to Vanity.

I'm meeting Riki up at the Cathouse tonight...better order a car to drive me there...I need to order a few things...I'm running low. I've had no toilet paper for a week. And I'm on my eighth day without a shower.

I am so into writing all this down. Sometimes when something is happening, all I can think about is getting this journal and writing. Crazy...

FEBRUARY 12TH 1987
Van Nuys, 5:10 a.m.

Tonight started off with a bang. I scored some old school loads from this black cat who sells porno out of his house in Van Nuys...he also had some china white. We headed out to the Cathouse and it was way cool. They only played glam rock from the early '70s. Hearing T. Rex blaring at that volume really puts a smile on my face. I remember seeing T. Rex at the Paramount Theater in Seattle as a kid right before Bolan died. Anyway...

Fuck, what a meat market that place is, girls galore and every sweet one ready for anything...so be it. Out to the limo and off with the clothes. A few lines up the nose and voila! Rock 'n' roll cliché 101. Back into the club, back out to the car with a different chick...on and on...

So how did it change? How did I end up crouched behind my bed with my gun?

WHAT THE HELL IS WRONG WITH ME??????

I'm glad nobody from the club came back here with me...who knows what might have happened.

Cocaine sucks but I love it. I need to have a couple of drinks and try to sleep. I'm supposed to meet the decorator tomorrow to look at some gothic English desk. I hope I'm not too hungover again...blah blah blah...

TOM ZUTAUT: I first realized Nikki had gone beyond the point of hard partying one night in 1983 when Roy Thomas Baker threw a big party for Mötley Crüe at his house after remixing *Shout at the Devil*. Nikki went for it all night–too much sex, a huge pile of blow and gallons of hard liquor, not to mention whatever pills he might have ingested out of his own pocket.

At one point I mentioned to Roy that it would be a bad idea for anybody to leave, as it was clear that no one was in any condition to drive. Roy pushed a button and I heard the sounds of a prison lockdown: doors closing, gates swinging shut and dead bolts clanging. RTB explained that he never wanted any of his invited guests to get hurt, so when everyone was too high to navigate home safely, he simply locked them in and insisted they spend the night and stay for breakfast.

Nikki decided he was going home, and must have come to me a dozen times asking me where the door was. Eventually he would find a door, but with the house in lockdown mode and Nikki barely conscious, there was no way he was getting out...or so I thought.

The next day we sat down for breakfast and only one guest was missing–Nikki Sixx. We found his car a few blocks away, wrapped around a tree, and eventually we found him at his apartment with his arm in a sling, a survivor who somehow had definitely beaten the odds, given the condition he was in that night.

No one knows to this day how he managed to get out of Roy's house that night, much less find his car keys and drive home. It made me realize that Nikki was willing to cross the line and put his life in danger with excessive drug and alcohol abuse. But that said, he also seemed to be indestructible.

Ragtime fast lane–another overdose
You know James Dean wasn't playing the role
I said hey, you, what-cha gonna do
When time runs out on you.

4 p.m.

Fuck. Just woke up...what's my excuse today?

Maybe I have the flu again...

FEBRUARY 13TH 1997
Van Nuys, 5 p.m.

Been listening to music and playing guitar all day.

Heroes—why do we look up to them? Is it their music or their lifestyle? For me it's both. I'm 29 years old, they say you grow outta loving rock 'n' roll but it's such a huge part of me. It feels like music raised me, adopted me, saved my life.

FEBRUARY 14TH, 1987
Van Nuys, 6:20 p.m.

I've decided I should do something for Valentine's
Day to mark the anniversary of the day that I died.
I think I'll call Vanity.

NIKKI: I had overdosed in London exactly a year earlier: Valentine's Day 1986. We had played Hammersmith Odeon, and the second we left the stage I caught a taxi with Andy McCoy from Hanoi Rocks. He took me to a heroin apartment in a real shabby neighborhood. I was drunk, and I remember I was very impressed that the dealer had clean needles. When he offered to shoot up for me, I let him. Big mistake.

The problem with street drugs is you never really know exactly how potent they are from dealer to dealer, so I OD'd on the spot. My lips turned purple: I was gone. The story I heard was that the dealer grabbed his baseball bat and tried to beat the fucking life into me. He couldn't, so he flung me over his shoulder to dump me in the trash, because nobody wants a dead rock star lying around.

Then I came to...and I guess I had yet another dark secret to never tell anybody.

Let me tell you, I felt like shit. When you die, every single muscle in your body hurts. Your body has closed down because it thinks it's done, and when it gets rebooted, every inch of you hurts. Plus I'd had the shit beaten out of me with a baseball bat. The second show at Hammersmith Odeon wasn't the happiest gig I've ever played.

TIM LUZZI: Nikki started taking heroin with Hanoi Rocks in Britain on the *Shout at the Devil* tour. Hanoi just weren't looking right; their eyes were off. But Nikki was a most willing participant. He was always destined to get hooked on heroin, and if it hadn't been with the dudes from Hanoi Rocks it would have been someone else.

FEBRUARY 15ᵗʰ 1987

Van Nuys, 2:15 p.m.

What the fuck was that about? Even by Vanity's stan-
dards, last night was insane. When I called her she
didn't want to come over, and invited me to her place
instead. I soon found out why when I got there. She'd
been smokin' coke for hours and looked pretty fucked,
so I thought I'd join in.

Vanity was doing her crazy Art shit and we ended up
doing base all night, then when it got light out she
told me she felt hungry. That seemed weird because
nobody gets hungry on coke but I said OK, and drove out
to get bacon and eggs and orange juice. Then when I got
back 10 minutes later, the guards wouldn't let me in
the gate to her complex...they said she wasn't there. I
was telling them fuck you when two black guys drove out
in a Cadillac...that was weird...there are no black people
there besides Vanity. She drove out 10 minutes later
and I chased her down in my car and asked who the black
dudes were. She said they were just friends.

Weird night. She always finds a new way to mess
up my head.

> NIKKI: I found out later from her sister that the two
> guys were dealers delivering coke. One more cute thing
> about Vanity back then: her car license plate said HO-
> HO-HO. When Prince had finished with her, he'd told
> her, "You ain't nothin' but a ho-ho-ho!" and she liked
> that because...she had a thing about Santa Claus. That
> sort of made sense in Vanityworld.

> EVANGELIST DENISE MATTHEWS: I was the glutton for
> punishment [with Nikki] and also the punisher punishing. It
> wasn't easy being high all the time and relating to another
> human being. He could have related better with a pet rock.

I won't pretend that I was always there. If our relationship had been examined by a professional at that time, his diagnosis might have read, "Intensive care is much needed for this mad, neurotic, paranoid, psychotic, disturbing relationship, with egos at large coming through the door."

I believe there is a whole phi-sod to the ph-sod of being an idol, don't you think? We take on the mysterious role of its origin. Everybody else traveled the same road so we might as well follow the drugs, the sex, trash the hotel, the crazy parties, grow your hair longer, look the part, wear the makeup and act crazy until it kills you. The rest is simple…boy meets girl, girl gets yucky, both get woozy and call it love, oh yes…sick!

LOST POETRY

Her love is like a swimming pool
Winter comes and it's no use to you
Her love is like a suicide
Lose your faith and it takes your life
Her love is like a merry-go-round
Spins you in circles then it knocks you down
Her love is like cheap alcohol
Morning comes and you don't remember at all
Her love is like a Cheshire cat
At first so friendly but at you it laughs
Her love is like a passionate kiss
At first so sweet then it takes your breath
Her love is like the stars above
Your guiding light always leaves you lost
Her love is like Jesus Christ
No matter how much faith
You still die on the cross

Van Nuys, 1 a.m.

Today I didn't drink, mostly because I'm pissing blood again. It will pass—it always does, right? I think I've done pretty good today.

I am reading a great book called Junkie by William Burroughs. I never really cared for Naked Lunch.

Van Nuys, 2:30 a.m.

Slash came over today. We were playing guitar and having a few drinks and watching MTV and I went for a piss. When I came back, Slash was looking at me funny. He asked me why I still have my Christmas tree up with unopened presents under it. That's a good question...

SLASH: My first memory of Nikki was seeing him playing with his band London at the Starwood. I was about fourteen at the time, and he was just this charismatic glam punk bass player who made a real big impression on me. Then I remember him coming to my high school and giving out fliers to a Mötley Crüe show at the Whisky A Go-Go to all the hot chicks.

Mötley Crüe was America's Sex Pistols. On a musical level they had some catchy songs and cool lyrics, but they were all about the attitude and the image. They were the

MÖTLEY CRÜE
DAY & SATURDAY, DECEMBER 11 & 12
WHISKY
FRIDAY DECEMBER 25
COUNTRY CLUB
1 SHOW ONLY CHRISTMAS NIGHT
...le For The First Time— Motley Crue's Dot...

only band coming out of the LA scene, apart from maybe Van Halen, who had any sincerity and took what they were doing seriously, and it was all down to Nikki. He just had this focus, a real sense of direction.

I hung out with Nikki at his house a little in '86 and I found a sickening allure in his lifestyle. My worst junkie years were behind me by then, but I was drinking like fuck: I'd start the day with a Jack and coffee. My junkie years were dirty and sordid, but Nikki seemed to me to have found a cool, glamorous way to be a junkie.

Guns N' Roses still hadn't taken off then so I was still a street kid, but let me be honest…if I'd had Nikki's money, I would have been living exactly the same way that he was.

FEBRUARY 19ᵗ 1987

Van Nuys, 6:15 p.m.

Just got back from antique shopping. Bought some old books. Tonight I'm gonna read one called Five Years Dead…it seems kinda fitting.

What is it about antiques that intrigue me? There's a feeling of history, a story not so plain to see, that seeps from the wood. It somehow makes me feel comfortable. I almost bought an old coffin today, but I couldn't think where to keep it in this house. The house is shrinking.

Midnight

I've lost so much weight. None of my clothes fit anymore.

FEBRUARY 20th, 1987
Van Nuys, 4 a.m.

So I've started writing a song called Five Years Dead. I guess it's another attempt at capturing what Aerosmith did on their first album...what a great record. It brings back all the best and worst memories from Seattle. How I survived those days I just don't know.

ROSS HALFIN: That was how Nikki got his song titles. He told me he used to just get old books and steal their titles. "Five Years Dead" was only one example— there were plenty more.

FIVE YEARS DEAD

Uptown downtown
Haven't seen your face around
Paper said you shot a man
Trigger-happy punk down in
Chinatown

FEBRUARY 21st 1987
Van Nuys, 2:45 a.m.

I wonder what my sister's doing right now. I wonder if she hates me for hating Mom. I wonder a lot of things...

1. Does my dad know who I am?
2. Does my band hate me and wanna find another bass player?
3. How's Lisa?
4. Will I ever have a family?
5. What would happen if someone found these diaries?

NIKKI: Lisa was my sister I never knew. After she was born, a year after me, all I remember was that my sister had vanished. I never knew where she'd gone until I was older. Lisa's whereabouts intrigued and troubled me all my life, but it wasn't until the late '90s that I discovered she was living in a sanatorium. I knew that she had Down's syndrome and other major health issues but, to be honest, it was all a huge mystery to me.

In a heart-to-heart conversation with my mom, I discovered where Lisa was just before I toured the *New Tattoo* album. When I called the people who had cared for her all these years, they told me they remembered me from when I was a boy. I said I was told that we couldn't see her because it would upset her, and it was better never to visit. They told me, "No, that's not true–we always wondered why you never came to visit." I said that I was a musician, and they told me Lisa's only pleasure in life was listening to the radio. She was living in San Jose, where we had played many concerts.

My heart sank and my anger soared. Oh God, I thought, more misinformation, and I arranged to visit her as soon as the tour had finished and vowed to do something to help change her life. By the time the dates ended, she had died, and all I could do was build an angel statue with wings in her memory. It's one of my life's huge regrets that I never knew her. I used to blame my mother, but now I know I had the power to force my way into Lisa's life.

I'll never forget holding her little hand in the casket and looking down at her sweet face. We had the same eye-brows. We never had a chance to be together. I cried harder than I ever had in my life.

DEANA RICHARDS: When Lisa was born, doctors knew very little about mongoloidism. All they knew was that mongoloid children had two genes instead of one. Lisa was a very extreme case of Down's syndrome. The majority of Down's syndrome kids reach a mental age of anywhere between three and ten years old. Lisa never reached that. She never walked, couldn't feed herself, nothing–she literally had the mind of a newborn baby all her life.

When Lisa was born the doctors told me, "Don't take her home, she will never be all right, she will never live." But when she was two months old I went to the hospital and took her out. The doctors said, "You can't do this, she is going to die," and I said, "Well, then she will die in my arms, at home." I took her home and tried to take care of her, but her father and I broke up, and I couldn't afford the constant care of the doctors and nurses and everything. I became quite ill myself trying to look after her, and Nikki was getting totally ignored.

I managed to find a little private hospital just outside Scotts Valley, California, that took care of Down's syndrome sufferers. They wanted Lisa there, but to get her cared for, I had give up my legal right to her and make her a ward of the state of California. I signed away my daughter, and the people who ran the hospital told me to walk away and never look back. I asked why, and they said, "Because it will only rip you apart. Lisa doesn't know you. She will never be anything but what she is today, and you will just tear your life apart."

I wouldn't listen and I made a lot of financial sacrifices to go see her every week, but it got to the point where Nikki, who was now three, was feeling so neglected that he would just sit on the floor and rock. I had to make a choice–it was Lisa or him. So I stopped going to see Lisa and started spending more time with Nikki. Things with Nikki started improving then…for a while, at least.

Nikki should not feel guilty about any of that. He never had any control over what happened to her, nor did I.

There would have been no point in him going to see her because she wouldn't have known who he was, and when strangers came in, she got upset. For years, I thought I had done something terribly wrong to deserve all that happened to Lisa. Then eventually I realized she was a special gift from God.

CECI COMER: Whenever Mom talked about Lisa she was always soft-spoken and heartbroken, and you could tell it was excruciatingly painful. She never denied us information but she was hesitant about visits–I remember asking several times if we could go see Lisa and it made Mom cry. She stopped visiting because it would make Lisa go into fits and be upset and withdrawn for days, and Mom was under the impression that complete strangers would have the same effect–or worse.

8:45 p.m.

I've been thinking for a while, why do I always buy such pissy amounts of dope? I just use it all right away, then I have to wait for Jason to come around and see his stupid face every day. Why don't I buy in bulk and just see him every week?

I'm waiting for Jason now. He's coming over with 1 oz of Persian and a 2 oz bag of blow...I should have done this a long fucking time ago.

FEBRUARY 22ⁿᵈ 1987
Van Nuys, 5:30 a.m.

Tonight may have been the worst of my life–which really is saying something. After Jason left I started shooting up, and the insanity kicked in right away. I don't remember going to my closet, but I was there, freaking out, knowing the cops outside had followed Jason here and were outside the house coming in...

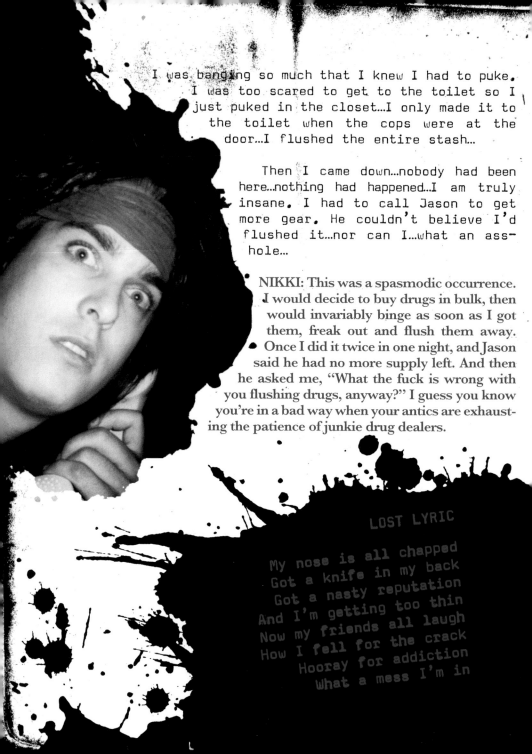

I was banging so much that I knew I had to puke. I was too scared to get to the toilet so I just puked in the closet...I only made it to the toilet when the cops were at the door...I flushed the entire stash...

Then I came down...nobody had been here...nothing had happened...I am truly insane. I had to call Jason to get more gear. He couldn't believe I'd flushed it...nor can I...what an asshole...

NIKKI: This was a spasmodic occurrence. I would decide to buy drugs in bulk, then would invariably binge as soon as I got them, freak out and flush them away. Once I did it twice in one night, and Jason said he had no more supply left. And then he asked me, "What the fuck is wrong with you flushing drugs, anyway?" I guess you know you're in a bad way when your antics are exhausting the patience of junkie drug dealers.

LOST LYRIC

My nose is all chapped
Got a knife in my back
Got a nasty reputation
And I'm getting too thin
Now my friends all laugh
How I fell for the crack
Hooray for addiction
What a mess I'm in

Van Nuys 11:30 p.m.

I felt hungover and strung out in rehearsal but Five Years Dead sounds badass and the album is gonna turn out OK. What does it say about me that I can write songs when I feel like I'm dying? I wonder what I would be writing if I were straight...

TOM ZUTAUT: Nikki was a pretty intense, driven individual, so when he first started dabbling, he seemed to be kicking back a little and finally able to enjoy the fruits of his hard work to get Mötley Crüe to the top. We didn't realize it was heroin at first–he just seemed a little dreamy, and nodded off on a few phone calls.

When I realized it was junk I voiced my concern to Nikki, and he assured me he was stopping and had it under control. When it didn't stop I mentioned it to the band's management, who told me they were dealing with it. Once I realized exactly how big his problem was, I was very worried about him–it seemed like the train was moving so fast and drawing in so much cash that nobody wanted to stop the cash flow by dealing with the abuse of sex, drugs and alcohol.

Van Nuys, 4:20 a.m.

Could I pay someone to kill my girlfriend?

Vanity came to rehearsal...Jesus, I try my best to look normal around the band and then she shows up like that. A year ago, I would have been ashamed at her cackling, throwing those fucking Prince dance moves and hanging off my neck while I was trying to play. Her eyes were fucked...she must have been freebasing all night. I told her to shut the fuck up and she got in my face and asked what I was gonna do.

What could I do? I just turned and walked out of rehearsal. Left her there with the guys in the band.

TOMMY LEE: There was something real crazy about Vanity. She would just turn up at a rehearsal and jump up on a road case and start dancing randomly, out of nowhere. We'd be trying to rehearse and Vanity would be doing this strange little burlesque show. When I first met her, she seemed cool, but then it all changed.

Nikki and I were freebasing a little back then. Vanity was into that as well, and Nikki claimed she got him started on it. But Sixx is a big boy—he can't blame Vanity; it was his doing. Back then Sixx was like a big spider's web, and he would bring others into his little fucking dark world. They would either a) never leave, or b) get so fucked up that they would panic, get out of there and leave him to it.

EVANGELIST DENISE MATTHEWS: Nikki and I had very different tastes in music, religion, food, movies—you name it. It made for a relationship built on chaos and confusion, like two people getting stuck in an avalanche that never stopped rolling downhill. Life was full of surprises, with too many bruises and not enough Band-Aids. The highs were too high and the lows were as deep as Hades, the home of the dead.

Was I happy? Well, happy is all that you know it to be when you're a kid parading, masquerading and raising yourself in this crooked, wicked world. Back then, it was like giving candy to a baby, or more like chocolate cake...all you can eat. Then the candles burn out and you burn out, and wake up wallowing on the plateau of stupidity.

I am happier today than I ever was. I am only unhappy when I am not paying attention and listening to God's voice for simple direction. The struggle is less because I quit fighting with God as much and now try to submit to his will (the Bible) faster. Life is a series of hits and misses and tests that never end, but the reward is when you win Heaven just because you gave it your best try.

True happiness comes when you obey the Scriptures. My morals and values have greatly changed and, because of my faith in Jesus, quite often pain and suffering breed growth. I dig doing what's right. I hate pain.

FEBRUARY 27th 1987
Van Nuys, 10:50 p.m.

Vanity left when Pete came over today. We have decided to have a party. I'm waiting for Jason now, and Pete has gone down to Sunset to pick up some girls from the strip clubs and bring them back here. It's never hard to persuade them.

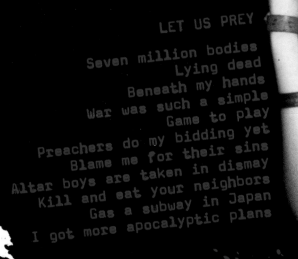

LET US PREY

Seven million bodies
Lying dead
Beneath my hands
War was such a simple
Game to play
Preachers do my bidding yet
Blame me for their sins
Altar boys are taken in dismay
Kill and eat your neighbors
Gas a subway in Japan
I got more apocalyptic plans

Before I
was so strung out, I
used to go out and pick
up girls and bring them
back myself. Now I'm too
reclusive to do it. Every time I go
out, somebody gets in my face and wants
something from me, and I just can't
handle it. It's not just the drugs,
it's the fame...it's overwhelming these
days to go anywhere. We're on the cover
of every magazine on the newsstand.

FEBRUARY 28TH, 1987
Van Nuys, 6:15 a.m.

Well, that was quite a night...until I brought it crashing to a halt as usual.

Pete came back around two with 20 girls and all hell broke loose. I was pretty drunk, and ended up fucking a girl in the bathroom while another girl banged on the door. Then when we were done, the second girl came in, got mad at me for screwing her friend, then fucked me as well. I'm pretty sure Pete fucked them both too. What about the other 17 or 18 girls? I can't keep track.

It was a cool night until about five, when the coke came out again. I was just gonna do a few lines, then suddenly I was wired and just wanted everyone out of my house. I couldn't bear them being here. So I told Pete to tell everyone to get the fuck out. I don't need anything but my drugs, my guitar and my journal.

TIM LUZZI: Nikki once showed me his heroin den in his closet. There must have been a hundred two-inch-by-two-inch pieces of torn aluminum foil covered in dark stains lying on the floor. He also took me in there once and shot up in front of me. He had the rig, the spoon, needle, cotton, flame, tie-off... that was wickedly sick. Nikki asked me to do it as well, but it wasn't my cup of tea.

LOST LYRICS:

Yuppies dressed up
as satanic clowns
Commit another suicide just
to please the crowds
And this anti-freeze is
how we shoot the breeze...
With this bottle and keys we'll
drive off in our disease...
Handsome dreams dressed up as a
scheme
And the reason for a gun is to
prey on the meek...
Last year's haggard housewife
scored a sedative as a lover
Sits on her kitchen floor and eats
from the same gun as her mother.
God bless the weak?

4:15 p.m.

I just had an outrageous memory
from last night. Right before I broke
out the blow and decided to end the
party, this big redhead girl I'd never
seen before dragged me into the bathroom
and gave me a blow job. She never said
a word until she was done, then she
said you'll never forget me, right?
I agreed, then I'd forgotten her 20
minutes later. I need to take it
easy for a few days...

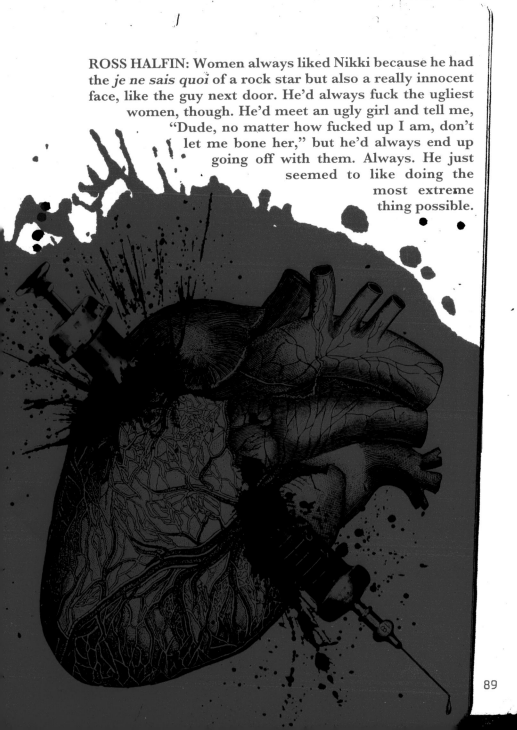

ROSS HALFIN: Women always liked Nikki because he had the *je ne sais quoi* of a rock star but also a really innocent face, like the guy next door. He'd always fuck the ugliest women, though. He'd meet an ugly girl and tell me, "Dude, no matter how fucked up I am, don't let me bone her," but he'd always end up going off with them. Always. He just seemed to like doing the most extreme thing possible.

MARCH 1987

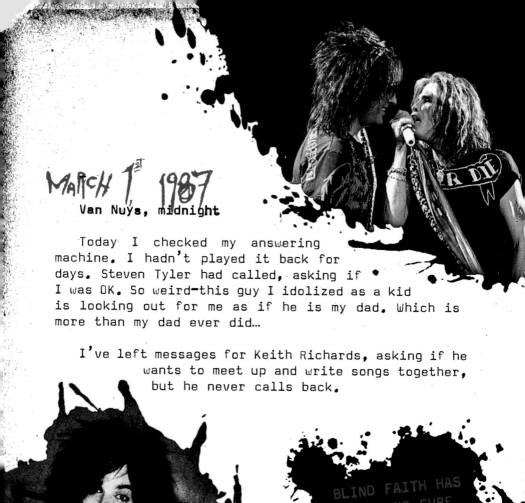

MARCH 1ST 1987
Van Nuys, midnight

Today I checked my answering
machine. I hadn't played it back for
days. Steven Tyler had called, asking if
I was OK. So weird—this guy I idolized as a kid
is looking out for me as if he is my dad. Which is
more than my dad ever did...

I've left messages for Keith Richards, asking if he
wants to meet up and write songs together,
but he never calls back.

BLIND FAITH HAS
NO CURE

    T-Bone came over after rehearsal. The usual routine...
chill out with a couple shots of Jack in front of MTV,
then I bring out the gear and we shoot up...why can Tommy
do the drugs better than me...why doesn't he get hooked?

    Tommy is the brother I never had. He has this energy
and positivity I just haven't got...I get off on that,
and I give him...what? Maybe a darkness and edginess he
doesn't have...and which in some twisted way he
admires...it freaks me out that Tommy has never mentioned
how I fucked up his wedding...I love him for that...

NIKKI: When Tommy had told me a year earlier that he
was to marry Heather Locklear, I'd replied, "Great,
dude! I'm so excited to be your best man!" Come to think
of it, he'd never actually *asked* me to be his best man.
Maybe I was jumping the gun a little there.

I was still with Nicole, and we checked into the Biltmore
Hotel in Santa Barbara for the wedding weekend. We had
decided to try to kick heroin again, so we took just
enough drugs to get us through the wedding. After that,
we were going cold turkey.

People were shocked by my appearance at the wedding.
Not only had I lost loads of weight and looked gaunt and
kind of yellow, but I also was not very lucid. I kept vanishing to the bathroom and I felt really uncomfortable
because I had simply forgotten how to socialize and be
around people. When it came to the best man's toast, I
had no idea what to say. Somebody told me to say, "May
all your ups and downs be between the sheets," and I
tried to, but I fucked it up. It all came out wrong. Heather
was from a very wealthy, conservative family, and they
must have been truly horrified at this junkie best man
swaying about at their daughter's wedding.

After the wedding, Nicole and I went back to the hotel, shot up our last bit of dope and threw away everything. We broke all the needles. We kicked at the Biltmore, and it was horrible. I was really sick, and the weirdest thing I can remember is that there was a *Little House on the Prairie* marathon on TV. Every time I came to from my kick before passing out again, it was on. I still can't watch that fucking show today: it brings back that memory too clearly. Years later I sat in an airport with a girl from the show and even that gave me the creeps. Not her–the thought of that damn show.

Eventually Nicole and I drove back from Santa Barbara to Van Nuys. For the first time in months, we were clean. When we got home we scoured the place, found all our dope and needles, and put them in the garbage can. They were out in the street for two or three days waiting for the garbage man to come.

Then on the third day I started getting a second stage of withdrawal. It's not as intense as the first stage, but it still hits you. Your brain tells you to just have a little: you'll be OK. So I said to Nicole, let's chip a little. She said, "I'd love to, but I

don't
want to
get strung
out again."
I said, "Me
neither, I can't
believe we're off
junk." So Nicole went
out to the trash, found the dope and the dirty needles,
and...that was it. We were strung out again like we had
never even stopped.

TOMMY LEE: When Nikki showed up at my wedding,
he was...transparent, dude. He wasn't white, or even
gray–I thought I could see straight through him. Nikki
couldn't have looked any worse if he'd been knocked
down by a Mac truck. He looked fucking terrible.

He was doing everything in his power to pull it together
and be a part of the day, but I'll never forget how bad
he looked. He was drinking everything in sight to try to
stay even, but you could tell he just wanted to get away
from everyone and get high: he had that look of panic
in his eyes. Then as soon as the wedding was over, he
was gone. I never gave him a hard time for it, but...best
man? He sure fucked that one up...

Midnight

Been playing a lot of open tunings on guitar. It's
interesting how I play with more rhythm. I think I'll
buy a piano and see where I go musically...I need
inspiration...I feel like I'm onto a different journey
sometimes. Metal is boring me. I'm being drawn to Tom
Waits, Rickie Lee Jones and Velvet Underground–I
guess it's the heroin. I wrote a song today called
Veins.

VEINS

I know I'm medicating
I know that you been praying
I know that God is waiting
Something tells me he can't save me

I know now I'm procrastinating
I crumble under cravings
I know that I'm novacating
God is laughing and he won't save me

Drug under the tracks again
I've lost another and it's my only friend

I miss my veins, I miss my everything
Collapsed and punctured have I gone insane?
I miss my veins, I cannot beat this thing
One more shot and I'll be just fine again

I miss my veins

MARCH 4TH 1987

Van Nuys, 11:30 p.m.

I'm finding it hard to find veins to inject into
lately. My arms are fucked and it's getting harder
and harder to find a good vein in my feet. Tonight
I sat in my closet injecting into my neck with a
shaving mirror.

Weird shit on the freeway today. Pete and I were driving down the 405 in my jeep, both in our leather pants and no shirts. Some redhead girl waved at us from her car and I asked Pete if he knew her. He said no, and I said I didn't either. Then she pulled alongside us and said, Hey Nikki, it's me! How you doing? I tried to play along with it but she looked furious, gave us the finger and drove off. This city is full of fucking insane chicks...

DANGER

Had wild dreams
Walkin' the streets
Hell, we were young
Never looked back
So we took our dreams
Ran like hell
Lived our youth
From the wishing well
Me and the boys
Made a pact
To live or die
No turning back
Scarred for life

MARCH 5TH 1987

Van Nuys, 11:40 a.m.

I just got woken up after one hour's sleep. When I answered the door some crazy woman started yelling at me and calling me an asshole...it took me a minute to recognize her as the freak who flipped us off on the freeway yesterday. I asked her what her fucking problem was, this made her go even more insane. It turns out she gave me a blow job at my party here last week and expected me to remember it.

Shit...this girl really doesn't know me too well.

NIKKI: When Mötley got big, we would fuck anybody and everybody, and usually did. Or rather, me, Tommy and Vince did: Mick always danced to his own tune. But I was always bored by girls and wanted them gone as soon as I was done. Sex to me was always about conquest. Girls were a form of entertainment, nothing more, and when heroin came along, it blew them away. The girls were like a crush: it was when I met heroin and freebase that I fell in love.

PRIMAL SCREAM

If ya wanna live life on your own terms
You gotta be willing to crash and burn

MARCH 6th 1987
Van Nuys, midnight

We were in the studio today and I heard Tommy playing a really cool lil piece of music on the piano in the other room. I ran in, sat down and joined him, and we wrote a gorgeous song that Barry fucking Manilow would be proud of.

I have the cassette with me now and I have a brilliant idea. I'm going to write this one for Nicole.

NIKKI: Nicole and I had finished after she came out of rehab clean in the middle of '86 and we discovered we'd had nothing in common except heroin. So no hard feelings, you might figure...but it wasn't that simple. I was convinced that Nicole had cheated on me while I was away touring *Theatre of Pain*. I was pretty sure she'd been fucking Jack Wagner, a pretty-boy actor from *General Hospital*. The fact that I must have cheated on her two hundred times during the same tour didn't even enter my mental equation. Jack Wagner had had a chart hit with a piece of slop called "You're All I Need." And in my twisted head it felt like the time for some serious revenge.

MARCH 7TH 1987
Van Nuys, 7:45 p.m.

We've finished You're All I Need, the song Tommy and me were working on yesterday. I guess it's a take on Taxi Driver in the sense that if you really love somebody, you would kill them so nobody else can have them, right?

The blade of my knife
Faced away from your heart
Those last few nights
It turned and sliced you apart
This love that I tell
Now feels lonely as hell
From this padded prison cell

So many times I said
You'd only be mine
I gave my blood and my tears
And loved you cyanide
When you took my lips
I took your breath
Sometimes love's better off dead

You're all I need, make you only mine
I loved you so I set you free
I had to take your life

You're all I need, you're all I need
And I loved you but you didn't love me
Laid out cold
Now we're both alone
But killing you helped me keep you home
I guess it was bad
'Cause love can be sad
But we finally made the news

Tied up smiling
I thought you were happy
Never opened your eyes
I thought you were napping
I got so much to learn
About love in this world
But we finally made the news

You're all I need, make you only mine
I loved you so, so I put you to sleep

I mean, I don't think I can ever really love anybody,
but murder is not out of the question...considering that
this fucking whore was fucking somebody else while I
was out on tour. How dare she cheat on me? So today
Vince sang the vocals, and I plan on hand-delivering
the cassette to Nicole tonight to see if she gets the
joke. If it IS a joke.

2 a.m.

Just got back from Nicole's house—it went like a dream. When I got there she looked kinda nervous, but I sat down with her and said, "We had a really nice relationship but we've had a hard time, so I've written a song for you about our time together." Nicole looked real emotional and reminded me that the last time we talked I told her I was gonna slit her throat. I'd forgotten that. I told her that I've changed.

I put the song on and Nicole looked touched as the beautiful piano kicked in. Then I sat there hiding my smile as the lyrics started to flow. When Vince sang, You're All I Need, I could see her thinking, That's Jack's song! Then when the song ended, she just looked at me and said, You're a fucking asshole, and you've always been an asshole. Nice!

I told her she could keep the cassette and as I walked out, I said, How's Jack doing, anyway? She said I had no idea what I was talking about. I said, Tell Jack to kiss his knees goodbye...

NIKKI: When I got home that night I phoned some local bikers and hired them. Their job was to wait in the bushes outside the TV studio and break Jack Wagner's kneecaps, then tell him Nikki Sixx sends his love.

WAYNE ISHAM: I shot Mötley's video for "You're All I Need," but at the time I never made the connection that Nikki saw the song as partly about him and Nicole. Nikki was so paranoid but his fears of her betraying him were totally unfounded. Nicole was a great girl with a real cool smile but Nikki took her down to the depths. Every time you saw her, you could see she was just being sucked into this vortex. It was too bad because she was a real nice person.

101

Taking the song to play it to Nicole is such a Nikki thing to do. He would enjoy doing it as well. He always had the Devil's wiseass smile in his eyes. I guess that's why he always wore sunglasses.

MARCH 8th 1987
Van Nuys, 3:50 p.m.

Nicole just phoned me screaming and crying and telling me that I was a sonofabitch for getting Jack's legs broken. I told her I had no idea what she was talking about, but it's fucking cool!

> NIKKI: This was a truly bizarre eventuality. Shortly after Nicole phoned, my contact called and apologized, saying they hadn't been able to get to Jack. I was baffled until it came on the local news that, by pure coincidence, Wagner had fallen over during filming that day and broken his knee on the soundstage! My head was so messed up, I thought it was divine retribution.

MARCH 9th 1987
Van Nuys, 11:30 p.m.

I did the stupidest fucking thing today...I still can't quite believe I did it. I called up Rick Nielsen to say hi. When he picked up the phone, I asked him to wait a minute then I went and drank a whole bottle of water, shot some blow, and puked down the Jacuzzi before I picked up the phone to talk to him. Rick had just waited the whole time. I must have sounded fucked 'cause he asked me if I was OK and if I was using. I said I hadn't touched drugs for months...

WHY DO I DO THESE THINGS? WHAT IS FUCKING WRONG WITH ME?

NIKKI: Rick Nielsen from Cheap Trick was an early hero of mine. I can't quite believe I was so fucked up that I phoned him, then made him wait while I shot up and puked before I talked to him. It's even harder to believe that I thought he wouldn't notice me behaving in this bizarre manner.

RICK NIELSEN: Nikki would sometimes call me at home and say he was having trouble. He'd call and say he was high and didn't want to be–or he'd tell me he was clean and I would know that he wasn't, because I would hear it in his voice. I'd tell him, "You can lie to your mom or your girlfriend or the priest, but don't lie to me!"

I used to tell him that he could tell me about anything–that he was doing drugs, or screwing a girl, or that his dick was going to fall off. A friend tells you the truth, that your breath stinks and you need a bath. An enemy tells you that you look great and you shouldn't change a thing.

I do remember one time Nikki calling, then going away from the phone for minutes. I figured he was just doing a line of blow. I had no idea about shooting up; I wasn't around that kind of stuff. Then he came back on the phone and could hardly talk, but he was telling me he hadn't done anything. It takes a fool to know a fool and, man, I heard a fool.

If Nikki called me when he was making no sense, I would say that I had to go, but he was often pretty lucid. I was flattered he wanted to talk to me, even if he was talking bullshit. Who else can a musician call? He calls his peers. He can't tell the other guys in the band he's in trouble because they'll tell the manager. Sometimes he'd call me all excited, saying he want-ed to get together and write, and I would say sure, when? Then he would get all vague. I'd tell him, be honest, try to do AA, take one day at a time...but he was pretty stubborn.

Before he was on junk, Nikki Sixx was a big teddy bear with a nice smile. He could barely play the bass, mind you, but that never stopped Gene Simmons. I wanted to help him but I guess ultimately you can only slay the dragon yourself. All that I could do was help him sharpen his sword if he needed me to.

MARCH 11TH, 1987
Van Nuys, midnight

I've been working on a little theory I call my hygiene maintenance theory. Basically, it's very simple...

1. Why take a shower if you're only going to get dirty again?
2. Why make your bed if you're only going to sleep in it again?
3. Why get sober if you're only going to get drunk again?

Showering is something you only have to do when the people around you can't stand the stink. The only reason to be sober is if you have to do something. When I've got a few days off at home, neither of those situations apply.

MARCH 12TH, 1987
Van Nuys, 3:10 a.m.

Tonight I realized something that terrified me. I was in my closet, worried that I could hear voices in the walls...then I went to lock all my doors at the security box and I realized that I only need to push a button to talk to West Tech.

Who is to say that they can't hear me whether I push the button or not? Who is to say they haven't got fucking secret cameras that can see me?

NIKKI: When I was high on cocaine, West Tech Security was the bane of my life and I was certainly the bane of theirs. They were a security company who had fitted all the alarms on my house and I also had a panic button that I could push to alert them in the case of intruders. When I was shooting or freebasing coke I invariably thought there were SWAT teams on the roof and storm troopers in the garden, and I often ended up phoning West Tech. Then when I got equally convinced that my security company was spying on me, it made our relationship very strained to say the least.

MARCH 13TH 1987
Van Nuys, 4:20 a.m.

Pete and me went down to the Cathouse tonight. I felt pretty cool. I wore my new tailored jacket for the first time, with the big Nazi armband on the arm. The Nazis may have been sick fucks but they sure looked cool. Riki showed us straight into the VIP bar and Pete and I hung out in a corner checking out the chicks.

I asked Riki to show me where the VIP bathroom was... he took me down there and I asked him if he had a bottle cap for some blow. Riki looked surprised but he got me a bottle cap and I pulled my baggy from my boot and shot up in the toilet. When I came out of the stall Riki's eyes were wide open. He looked disgusted...fuck, he'll get over it.

MARCH 15th 1987

Van Nuys, 2:30 a.m.

It's getting to the point where life only makes sense to me when I'm here, in my closet.

People don't make sense to me...I have no comfort zone. I don't know how to live. I feel like an alien.

When people talk to me, I can't hear them. When I go places, I feel alone. I see messages in the TV shows...I hear things other people don't hear...I decipher what they say wrong...

Am I insane? Sometimes it seems like suicide is the only solution.

TOMMY LEE:
I only realized how uncomfortable Sixx was in his own skin when I saw him sober. If he was sober, he would not leave his house. He was so antisocial that he couldn't be around people for more than two minutes. A sober Nikki Sixx would never enter a room full of strangers—no fucking chance. I would look at him and see his face scrunch up, and I could see he was

sweating and thinking, I've got to get out of here; I don't know how to act or what to say. I could see it all over him, and I'd predict to myself, Just watch, Sixx will be out of here in one minute! When he was high, he was fine with everybody, but as soon as he sobered up, he had major issues about being around people.

MARCH 16TH 1987

Van Nuys, 7:35 p.m.

Having no needles left when you're jonesing is the worst thing in the world. Last night I was shooting up with my last syringe and it broke. The needle snapped right in two. I was dying for the fix so I was just trying to cram the broken stub into my fucking vein… gouging and ripping at my skin trying to force it in. The blood was spurting all over the closet and I was just slamming the drugs any place under my skin, praying they would take the pain away. Thank God that they did.

DOC McGHEE: By this stage, Nikki wasn't taking heroin to get high—he was taking it to try to stay normal. That's the way it is with junkies after a while: they use it in order to not get sick. It takes away the withdrawal symptoms, the aches and the pains, and it's clear to me now that Nikki was taking heroin to stay out of the pain that he was in every day of his life.

MARCH 17TH 1987

Van Nuys, 3:40 a.m.

I found myself thinking about Lita today… we were pretty cool together…

Maybe if I'd met her later in life we'd have worked out, but I wasn't ready for settling down back then.

But we had some good times. When I met her just last December, I could see she was shocked at the state I was in. Maybe I was too, but she never said anything. For some reason, people hardly ever do.

They can all see how strung out I am—why don't they fucking say something?

NIKKI: I'd met Lita Ford in 1982 at the Troubadour in Los Angeles. She'd walked up and introduced herself by putting half a quaalude on my tongue, and in a matter of days we were living together. But back then I was in full-on party animal mode, and after Mötley finished the *Shout at the Devil* tour, I moved out from her place to live with Robbin Crosby from Ratt.

We met up again just before Christmas '86 when I wrote a song, "Falling In and Out of Love," to go on her album, and she was horrified at my condition. I was waif-thin, out of my mind, doing drugs non-stop, snorting off the piano as we were trying to write. I'd taken things much further than she'd ever dreamed, and she felt she didn't know me anymore. Lita liked to party, sure, but I had become a full-blown addict.

MARCH 19TH 1987
Van Nuys, 1:15 a.m.

I just took a shit and realized yet
again that I haven't bought
toilet paper in weeks...

ODE TO MOM

I woke to the sound of screaming in my head
There was a dead body laying next to me in bed
A knife had so neatly cut out her heart
Ripped and tore and shredded it apart
I hadn't had a drink, hadn't left the house
So I was scared half to death,
trying to figure this out
I tried to scream, but my words came out low
I was drowning in confusion, panic without hope
Then the sound, a blessing I swear
My alarm going off, waking me from fear
I opened my eyes, a nightmare I gasped
Then I realized I was holding
a knife in my grasp
I get out of bed, following a trail of blood
There lies mother, no heart
But looking good.

MARCH 22nd 1987

Van Nuys, 11:30 a.m.

Last night it happened again.

I remember going into my closet and pulling out my Dom Perignon box. I love it when that box is full. Some might see it as opening a casket and peering at death, but to me it's like seeing a hole in the sky with a ray of light from God coming in. Whenever I open that box I know I'm gonna feel good in just a matter of seconds...

Then I shot up the coke, into my neck, my leg, my arm or even my cock...and then it started. I knew that West Tech was listening in on me, that they could hear my heart beating, that they had cameras spying on me. I stood with my ear to the security box, not daring to breathe, and I was terrified. Did they have police coming to get me, or guys with straitjackets? They know that I'm insane, right?

Then I realized I was wrong... West Tech isn't my enemy—they are the ones who can save me from the people outside, trying to get in...so I pushed the panic button. Then I didn't know—had I pushed it? Or did I just *think* I'd done it?

So there I was...naked, strung out, my shotgun loaded, knowing people were about to break into the house...were they coming to save me, or to get me? So I quickly flushed my drugs down the toilet and waited for what was about to happen. My biggest decision was this...do I go quietly, or shoot to defend myself?

Now I wake up to discover it was just another night of insanity. I didn't press any button and nothing happened...except I flushed all my fucking drugs down the toilet again.

Noon

I hate mornings like today, when I wake up or come down...whichever comes first...and I have these memories of things that I've done that feel like they were on TV or I read them in a book. It's getting harder and harder to know what's real.

MARCH 23rd 1987
Van Nuys, midnight

Well, today we finally wrapped up the Girls album. All in all I think it turned out pretty good...of course you always say that when it's your newest album, don't you?

We're leaving for New York tomorrow to master the record. Mastering always brings out all the life and sparkle...so I will reserve judgment until the master to decide whether this is a great Mötley Crüe record or just a good Mötley Crüe record. But the fact that we've managed to finish a record is amazing to me.

NIKKI: Tommy and I flew out first class to New York to master the album. Our engineer and mixer, Duane Baron and Pete Purdul, weren't flying out until the next day. So what did Tommy and I do in NYC with a night off to ourselves? We went out to the sickest underground dance club we could find. All was well as far as I was concerned–I was a few thousand miles away from my junk and our album was done. But as usual the devil wears many masks…he kept on and on in my ear about how we should get some junk…finally I set out to find some, only to come back with pockets full of cocaine. Thank God–but, of course, none of us slept before mastering the album.

MARCH 31ST 1987
Van Nuys, 9:15 p.m.

Just got back from mastering the album. I forgot to take you diary, but if I had, I doubt I'd have written anything in you. They say New York is the city that never sleeps. I guess if we did nothing else, we fucking proved that one…I need my bed…

113

APRIL 1ST, 1987

Van Nuys, 6:40 p.m.

I just had a surprise visitor. It was the last
thing I expected. Randy Rand turned up at my door
out of the blue…I hadn't seen him in months. When
I opened the door his jaw literally fell open in
shock, like he had seen a ghost. He told me that
I'd lost 50 lbs since he'd last seen me. I'm
pleased about this, but Randy didn't seem to see it
as a good thing. Then when I invited him in, he
shook his head and said he had to go…does my illness hang off me like a fucking smell?

I'm waiting for T-Bone to come over.

**NIKKI: Randy Rand was in the band Autograph, who
had supported us for a few dates on the *Theatre of Pain*
tour. I once stole his bass head from a rehearsal room in
Hollywood because it sounded better than mine. He is a
great guy…he never did bust my chops about it, still to
this day…**

APRIL 2ND, 1987

Van Nuys, midnight

I went fishing today with
Tommy and Duane Baron.
We did coke all night
until it was time to
leave for the lake. We
sailed out then came back in
for more beers when Doc McGhee came
to meet us. We were out on the lake
playing the mastered *Girls* album over
and over on Tommy's little blaster.

Doc told us that Jon Bon Jovi thinks we've written the greatest song of our career. I asked him which one and he said You're All I Need. I asked if Jon had ever listened to the lyrics and Doc said, Why, what's it about? I snickered and told him, and Doc told me that I'm an asshole and a sick fuck...fair comment, I guess.

NIKKI: Tommy and I were so high on coke that night that in our minds the tent was flying like a magic carpet ride. We actually believed we were flying through the air around the lake in the tent. I remember Tommy telling me to stare at him and not move. With my hair all in tangles and the shadows from the lantern dancing across my face he kept imagining I looked like this wicked witch. He was getting so into it, I remember at one point thinking, OK, who's more insane here? Me for sitting here for hours motionless, or Tommy for having me sit here so he can hallucinate? I don't think we caught any fish on that trip but we sure had one hell of a magic carpet ride...

TOMMY LEE: Here's a "There Goes the Neighborhood" memory! Readers, picture this—a packed family campground with kids, bikes, fishing poles, water skis, campfires, etc. Then, just when you think it's safe… here comes the badass black super-stretch limo from hell! It's not something you normally see at any campground you go to, but then again you never went camping with me and Nikki! I know you are thinking: God, these dudes are so spoiled and that the limo is there to take them home right?? NOT! The cocaine has been delivered by limousine! Imagine us crawling out of our dark tent into the daylight to pick up more blow—not a good look! That poor limo driver ended up making a few more round trips up there to keep our magic carpet ride afloat.

APRIL 4ᵗᵈ 1987
Van Nuys, 2:20 a.m.

I think things are looking up. Pete and me have now got porn stars doing our drug runs for us…Lois came over earlier. She's an interesting character. She came in and we had a few beers and then she said she wanted to show us her new video…we said sure. So she walks over with the VHS tape, sticks it in the machine and voila! It was eight black guys coming all over her face. Even I was shocked, but Lois is proud of it…says she thinks it's some kind of world record…

More importantly Lois has agreed to go down to Watts for us to score some loads. Let's just say it's not the best place for a tattooed white kid to go to score. But after seeing her video, maybe Lois has a special relationship with the dealer down there. Hey, practice makes perfect…

These pills are my new fave drug. I love them. You can't even fucking move on them, completely comatose! They're like heroin on steroids. I can't wait…

NIKKI: Loads were a combo of two different kinds of pills. You took three of one kind and two of the other and literally in ten minutes you were so high you couldn't even stand up. We had a very scientific approach to mixing it with blow to somehow even out the effect enough to at least somehow function. When I was a teenager, we used to take elephant tranquilizers. The effects were similar.

3:30 p.m.

After Lois got back with the loads last night, things got kind of...warped...

When she came back she had some other girl with her. I recognized her from some porn movies Pete had. I don't remember what her name was ...did I even know it? but she left a few minutes ago. Anyway, after I took a second dose, and not enough cocaine to bring me out of my stupor, this girl decided she was going to spend the night with me...who was I to argue?

The only problem we had was that my dick didn't seem to be aware that she was there. She kept asking me what was wrong, and I was so out of it that I thought she meant what was wrong with the world, so I started talking about global poverty and shit. I'm not surprised she left...I suspect she won't be coming back.

APRIL 5th, 1987
Van Nuys, 1:45 a.m.

Went to a bookstore today and bought some cool books on performance art. Also got a book my grandmother sent me to read when I was 17, called Autobiography of a Yogi.

APRIL 6th, 1987
Van Nuys, 2:40 a.m.

Today I was thinking about coming back from Tommy's wedding last year and finding that letter from Chuck Shapiro telling me that I would go bankrupt if I carried on getting wasted at the rate that I was...fuck, that I still AM. The funny thing is, even if I was broke, and kicked out of the band, and all I had was a room like this closet, and enough gear to stay under the warm blanket...forget Mötley and the fans, forget the music even. I think I could be happy...I think.

NIKKI: Chuck Shapiro was the band's accountant. On the day in '86 that Nicole and I got back from Tommy's wedding, Chuck left me a hand-delivered note. It read,

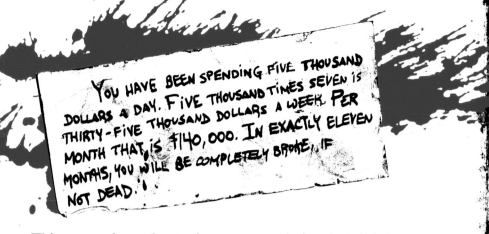

You have been spending five thousand dollars a day. Five thousand times seven is thirty-five thousand dollars a week. Per month that is $140,000. In exactly eleven months, you will be completely broke, if not dead.

This was quite a chastening note, so obviously I did the only thing that I could in the circumstances. I ignored it completely.

Steven Tyler told me once he didn't think he would ever be off heroin. At this point in my life, I remember thinking the same thing. The feeling of completely giving into your demons is hopeless, but when you can't climb your way out of such a hole, you tend to crouch down and call it home.

APRIL 7ᵀᴴ 1987

Van Nuys, 2:30 a.m.

Jason is coming over with some real pure china white rather than the usual Persian...Persian is OK but you have that whole routine with lemons and the extra cotton. China cooks up clean and dissolves so much easier, and when I put it in a syringe with some coke...man, that's the fast track to heaven.

The thing about china is it looks like coke and you can snort it easy. Sure, you can snort Persian, but it kinda stinks like dirt and it's a dead giveaway snorting anything brown. So nobody knows you're snorting heroin. They assume it's something harmless (Ha!) like coke.

I hope he doesn't bring his damn girlfriend. She sometimes will be talking as I nod off and when I come to she's still talking. It's usually about her so I can jump in right where I was before...not caring.

NIKKI: There were such different levels of addiction during this year. Sometimes I felt I had it under control and I was just having fun. Unfortunately the fun never lasted. If you're gonna play with the dragon, you're eventually gonna get burned.

BOB MICHAELS: Sometimes Nikki would take heroin really openly around me and ask me to take it with him. At other times he was real sneaky. He would go to the bathroom, shoot up, puke, then walk back out and sit by me to watch a movie. The whole thing would take ninety seconds and I would have no idea he had done it. Nikki was a very good actor.

APRIL 8th, 1987

Van Nuys, 11 p.m.

So here I sit. Alone again. Needle in my arm. Playing the fucking victim yet again—or is it the martyr?

As much as I love my band, I also hate them, because they are with people that love them. I don't understand why, as big as my heart is, I'm alone.

Maybe I just choose to be this way?

Maybe I don't have a choice?

Maybe I don't know?

Maybe I'm just asking myself questions to hear myself talk?

3 a.m.

How could my parents treat me the way they did?

How could my father just vanish, and not care about the son that he brought onto the Earth?

How could my mother love me, or say she loves me, then send me away for months and years at a time every time she got herself some new fucking boyfriend?

I don't have a mother...I don't have a father...I don't have a friend. And they made me the way I am. They made me like this.

> BOB TIMMONS: In my opinion, Nikki Sixx was suffering from depression during the time of his addiction. There was a lot of sadness: he told me many times that he felt people wanted to be around him only because he was famous, not because of who he was. Addictions are just symptoms of underlying issues, and in my view Nikki self-medicated the emotional pain of his childhood, and being away from his mother a lot, through drug use. What did he want? Ultimately he wanted to be able to create love for himself as a person.

THE TROUBLE WITH ASKING QUESTIONS IS YOU SOMETIMES GET ANSWERS YOU DON'T WANNA HEAR.

11 p.m.

Jesus, it's such a hassle to go out nowadays. I can't walk down the street or go to the store without being surrounded by fans, wanting to talk, or wanting my autograph, or to come home with me. I mean, I love our fans, but fuck...

I'm gonna go back to the bookstore 'cause I think I might have depression. Maybe something there can help me? I can't control my moods. I feel like I'm coming apart at the seams...even when I'm not on drugs. If only they knew.

It seems I'm always falling apart, always falling apart at the seams...

APRIL 10, 1987

Van Nuys, 5 a.m.

I pushed the panic button again tonight. It wasn't my fault. Every time I dared to peer out of my closet, I could see faces at the window and I heard voices at the door. It's probably 50 feet from the closet to the security box but it took me an hour of shaking to run there. I felt like I had to run the length of a football field.

Then when West Tech arrived I wouldn't let them in...I just kept shouting at them through the door to get away from my fucking house or I would shoot them. Eventually they went away. Thank God I had a little junk to bring me down.

DOUG THALER: It was about this time that I called Nikki at home one day. He could never wait to get off the phone, and on this particular occasion, he told me after about a minute, "Well, I've got to go now." I asked him why, and he said, "Doug, there are Mexicans carrying guns climbing over my fence."

3:15 p.m.

Doc McGhee just phoned. He says he had a call from West Tech security about last night. Their guy claimed that when he showed up here I was naked and waving a shotgun at him, and accusing him of bugging my house. Seems they're worried about their "personal safety" and threatening to cancel our contract. Luckily Doc talked them down and smoothed things over.

That's what a good manager is for, right?

DOC McGHEE: Nikki was always seeing Mexicans and midgets running around his fucking house. His blow paranoia was totally out of control. I would get calls from West Tech saying he had set all his alarms off and was in the house refusing to answer the door. Or the police department would call me because Nikki's neighbor had phoned them to report that Nikki was crawling around in his garden in the middle of the night with a shotgun. It would be bad enough if it happened once, but this shit was going on at least twice a week.

APRIL 12th, 1987

Van Nuys, 3:15 a.m.

Went around strip bars with T-Bone and Wayne to scout out locations for the Girls Girls Girls video. I think this one is gonna be good. Wayne gets where we come from…it's just a shame that the bastard steals our ideas for Bon fucking Jovi…

WAYNE ISHAM: I shot a lot of videos with Mötley but I first met them way before I was a director, when I was stage manager at the A&M soundstage in LA. They came in to film the "Shout at the Devil" video. I had a little office next to the dressing room, and could hear them complaining to each other that they needed a drink before they started shooting. I told them I had some Jack, and they all came stomping into my office with their huge hair and platform boots and drank it all.

My first Mötley video was "Smokin' in the Boys' Room" right at the start of my career. I met Nikki and Tommy and talked through the shoot the night before, then they said, "OK dude, let's go out!" I was saying, "No, no, we have to work tomorrow," and Nikki said, "Are you some sort of pussy?" They had this real, um, enthusiasm for life.

We all partied so hard back then, drank so hard and did so much blow, I guess we felt indestructible. Nikki never seemed worse than anyone else, although when we made the "Home Sweet Home" video there were a couple of times he had to be carried on and off the set for his close-ups. That was the first time I thought, Are you rocking this, or is it rocking you?

Nikki was a real Jekyll and Hyde character. One minute he would be coherent, friendly and articulate, the next he'd be out of it and a real sardonic wiseass and insulting motherfucker. He had this positive energy, then he'd just turn the page and be a real asshole–and there was a real meanness in the way he chastised me.

Nikki hated Bon Jovi, and he was always busting my balls and calling me a traitor for working with Jon. He accused me of selling out by making Bon Jovi videos and told me I was ripping off Mötley's style–well, pardon me, but I thought that was a universal style, not just

Mötley's! He'd always be in my face, saying "Fuck you," and one day he grabbed me and sucker-punched me real hard. You kind of got used to it.

NIKKI: I always dug Jon—I just hated his band's music. It was the opposite of everything I loved and believed in. I would bust his band's chops in the press then we would sit down over dinner and he'd say, "Thanks" and we'd both laugh. I think he liked to be around a true rock 'n' roll asshole who didn't give a fuck about anything.

When they first got signed to Doc and we were both in Europe, Jon and I went to a brothel together in Germany. We were in this room with two twin beds and we each had a girl. We were both drunk off our asses and I looked up above my head and there was this Mick Jagger poster and the same one above Jon's bed.

The girls were doing their job but Jon wouldn't stop telling jokes in his New Jersey accent and I couldn't get it up. Finally I said, "Bro, can you stop talking?" He said OK and kept on rambling. To say I didn't get my money's worth would be an understatement unless I was paying Jon Bon Jovi to tell me jokes, in which case I got a pretty good deal.

APRIL 13th, 1987
Van Nuys, 4:20 a.m.

Shot the video for Girls tonight. We had a blast. I even brought me a little souvenir home...dunno what her name is. Did me good to get out tonight.

WAYNE ISHAM: When Mötley told me the concept behind "Girls Girls Girls" was strip clubs, I naturally did some meticulous multiple-night research to discover which establishment was the most appropriate. We wanted to use the Body Shop but that was all-nude and didn't serve alcohol, so we ended up with a place called the Seventh Veil. Nikki and Tommy came with me one night–I remember us heading from club to club with a load of strippers in tow.

We were in the same mind-set on the video–we just all kept saying to each other, "Can you *believe* they are paying us for doing this? We should be paying them!" This was the heart of Mötley–they were fun guys, and I don't think the video was exploiting women. It was more a celebration of them, like a burlesque thing. But we got censored a lot by MTV because it was seen as scandalous back then.

By the time we finished filming in the Seventh Veil, none of us were functioning properly. We left the club in a few cars to go to my studio nearby to film inserts. Tommy was in my car with me, and I suggested we should stop off at a Mexican restaurant on the way for a couple of secret shooters. When we got in there, Sixx was already in the bar, doing a line of shooters. He just looked at us and said, "What are *you* guys doing here?"

When I look at the video now, Nikki's eyes have that droop...there's a real buzz going on. Look at the part where he gives the camera the finger...I think it's fair to say that he is coasting there. But I can't claim I noticed at the time. It's like Hillel Slovak from the Chili Peppers—he was a fun guy, and the first time I noticed that something was at all wrong was when he went and died.

APRIL 16ᵀᴴ 1987
Van Nuys, noon

I'm sorry I haven't written for a few days but things have been kind of crazy. You know how it can go sometimes.

Vanity showed up unannounced a few days ago. It's so fucked with her...I don't see her for weeks, then suddenly she appears and we don't leave each other's side for...how long was it this time? Four days? Five? It can't be healthy...but then I guess me and Vanity have never exactly been healthy.

So she turned up with this huge baggy of coke, just like she always does, and we've been living in a blizzard for the last couple of days. But somehow I never go quite as insane when Vanity is with me. Maybe I hate her too much to let her ever see me at my most wasted and vulnerable.

I never shoot dope or go to my closet with Vanity but it still gets fucking crazy. Yesterday we were lying on the bed and I could hear voices...people moving about the house. I started shouting, then fired my .357 through the door at them. Of course there was nobody there. It was the radio, and I shot a hollow point clean through my new speakers I bought off Bob Michaels...fuck.

She just left and as she went she said the most fucked up thing I've ever heard. She said we were soul mates and asked me to marry her…I don't know how I kept a straight face, so I said something equally stupid…I said yes. I couldn't face her going crazy and starting another argument, and what does it matter what I say? My funeral will come before the wedding.

BOB MICHAELS: Nikki called me one night when he'd shot a bullet through his bedroom door and into a JBL speaker he had bought from me. He was hallucinating that people were trying to break in and the police were there, and he and Vanity had barricaded themselves in the master bedroom in the middle of the night. He called me again the next day and they were still barricaded in there.

EVANGELIST DENISE MATTHEWS: My help could only come from God. None of my relationships, including with Nikki, were capable of finding any kind of love or happiness because I would never look at the root of my problem, which undoubtedly was me. I was very messed up and it was time to change or die.

We paint the outside of our bodies beautiful but the inside is like dead men's bones. The hurt topples on top of itself until our hurt gets so big and ugly, growing like a cancer worm, webbing around the walls of our heart, which ultimately turns cold and callous and dull of love. We mistake lust for love and pop more pills, slam more drugs, drink ourselves silly or end us, as I did, scraping the inside of a pipe just to hit the resin and flush life down a toilet.

Personally, I hated every second of being alive in this collapsible body. I wanted a new body inside. I wanted to remove my mind altogether–especially the part that hurt. Jesus did that for me.

LOST LYRIC
VAMPERILLA

Can't say I'm happy
Can't say I'm sad
But I can sigh in relief
That I don't have that
Black-skinned bitch
Drawing her nails across my grief

Just do me a favor
Before you draw the razor
Next time across your wrists
Tell me again
I'm your white boy flavor
And how we will live in bliss
A little hidden sanctuary
Only seen in this Hollywood tabloid hell
Living in loyal matrimony
I guess didn't mean loyal to me
Oh well

Vamperilla
Now you might as well go fuck yourselves
Everybody else has for sure

I guess you had to lose
So the rest of us could win
Your only fame and fortune has left you
And he's holding this paper and pen.

Slash came over earlier...I haven't told him this, but last year Tom Zutaut asked me if I would produce the Guns album. I just turned him down flat. I was way too strung out to take it on. It was all I could do then to focus on Mötley and staying alive...

It's a good thing that I didn't do it. I know I could produce a great album for them but not while I'm on drugs...I'm too fucked up even for those guys.

NIKKI: Tom Zutaut had told me I was being considered to produce *Appetite for Destruction* for Guns N' Roses. I went to see them play at the Roxy, but I didn't think they were all that great. The truth is that I was so out of it that I had no idea who was any good and who wasn't. Fuck, at the time the most I would have been able to do as producer would have been pressing PLAY on the tape machine.

TOM ZUTAUT: I was like a dog with a bone trying to get Nikki to produce Guns because I thought they were the next-generation Mötley, but more rooted in the Sex Pistols and Zeppelin than Mötley's New York Dolls-meets-Kiss. In the same way that Nikki understood the role of each of the members of Mötley, I thought he might be able to do the same for Slash, Axl, Izzy, Duff and Steven. I hoped G N' R might learn something from Nikki since he had crawled from the bottom of the dirtiest street in Hollywood (which was also their birthing place) to the top. But Nikki was in his strung out narcissistic asshole days and he kept blowing me off and not even watching the video of G N' R that I had sent him.

Do I think he would have done a good job of producing the album? Given the state he was in, probably not.

SLASH: That's funny…I never knew about any of this. It is true that Zutaut was desperate to find somebody to produce *Appetite for Destruction* who would be able to deal with us. I remember that Paul Stanley from Kiss came down at one point, but we were way too much for him.

APRIL 19, 1987
Van Nuys, 4:50 p.m.

I realized something yesterday that when I'm high on coke, only to come down and realize again that I was on the fringes of psychosis, I'm starting to feel a friendship with those voices. I actually look forward to hearing them as I'm tying off. Ah yes, my friends the demons…

I need to get out. I've arranged to meet Andy McCoy at a club tonight.

APRIL 20, 1987
Van Nuys, 4 a.m.

Well that was a fucking disaster of a night.

I met Andy at the club and he was with a lot of other people. I felt uncomfortable and awkward from the start so after about half an hour I was saying to Andy, come on let's go, let's get out of here. Everybody around him was freaking out because Andy is clean now and they know I'm not, and he's always on the verge of getting strung out again. But I didn't care about that, or about anything…I just wanted to get back here.

I brought Andy home and showed him my closet. I got all my shit out and said, Come on, let's get high. He just stood there in all his gypsy clothes, and told me, You've got a habit! You're strung out. I tried to say it wasn't much but this dude has seen me die once, he knows the truth. Then he left.

One by one my friends are abandoning me.

APRIL 21, 1987
Van Nuys, 9:30 p.m.

Pete just called to see what I was doing...What does he think I'm going to be doing? The usual...walking around this mausoleum, waiting for Jason, thinking about shooting up, hating the security box, going quietly insane...

Pete was calling from a strip club. He's going to come over with some girls. It might be nice to make a few new friends. I just called Slash and Steven as well.

APRIL 22, 1987
Van Nuys, 1 p.m.

I woke up this morning and the house is littered with bottles and empty bindles and cigarette ashes...it's a disaster zone. There are people lying around, some naked, some partially naked...I walked into the bathroom to find Steven Adler fucking that girl we like to call Slave...and Slash pissed in the spare bed in his sleep. It's at times like this that I wish all these people would go away...

There must be something wrong in my blood sugar or my chemical DNA, because I can go from being completely the happiest guy in the world to being the most pissed off, angry motherfucker in no time at all. Last night I could think of nothing I would rather do than this. Now I hate it...

I hate it...

I hate it.

SLASH: Man, I remember that party...there was *so* much blow and whisky. I fucked a lot of girls, and the next morning I woke up in Nikki's spare bedroom with some chicks. I was hungover, my shit was strewn all over the place, and I had to be in the recording studio in twenty minutes. Fuck knows how I got there, but I did.

I can't deny it–I used to get so drunk that I wet the bed. Nikki's place wasn't the worst time. I remember once waking up in a hotel lobby in Canada. I was lying on a couch and I'd pissed myself. Then I found that not only was it not the hotel I was staying in but I had no idea where my hotel was or what it was called. I had to walk around in the freezing cold for hours. The wet pants didn't help.

APRIL 24ᵀᴴ 1987
Van Nuys, 1:40 a.m.

I feel like a rat on a wheel. At first I embraced
this, then I wanted to get off, but it's like somebody
is turning it faster and faster. I fall and it throws
me around and I just can't stop...

We have some time off, so what are we doing? Vince
is cruising around the Caribbean and singing guest
spots with Bon Jovi. Tommy is playing golf and riding
his dirt bike. Mick is content to buy guns and hope
for World War III...and Sixx? I'm losing my mind trapped
in this tomb...

APRIL 25ᵀᴴ 1987
Van Nuys, 10:10 a.m.

This is how low it gets...at 3 this morning I was
crouched naked in my closet thinking the world was
about to burst through my door. I peered out the closet
and saw myself in my mirror. I looked like an
Auschwitz victim...a wild animal.

I was hunched trying to find a vein so I could
inject into my dick. Then the dope went in my dick and
I thought I looked fucking fantastic. I can't keep
doing this, but I can't stop.

26 and I've never even lived
I've been too busy slow-dancing with death
Maybe a bullet to my head
will make somebody love me
Maybe a bullet in my head
would make somebody care.

APRIL 27, 1987

Van Nuys, 10:30 p.m.

I sat behind my bed last night with my grandfather's double-barreled shotgun. I had it aimed at the door, and I knew people were coming in. I can't bear all these windows being open to the street so everybody can see in. Today I called a shutter company and tomorrow they are coming to fit heavy wooden shutters on every window.

I'm thinking about going to rehab, but I have too much to do right now.

APRIL 28, 1987

Van Nuys, 11:40 a.m.

This morning I woke up with my shotgun in bed with me. The girls have stopped coming around, and now I'm sleeping with a gun. Then I remembered putting the gun in my mouth last night and considering pulling the trigger just to stop the insanity...I want to shut my head down and make it stop.

Somehow I've gone from a person who laughs at people considering suicide to a person who is considering suicide himself...some fucking progress...

Midnight

The new shutters are fucking cool.

BRYN BRIDENTHAL: I was Mötley Crüe's PR for many years–I first met them the day they signed their record contract with Elektra. I could see immediately that there was a special light on in Nikki's eyes. He knew where they were going: he had the whole idea, every album fleshed out in his head. Tommy was just a big cocker spaniel, Mick was real quiet and as for Vince...well, let's just say that Nikki Sixx *was* the brains of Mötley Crüe. I'm sure he still is.

One of the early things Nikki used to do was set himself on fire during interviews. I remember he did it in Mötley's first ever TV appearance. I was always terrified the flames would ignite his hair spray and he'd totally go up, but Nikki never seemed bothered by that: he thought he was invincible.

Nikki was a brat and he was very smart, but he had a great big hole inside. Money didn't fill it, nor did success or power: what he really wanted was respect for his songwriting. But I spent so much time with him, and I had no idea he was doing all the dark stuff he was. When he was bad, he was very, very bad, but I never thought he was doing any more drugs than everybody else was back then.

At the time, I didn't know much about junkies. Since then I've worked with Nirvana and Courtney Love, so I'm rather better informed. But the '80s were the days that I'd regularly go into a record label executive's office and find white powder all over his desk. Heroin seemed like just one more temptation–no better and no worse than the others.

Nikki Sixx never struck me as dysfunctional. He had so much drive and energy and certainly wasn't drooling or living in the gutter. He hid everything so well: he can dance fast, that one. I guess junkies can just be so cunning.

APRIL 29TH, 1987

Van Nuys, midnight

For reasons unknown to me I believe I am not meant to live much longer. I am dying a slow, unhappy death shrouded in confusion and questions. I am confused as to how I have become the drugs and the drugs have become me...we live together in complete harmony.

What was once a question, an inquisitive interest, a curiosity even, has finally answered itself. It's a death wish I cannot will away. I cannot or will not escape this prison until I have completed this journey. It ends as it began, with me alone. Like birth, death is a solitary experience.

Like Hemingway said, the only thing that could spoil a day was people. I am the person who has spoiled my life...

I have lost all track of time in here.

APRIL 30TH 1987

Van Nuys, 5:10 a.m.

When Jason left last night and closed the door, I had the feeling he was closing the door on a crypt. It's so fucking dark in here...I feel like a ghost. So I got a hammer and ran around the house tearing the shutters from the windows and throwing them into the yard...they were making me feel like I was in a cage.

I'm not doing any drugs when I wake up today.

HE ASKED ME TO GET ON MY KNEES AND PRAY TO GOD TO LOSE THIS OBSESSION WITH DRUGS.

MAY 1ST 1987

Van Nuys, 3 a.m.

Today I did something that I never thought I'd do...I called Bob Timmons and asked him to help me. Bob came over and I told him I just can't stop bingeing on cocaine and heroin. I think the blow speeds up my heroin addiction ten times. Bob agreed and said he knew how strung out I am. He asked me to get on my knees and pray to God to lose this obsession with drugs...I wouldn't do it. Fuck that! I won't get on my knees. Bob said he's got on his knees with guys a lot tougher than me, like the president of the Hells Angels, but he can forget it.

BOB TIMMONS: Part of the twelve-step program for curing addiction is accepting there is a greater power in the world than you. It doesn't have to be God, it can be anything–but Nikki was always too stubborn to take that step. He was simply too self-centered, and wouldn't let me in to help him. That was Nikki Sixx–he always had his armor on.

MAY 2ND 1987

Van Nuys, 4:40 p.m.

OK, I've got to wean off the heroin and coke before we go on tour. I can't go out on the road like this...it will kill me.

The weird thing is, the coke is the worst part of this, but you don't go thru withdrawals if you can't get blow. Smack is a different story. I'm so strung out right now...I couldn't go a day without it. I would have to take so much on the road with me or have it FedExed in every week, which is crazy...what if I missed my delivery? How would I play?

How do some guys tour and stay strung out? I do not wanna know. I'm gonna quit, I have to. This is gonna be bad, but it will be over soon. I hope I don't have to call Bob again. I have a plan and I've just called Jason...

7 p.m.

Jason has just left and it went pretty well. I explained to him that I have got to get clean before Mötley goes on tour next month. I reckon I'm doing $500 or more of smack a day now...the coke I'm just gonna stop. My plan is to do less and less each day, then when I'm low enough go on to methadone and get off completely. So he got his scale out and we made 30 bindles, each one smaller than the one before, each with a fresh needle next to it. It took us an hour...it should take me about a week to wean down. When we were done, it looked like a regiment of drugs, a regime...it looked like an army.

The brave new world starts tomorrow...when Jason left, he shook my hand and said he hoped I'd be able to do it. Ya, right...

DOC McGHEE: Nikki was always dreaming up fantasy ways to kick drugs that didn't involve going into rehab. One time in 1986, he decided that he and Nicole, his old girlfriend, would detox for five days at my house. Those five days felt like a fucking year. Nikki was just so sick–I had to keep carrying him from the house to the hot tub because he was cramping up so bad.

143

And Nicole was something else. She kept thinking Nikki wanted to kill her. One night Nikki came into my bedroom at three A.M. and said, "Dude, you've got to go and see Nicole." I went into their room and she was putting her makeup on. She said, "I've got to go to a photo shoot," and I said, "Look in the mirror–who wants to take a photo of *that* at three in the morning?"

She looked at me and started sobbing, and asked me for a sewing needle, just a sewing needle, because if she stuck it into her arm, it made her feel better. That was on the second day of the five–and, believe me, it didn't get any prettier from there.

BOB TIMMONS: I remember the attempted detox that Doc is describing. As we both predicted, it was a dismal failure. Nikki seemed to have this strange idea that he could just go to Doc's, sit in the hot tub and eat candy, and be off heroin in two days. I'm a former junkie and believe me–it's a lot harder than that.

MAY 5TH 1987
Van Nuys, 8 p.m.

I feel pretty good considering how much I've cut down. I've been buffering my itch with Valium and vodka-and-cranberries...

MAY 7TH 1987
Van Nuys, 9:30 p.m.

Tom is coming from Idaho to stay for a few days. I feel frightened about it. I love Tom and I always love to see him, but I can't let him see me as strung out as I am now...but it's cool that he's stayed close and never given me a hard time about missing Nona's funeral. I respect him for that. I'm going to be strong for him.

I used up more of my stash than I thought. I'm running low.

NIKKI: I spent months and even years as a kid living with my grandfather Tom and my grandmother Nona in Idaho and Texas, when I felt my mother couldn't be bothered with me. Tom is hard but fair, a good man, and I was incredibly close to Nona, who loved me and was better than a mother to me. She always forgave me, and I could be a pretty fucking wild kid.

Nona had been ill in 1986 and I'd ignored it. When she died and Tom called to tell me, the bottom fell out of my world, but I was so fucked up that I couldn't even cry. I was going to fly to the funeral but I was too strung out and wasted that day to get on the plane. I would have had to confront my past, confront my mother and spend time with the family that I had run away from. There were too many issues. They had abandoned me and I had abandoned them.

People were calling me saying I had to come, but I never went. I loved my grandmother and she was very important to me, but I couldn't face it. Instead I got wrecked in front of the tube, feeling ashamed and guilty, and I wrote "Nona," a song for her, which we included on *Girls Girls Girls*. In my fucked-up state, that was the best that I could do.

DEANA RICHARDS: It breaks my heart when Nikki thinks I couldn't be bothered with him as a child. I loved him more than life itself, and I still do. I've wanted to tell him the truth all my life, but I have just never had the chance—and the truth is that my own family, my mom and my sisters, plotted against me to take Nikki away from me.

I didn't know at the time what was going on. I was so naïve. You can't fathom that your family would do such a thing, but they took Nikki away. They did it slowly. It started off with them telling me to send Nikki to stay with them for the weekend. Then they would ask me to send him for a couple of weeks, or for a month, because they would say he needed to be around a man and have a man's influence.

I missed Nikki so much but I thought they were trying to help me, and he would soon be back with me, even when he ended up spending whole summers with them in Idaho. But they were telling him I was wild, and then they started telling me that they weren't sending him back to me because he didn't want to come.

I didn't realize they were poisoning him against me until one day when he was around ten. I was just sick of him being away, and I called him to say, "Nikki, it's time for you to come home." And Nikki told me, "No. Once you get some roots and a dependable life and can take care of a child, *then* I will come home." This out of a child's mouth–well, it wasn't too hard for me to figure out who put those words into the child's mouth.

Then when my mother died, Tom and my sisters didn't even tell me when she was being cremated. Tom only told me afterwards, when my sisters had already been to the house and been through her things and taken everything they wanted.

TOM REESE: Bullshit! Nona and I never said anything against Deana around young Nikki. We were very careful what we said about her. If she had pulled some damn thing on us, we'd make sure we got well away from Nikki before we talked about her.

Whenever Deana would call for us to send Nikki, we would leave it up to him. We'd never try to run that boy's life–he stood on his own two feet. If Nikki wanted to go see his mother, we'd pay his way for him and pay it back again. If he didn't want to go, he didn't go–but he always *did* go, every time until he got to be about thirteen.

Deana would throw him out every time. She threw him out of LA and every damn place she went to. We'd get a call from Nikki saying, "Grandma, can I come home?" and we'd get money to him to get a plane home. One time, Deana just left him with some woman in Sparks, Nevada, and went off with a guy. The woman phoned us, saying, "What am I supposed to do with this boy?" and I had to drive over and fetch him.

Deana has a screw loose and it's drug-induced. You name it–LSD, marijuana, she used to take it. She was taking drugs before Ceci was born, before Lisa was born–even before Nikki was born. She was flying half of the time.

Nikki was very loyal to his mother for years and years, more than she deserved–when he asked us for anything, we used to give it to him. If he asked Deana for anything, she told him to go to hell. Nikki did pretty good with her until the time he went to live with her in Seattle when he was about thirteen, and she threw him out of there too. After that, he would absolutely have nothing to do with her. I guess he just decided that she didn't care.

NIKKI: Which side of the blade is sharper? The lie or the truth? It all seems irrelevant when your jugular is sliced open and you're lying in a pool of blood for the whole world to see.

MAY 8th 1987

Van Nuys, 10 p.m.

Tom is here now and I think it might be a good thing for me. I can't get wasted in front of him, so I just do my little maintenance shots in the bathroom.

Tommy came over tonight. We did a couple of shots of Jack with Tom and made small talk. Tommy can tell I'm sick. Tom asked me if I wanted to go to the doctor, I said it's just a really bad flu...if I went to the doctor and they saw my veins they would call the police in a New York second!

I'm gonna go to the clinic in Burbank tomorrow and register for a 30-day program but I'm only gonna do it for three or four days then just cold turkey out from there...

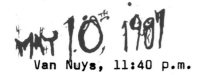

MAY 10th, 1987

Van Nuys, 11:40 p.m.

DAY ONE COKE AND DOPE FREE

Went to the clinic today and got my first dose. I'm outta dope. I threw all my rigs away, even my Dom Perignon box. I gotta tell you I'm fucking sick. I got an illegal scrip for Valium and percs from this quack we all use. They always help ease the pain.

I'm shitting and puking so much but I'm trying to keep it together for my grandfather...Thank God for him...

NIKKI: I remember Tom coming out to the Heroin House. When you're in the middle of a crisis it's not easy to notice other people's pain. Looking back, my grandfather had to be dealing with a lot of pain. Losing Nona was the hardest thing he ever had to go through, and on top of that the boy he raised was in a tailspin and heading towards an early death. He probably saved my life and I'll always owe him for that. I will forever regret not being there for him in return.

TOM REESE: When Nona died, Nikki was devastated, but he was also pretty fucked up. I went to stay with him once or twice, and the way of life he had was not to my liking. And he was so skinny! A good gust of wind would have blown him through a knothole.

Nikki didn't inject in front of me, but it was obvious he was doing it. He would sit around with his buddies talking, and their drug talk might have made sense to them, but to me it sounded like gibberish. I used to see people in the same state in my years in the military. It never held any appeal for me.

While I was staying at Nikki's, I'd often answer the door for him. Sometimes it was girls; I'd let them in except for the real young 'uns, who I'd send packing. I never let the drug peddlers in. One guy was kind of persistent, until I waved my shotgun in his face, and then he never came back.

I was worried for Nikki and I told him what I thought, but it just went in one ear and out the other. Stopping Nikki was like trying to stop a tornado. I couldn't do anything except look out for him…and hope.

DANCING ON GLASS

Can't find my doctor
Bones can't take this ache
If you dance with the devil
Your day will come to pay
My fuel injected dreams
Are bursting at the seams
Am I in Persia
Or lost in Spain

I've been to hell,
hope I never make it back
To dancing on glass.

MAY 11TH 1987
Van Nuys, midnight

DAY **TWO** COKE AND DOPE FREE

I can't believe it's been two days without any junk! Went to get dosed today, saw a few guys I know. Fucking smack...just ruins people's lives. At first it seems so sweet, then one day you wake up to a monster.

See you tomorrow...too sick to write. I have to go lay down...I haven't slept much...

MAY 12TH, 1987
Van Nuys, 11:30 p.m.

DAY **THREE** COKE AND DOPE FREE

I haven't had anything for three days now. This withdrawal is the most painful, intense one I've been in, like shock therapy. My guts are ripping, I'm puking and shitting, I'd do anything for a fix, but I won't give in. This is the worst day so far. It always is...day three and four is when most guys give in. I can't sleep for the pain.

I've heard stories about hookers who will blow a fucking donkey for a fix rather than go thru this. That's how much this fucking hurts.

Today was my last dose...maybe one more day, but I don't wanna get strung out on methadone. If you're hooked on that, it's almost impossible to get off.

I'm so sick. Thank God I'm getting dosed or I would definitely die from this one. I'm so sick I'm even sick of writing that I'm sick in this diary.

MAY 13th 1987

Van Nuys, 10:20 a.m.

DAY **FOUR** COKE AND DOPE FREE

Last methadone visit this morning. I haven't eaten
anything but candy. I'm too sick to go into the store
and face people. Pete brought me a bag of candy and
ice cream...every time I've kicked I go thru this sugar
thing...what's next? I'm gonna fucking get fat? My whole
body feels like it's cracking into pieces-
fragile doesn't even come close to describing how I
feel.

MAY 14th 1987

Van Nuys, 4:35 a.m.

DAY **FIVE** COKE AND DOPE FREE

Had to go to the album listening party. I'm still
sick as a dog but a handful of painkillers and a lot
of whisky got me thru. Vanity showed up, I was talking
to this black stripper and Vanity got all weird and
abrasive. I'm so dope sick I feel brittle. It wouldn't
take much for me to shatter in a million pieces.

P.S. Speaking of dogs, I forgot I put money down on a German short-haired pointer. I couldn't get him at the time, because he wasn't old enough, but he's getting delivered tomorrow...I'm gonna call him Whisky.

NIKKI: The *Girls Girls Girls* listening party was at the Body Shop, a strip club on Sunset. The band posed for photos with five strippers whose panties spelled out MÖ-TL-EY CR-ÜE. Vanity lost her mind when she came in because the stripper standing next to me was a black girl. The other thing I remember about the party is that asshole Yngwie Malmsteen showed up. He'd been dogging the band in the press yet dared to show up to our album listening party, so we had security throw him out on his ass on the curb. But I was so sick from junk it was all I could do to hold it together.

MAY 15TH 1987
Van Nuys, 5 p.m.

DAY SIX COKE AND DOPE FREE

MTV has said no to the Girls Girls Girls video because of the topless strippers in it. We sent them one that was so out there so they would be happy with the one we really wanted them to play. If we sent them the one they approved first, they would of made us tame that one down...suckers.

Tom left today but I think I might still be OK getting cleaned up for the tour. It helps when I have things to focus on like my new dog Whisky...he just came today. Tom loves him.

It's when I'm left to my own devices that I go fucking insane. I've always been too good at making my own entertainment. I can safely say I'll never use heroin again...it's just a nightmare. I feel so much better but my sheets on the bed stink from the gallons of toxic sweat that have poured outta my body. I have a pile of clothes in the closet with shit all over them from the first few days. I've been able to get a few hours of sleep at a time now and I can hold down something other than sweets. I feel hopeful.

RANDOM THOUGHT
Cleaning up is dirty work.

DOC McGHEE: Nikki used to sometimes have these dogs that were kinda messy and sloppy. I used to call them the heroin puppies. Can I tell you something that's not too nice? I used to think of Vanity as a heroin puppy as well.

MAY 16rd 1987
Van Nuys, 8 p.m.

DAY SEVEN COKE AND DOPE FREE

So another Mötley Crüe album is set to come out and we kindly donate another fucking chunk of profit to Neglektra Records. Why should they own our music?

This industry is the most fucked-up business ever. Musicians spend their childhoods learning to play instruments in their bedrooms, then they spend their lives in a recording studio creating music...then some fucker in a suit comes along and says if I can distribute what they've done to enough people, I'm going to sell PRODUCT to create CASHFLOW for my CORPORATION...at which point I ask myself, Where did we lose the music?

We write the music. It's our songs, our vision, our message, our angst, so how can some record company OWN Mötley Crüe or Aerosmith or Led Zeppelin's music? I mean, what the fuck? This system is slavery. It's our music, our business...we should own it...

I can't believe I'm clean. I feel lucid, alert and alive. I hurt like hell and my nerves are on edge but I'm clean-just in time for the machine to fire up...

MAY 17ᵀᴴ 1987

Van Nuys, midnight

DAY EIGHT COKE AND DOPE FREE

Slash came over and we just hung out, played with Whisky and played guitars. Then we got out of here and went to lunch...Slash even told me that he thinks I'm looking better. I told him I just got outta a real bad kick and I was done with the worst of it. He said he knows how hard it is.

Vanity kept calling but I let the answering machine take the strain. I'm not ready for her right now. I'm making progress but I'm still fragile-more emotionally than physically now.

UNUSED LYRIC

South Street Sam sells it by the box
Half-price murder and double-price rocks
Easin' in 20, he's looking 85
He'll be pushing up daisies
By the time he's 25

MAY 18th, 1987

Van Nuys, 9 p.m.

DAY **NINE** COKE AND DOPE FREE

I ran into Jason today while I was shopping on Melrose and basically ignored him. He saw me and came over and asked why I hadn't called him lately. I just said that I had his number if I needed it, but I was planning not to use it. The parasites are panicking because their free meal is over!

> **NIKKI:** When I read these diary entries, it boggles my mind how much power I had when I finally decided to quit. I don't know if it was fear or greed that eventually got me to that point but whatever it was, it seemed to be working...temporarily...

MAY 19, 1987

Van Nuys, 11:20 p.m.

DAY **TEN** COKE AND DOPE FREE

Had a meeting with management earlier. They want to hire a jet for the tour so we can leave right after shows and base ourselves in a city for a week or so at a time while we play all of the nearby dates.

Doc said it would save us money, but I'm not stupid...I know the real fucking reason. They are terrified of me and Tommy and Vince heading off to clubs and getting wasted after every show...they think they can keep an eye on us this way, and we can't get up to too much bad shit up in the air every night.

I see their plan,
but I went along with it...
it might even be what I need. I
said we would only do it if the
jet was painted black with a big
naked chick on the side. Doug went
pale but said he'd see what he could do.

They seemed amazed that I had color and had gained some
weight. I've even been lifting a few weights in my garage.

NIKKI: My suspicion of our management's strategy was
entirely correct. Their plan was an honorable one, but
overlooked one major flaw: being based in a city for
seven nights at a time, rather than one night, would give
us plenty of time to track down all the local services and
supplies that we *shouldn't* be tracking down.

DOC McGHEE: It was always way easier to tour Mötley
Crüe on private jets than on buses. We could get the
journey done in one hour rather than five or six, and on
buses they were a fucking mess. They were always
running around drunk or biting people. And considering
the state Nikki was in at that stage, we wanted to have
him somewhere we could keep an eye on him.

Van Nuys, 9:30 p.m.

DAY ELEVEN COKE AND DOPE FREE

Been down in the garage lifting weights and riding my exercise bike every day. It's nice that for once my muscles are aching for a good reason. One bad thing about coming off drugs is putting on weight. Which is worse? Being strung out or fat?

Van Nuys, 11:30 p.m.

DAY TWELVE COKE AND DOPE FREE

Not much to do again today except a few phone interviews for the album. All the journalists are the same. They all ask identical questions as though they're the only person to have ever thought of them. I hate the press almost as much as they hate me…ha ha…but really, when are they going to ask about the MUSIC? What's the meaning behind the song "Nona"? Or did I know that Girls Girls Girls was an Elvis Presley album? Duh…

I'm really happy to be off dope. I can't believe I finally did it—on my own, no less. To be on a journey that you see no ending to, and then you finally get where you're going, feels soooo good. Like the insanity has stopped. I'm really happy.

Pete is still strung out and I hear King is too. I can't be around anybody who uses junk, I just can't… even if they're my best friends.

MAY 22ND, 1987

Van Nuys, 11:20 p.m.

DAY THIRTEEN COKE AND DOPE FREE

T-Bone has just left. My head is still buzzing from talking to him. He had a dream last night that he was playing the drums upside down, and he wants to turn it into reality. So he's told management he wants them to design a kit that can spin around like a gyroscope while he's playing it...they're looking into it.

Tommy is so enthusiastic and I hope it happens, but rather him than me. When I'm trying to survive a hangover, the last thing I'd want would be fucking spinning upside down. I hope the front row likes the taste of projectile vomit....

P.S. You know what's weird? I don't even know where Vince or Mick lives.

MAY 23, 1987

Van Nuys, 11:50 a.m.

DAY FOURTEEN COKE AND DOPE FREE

Days like today are beautiful. There's nothing to do, nobody is on the phone, the sun is out, the doors are open. I'm lying on my back patio right now writing to you, soaking up the sun, listening to Aerosmith and Bad Company.

I'm not strung out and that feels good. I feel like I've finally got the monster under control. I'm excited...what a perfect day.

MAY 24th 1987

Van Nuys, 5:45 p.m.

DAY FIFTEEN COKE AND DOPE FREE

Today we went to look at the plane we are hiring for the tour, but it seems management "forgot" to tell them about the little adjustments we need—the Mötley Crüe accessories.

So I patiently explained to the guy that we need it painted black, and we need a naked girl painted on the outside. He started stuttering that they couldn't paint it black and I just gave him a look and said, Oh, that's a shame, we can't take it then. He said he'll see what he can do, and get back to us. We agreed on a compromise—the girl can be riding a bomb on the side of the plane.

Fuck—sometimes people don't seem able to handle the simplest requests! No is not a word I think should be in the dictionary when it comes to creativity.

P.S. I did it...totally clean...amazing. I'm not even the same person I was two weeks ago. I've been playing so much music, practicing, writing, getting all the ideas together for the tour. Shows, planes, hotels, food, stage clothes, new basses, amps...yes...I'm back!

Band reh today. I'm so excited to play. Pete wants to go out after but I can't hang out with him anymore. He's on methadone but still I have to stick to my guns. I feel sorry for him 'cause I am his only friend and he knows why we can't hang out anymore. Junk ruins lives and friendships. I hope he gets clean too.

MAY 27TH 1987

Van Nuys, 11 p.m.

Last night I went to the Cathouse on my own. I always know plenty of people there. I had loads of Jack and tequila shots but no more than a few bumps. I fucked a girl in the bathroom and brought another one home, but this morning I can't remember her name and I can't wait for her to leave...

Girls do their best, but they're never gonna take the place of drugs, 'cause drugs don't talk back.

Short reh today but we sounded good...I was a bit hungover and that felt bad after feeling so good for the last two weeks.

DEANA RICHARDS: After Nikki moved to Los Angeles I hardly heard from him. He would occasionally call me, very late at night or in the middle of the night, demanding money. I would gather up all I could and send it to him, and then I would never hear from him again unless he got in really bad trouble.

When Mötley Crüe started getting big, I was proud of Nikki but I could see what a toll it was taking. I was so scared for him because I knew it was killing him. It was obvious he was taking drugs and I tried to talk to him twice about getting help, but he wouldn't even discuss it. He said he didn't have a problem—*I* had a problem.

Then later on, when he was married for the first time and I went to see him in Los Angeles, he told me that the only reason he had started taking drugs was because I had been drinking and drugging for years. Well, I never took drugs—and I didn't start drinking until after Nikki left Seattle and refused to come back.

SELLING MY SOUL WOULD BE A LOT EASIER IF I COULD JUST FIND IT.

MAY 29ᵀᴴ, 1981

Van Nuys, 11 a.m.

Just woke up. Phone was ringing. It was Gene Simmons, reminding me that we're getting together to write music today. Glad he called, 'cause I'd forgot...

10 p.m.

Gene came over in his new black Rolls. When he was leaving and backing out the driveway he got too close to the wall and was freaking out 'cause his car was about an inch away from getting scratched to fuck. Me and Pete just laughed—it serves him right for what he said about my lyrics.

Oh yeah—Pete came over this afternoon. He looks better than I've seen him in a long time. He's almost clean—no junk, just getting dosed.

NIKKI: Gene Simmons and I wrote a song together one time but when I showed him the lyrics he said they were "too radical" and wouldn't get played on the radio. Later, I used the same words on the "Girls Girls Girls" single and radio had no problem playing it. He was always a weird guy. I remember the first time he came over to my house. I did a line and took a quaalude and was drinking, and asked Gene whether he wanted anything. He said he didn't do drugs or drink. I asked him what he did instead. He said, "I fuck." So I asked him, "What do you do after you fuck?" He said, "I fuck again." And I asked him, **"Why????"**

Because Rule Number One:

CHICKS = TROUBLE

163

MAYBE HAVING THESE DEALERS FOLLOW US IS A BAD IDEA.

JUNE 1ST 1987

Van Nuys, 12:50 a.m.

Rehearsals were a kick today. We've decided to hire background singers for the tour. As we progress as a band we've naturally started to use more background vocals but it can be hard to cover them live (and boring to be stuck on the mic all night), so we've decided to use female background singers like the Stones. We'll be auditioning girls all week at rehearsals. Should be interesting.

The band needs less reh this tour than usual. The old stuff is tight and the new stuff isn't far off. I think the new stuff is simpler and more bluesy at times. It just falls in the pocket easier. There's the usual excitement about tour production going around like a virus. I love this part...the part where the visual meets the music.

We're having the stage show evolve...more on that later. My ears are ringing. Off to bed...working out in the morning...

NIKKI: When you're sitting on a plane 40,000 feet up in the air, looking out the window, dreaming of your future and how bright it appears to be, or maybe just watching the drops of rain being pushed into different designs from the force of air at 400 mph, well, life feels good. It feels safe, your seat belt is on and your feet are up. Then the oxygen masks fall, the plane jumps, snaps and jolts. People start to scream, babies burst out crying, people start praying all in time to the overhead announcement that we're gonna crash. Right then, as your life flashes before your eyes, you hear yourself say, "God, if you get me outta this one, I'll stop [insert lie] forever." Right then the nose of the plane pulls up and the captain says, "Wow, that was a close one, folks. We're OK, we'll be landing in thirty minutes and we're all safe and sound…sorry for the scare…"

That's how getting hooked on junk is, and when the kick is over you can't believe you ever got on that plane in the first place. The question is, Will you ever fly again?

JUNE 3RD, 1987
Van Nuys, 10:45 p.m.

We met about ten singers today. Some of them could sing and some of them could dance. The ones that could sing couldn't dance, the ones that were pretty couldn't sing, the ones that were ugly sang like Janis Joplin. What a nightmare!

We have more tomorrow. This one girl was dancing in front of us grinding on the mic, and then went over to Mick and was singing in his face. I had to look down and away so I didn't burst out laughing. I almost pissed my pants laughing after she left...good times.

Mick is playing his ass off. I haven't seen that fire in him for a while. I think the break did him good.

JUNE 5TH, 1987
Van Nuys, 11:20 p.m.

We finally picked our background singers—a girl named Emi and one named Donna. I told the band the first rule of the tour—nobody fucks the background singers. These tours have enough dramas and problems without us importing dysfunctional relationships right into the fucking heart of them. But it was amazing to hear the vocals on top of all the guitars and drums. It took it to another level...badass!

Of course, I foresee problems. I mean, chicks = trouble.

A lot of phone calls today with management about last-minute details for the tour. If we have one more meeting at reh I think I'm gonna lose my cool. They seem to think since we're all together it's their time to trap us, and we end up not getting to reh as much as we should.

I dunno, maybe that's not a bad thing. An over-rehearsed rock band can sound sterile.

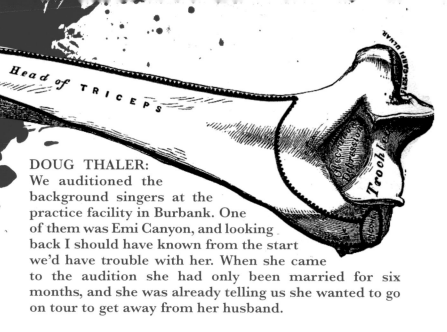

DOUG THALER:
We auditioned the background singers at the practice facility in Burbank. One of them was Emi Canyon, and looking back I should have known from the start we'd have trouble with her. When she came to the audition she had only been married for six months, and she was already telling us she wanted to go on tour to get away from her husband.

Nikki laid down the law about nobody sleeping with the backing singers, and the band all agreed, which was highly ironic, given that Vince had already tried his luck with both of the girls at the audition and been knocked back. But when Emi later turned her attentions to Mick, it was a very different story.

JUNE 12ᵀᴴ, 1987
Van Nuys, 9:30 a.m.

I just realized I haven't written in here for a week…maybe 'cause I've just been getting on with life, like other people do? Reh has been going great, I've not been drinking more than half a bottle of Jack a night. Even Jason has given up on calling me. This is like a health kick. Maybe there are two things I do when I'm falling apart—write in this book and phone Vanity, ha ha…

Now for the hard part—holding it together on tour.

JUNE 15th 1987

Van Nuys, 11 a.m.

So today I'm packing for the tour. I'm making a list (and checking it twice)…

- KNIFE
- TWO PAIRS OF LEATHER PANTS
- EIGHT T-SHIRTS
- BOOTS
- RUBBERS?
- BLACK NAIL POLISH
- BLACK EYE MAKEUP (GET AT SAV-ON)
- $3000.00 IN CASH (GET OFFICE TO DROP OFF)
- TWO GRAMS
- NO SYRINGES
- SLEEPING PILLS
- CANDLES & INCENSE
- FLASK
- DIARY
- BLANK JOURNALS
- HAVE WHISKY PICKED UP FOR OBEDIENCE CAMP

Now for the killer question—how long before I can dump the psycho girlfriend? All will be revealed. Follow me…

JUNE 16th 1987

Sheraton Hotel, Tucson, Arizona, 2:30 p.m.

Got into the hotel from LA an hour ago. We're all
going down to the arena in a while. Can't wait to see
the stage set. After all our bombastic sets in the
past and all the cheap imitations that have followed
our every move, our direction is simpler this time.
It's raw, stripped back, but huge…a lot of the power
will come from the lights, pyro and our wayyyyy too
big PA.

We shoot the Rolling Stone cover tomorrow and I
want to see what's around there for the shoot. Since
I'll be doing my best to keep my nose clean on this
tour I'll try to write a lot every day. Someday maybe
I'll have kids, and they can read these diaries…or
no, maybe not.

The Rolling Stone writer is hanging around asking
us questions. I wish he would leave us alone. He
doesn't know shit about rock 'n' roll. The same typical
stupid questions: how many girls do we fuck? How much
do we party? No questions about music, spirit,
lyrics, soul, no questions about the Dolls or Angus
Young, just the same old bubblegum magazine bullshit…

JUNE 17th 1987

Sheraton Hotel, Tucson, Arizona, 1:40 a.m.

Wow, the set turned out amazing. It's exactly what
we intended it to be. It has so many levels and
different looks. Tommy's solo is insane, the drums
flip all the way around. In fact, I think he's
insane…Thank God!

I have to tell you, if you ever have to come to Tucson in June…don't. It's fucking hot. I mean the kind of hot where rattlesnakes won't even come out. You walk outside in the day and a wave of heat slams you in the face. It feels like you've stuck your head in a fucking oven.

All the usual suspects came around tonight. I said no to all but two lines and a few shots. I'm not starting off the tour with a hangover. I can't believe I'm off junk—what a horror story that was. But I have to watch it 'cause the junkies just seem to sniff me out. The word's on the street that I'm clean and they don't like it.

I want to help out Slash and give his band some shows. They're not worth any tickets but I believe in them. Cool new band but the singer can be an asshole—but what's new? I can see him and Vince bumping heads.

It's good to see Fred again, with his perfect hair and Grizzly Adams beard, covered in tattoos. He always wears this devil's smirk which somehow yields him more pussy than the guys in the band. As soon as Fred walks into the room I know we're REALLY back on the road again. Everybody is hired, the

plane is on the runway, trucks and buses are all warmed up, and the hanger-ons are floating outside the arena.

So let the madness commence...because I know it will...

FRED SAUNDERS: I was tour security for Mötley Crüe ever since the *Shout at the Devil* tour. When Doc McGhee first hired me, he said the band was so wild I should do whatever it took to keep them in line. In fact, he said he'd give me a bonus every time I hit them. I told him he'd got himself a deal.

I hit Mötley a lot. I once broke Tommy's nose in Indiana, I broke Nikki's ribs and I beat the shit out of Vince many times, because...well, because he's an asshole. I think I even hit poor Mick once. That was just to complete the set.

Nikki was always the strongest of the guys. He was the brightest and had the biggest ideas. Vince had just got lead singer syndrome, and Tommy was a typical drummer–he's always 100 mph and everything is fine by him. Mick just always wanted to drink his wine and not be bothered with anything. So it was always Nikki's moods that shaped what happened with Mötley.

Nikki and I became friends and had a good relation-ship–on the whole. We'd get fucked-up drunk together, cut our hands and swap blood to show that we were blood brothers. But Nikki was a very wild, unpredictable guy. He had so many façades–he'd rarely show his true personality. I also worked with Ozzy Osbourne a lot, and there are many similarities between those guys.

ROSS HALFIN: Fred was this big ex–Hells Angels guy and part of his job for Mötley Crüe was scoring cocaine. They used to call it krell, from that movie *Heavy Metal*, where monsters from the planet Krell came down with big noses and snorted Earth. They'd say, "Where's the krell man?" and ask Fred, "Dude, are you gonna krell me?"

Fred's other job was stopping them getting smashed up and getting into fights. One thing about Mötley Crüe is they will never turn away from a fight. Vince, Nikki and Tommy are fearless. If there are fifty people, they will fight them—you have to hit them with a brick to stop them. They will take on the world.

9:20 a.m.

What the fuck is wrong with housekeeping? They just keep knocking on my door. Now I can't sleep...fucking great. It's going to be a long-ass day.

2:40 p.m.

Just woke up. Finally about 10:30 this morning I ordered two shots of Jack for breakfast so I could go back to sleep. The room service lady was about 65 and she gave me that grandmotherly look of disapproval. The fact that I had on more makeup than she did probably didn't help.

Vanity is coming in today and I'm dreading the drama. Why do I put myself in these situations? I really need to learn to say no. She will

1. embarrass me
2. be a bitch
3. be over-hyper
4. complain
5. get high
6. stumble around drunk

I mean, isn't that MY fucking job? I'd rather sleep with the grandma room service lady.

JUNE 18th, 1987

Sheraton Hotel, Tucson, Arizona, 4:30 a.m.

Vanity is asleep in the other room. Laying in bed, her hair is all over the pillow like a seductive Medusa, skin like milk chocolate against the white white sheets and goose down pillows. You'd think she was a gift from the gods but somehow we are like fire and ice, oil and vinegar, and mostly it's painful. We argue a lot, not all the time, but a lot...let's just say, everything ends in an argument, usually over some stupid stuff. Somehow I always feel like I'm in high school when we're fighting, 'cause nothing that we ever fight about is even important. I'm sure she feels the same—in fact, I know she does, 'cause she told me so right before she told me to fuck off and went to bed last night.

I just took a celebration shot in the bathroom (OK, I admit to having brought a small bindle of gear). God, I love that warm feeling that comes over me (OK, I admit I brought one pack of rigs). It's the best feeling in the world as you slump back and everything in life feels perfect...

I know I said I wouldn't use again but this was just a final kiss goodbye...just a pat on the back for being off dope, right?

Now I'll sleep like a baby. Oh ya, we did the cover shoot for Rolling Stone today. First show tomorrow. Better get some sleep...life is good...

P.S. I got the dope from Pete. He's back on.

NIKKI: You know what I think now when I read this entry? I guess you know you're insane when you are lying to yourself in your own diary.

BOB TIMMONS: I always thought Nikki and Vanity had an extremely unhealthy relationship. Basically, they were co-addicts. Whenever Nikki got attention, Vanity would act out her jealousy. If he was in a room talking to people, she would get up on a table and start dancing. There was no support for Nikki at all because essentially they were always in competition with each other.

EVANGELIST DENISE MATTHEWS: Live hard die young. That was where my vision was taking me until the reality of staring down that dark pit of death woke me up in shock. That is when I cried out to Jesus to save me lest I die. I was suffering in the bottomless pit playground of cocaine addiction. Lifting me higher and dropping me like a steel beam...I'd smoked enough rock that you could lift me up and stick me in the nearest cold grave.

Sinking down into deep depression, I camouflaged my pain with even more makeup and a false smile. I have a shocking medical history of high blood pressure of 250 over 190, plus a heart attack, stroke and kidney failure due to my addiction. I had blood clots in my brain and had only three days left to masquerade this miserable lifeless creature that I had become. That was fifteen years ago. I said, "Do whatever it takes, Jesus, just don't let me die."

7:35 p.m.

More reh today and a lot of "hurry up and wait." Beats the hotel...Rich Fisher is still trying to get the jet together but I guess painting it black is taking longer than we thought. We'll probably have to lease a Lear jet for a few days.

It feels so good to be out of LA and all the temptation
and losers who creep around...I feel so guilty that I did
some dope but it's gone and I'm OK. I need to load up
on some music. Better hit a music store. I'd die without music...I feel like I'm getting my life back.

I gotta say the band sounds killer. We always pull
it together right before the tour. Reh back in LA
seemed to drag on forever...playing the songs in a dingy
lil sweatbox just doesn't have the zap it used to. As
soon as we have to rise to the occasion we always get
energized and sound tight as fuck.

But one thing is bothering me—Vince isn't the same
guy he used to be. Since the accident he seems bitter
and withdrawn. I can feel him slipping away from all
of us. He seems to not want to be in the gang. He's
marching to his own drum, which is fine but I'm assum-
ing the drift is a resentment he has towards us since
he went to jail...can I blame him?

OK, I gotta get outta here right now. I'm off to a
Mexican dinner with Fred and some of the band and
crew. No drugs today...first show tomorrow...

VINCE NEIL: Nikki and Tommy were complete fucking
assholes to me on the previous tour, *Theatre of Pain*. At
the time I was not allowed to drink or use drugs because
of my vehicular manslaughter conviction, but we'd be
sitting on our jet and they'd think it was real funny to say,
"Oh Vince, pass me that coke, will you?" I was supposed
to be sober, and nobody gave a shit–they were just drinking and having fun. Everybody was out for themselves,
and Nikki was the most spiteful of all.

So Nikki and I didn't have much of a relationship on the
Girls Girls Girls tour. Nikki and Tommy had a relationship
and whatever they did, I made sure I did the opposite
thing. I wasn't included in a lot of stuff they did, and I

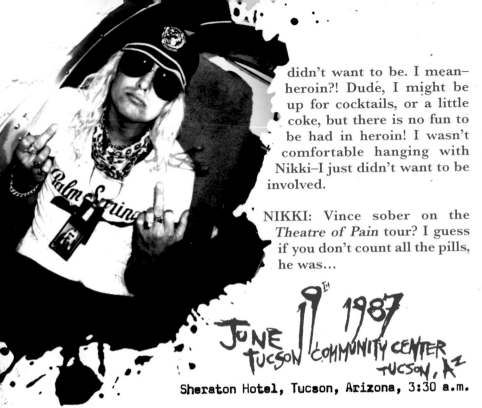

didn't want to be. I mean—heroin?! Dude, I might be up for cocktails, or a little coke, but there is no fun to be had in heroin! I wasn't comfortable hanging with Nikki–I just didn't want to be involved.

NIKKI: Vince sober on the *Theatre of Pain* tour? I guess if you don't count all the pills, he was...

JUNE 19TH 1987
TUCSON COMMUNITY CENTER
TUCSON, AZ

Sheraton Hotel, Tucson, Arizona, 3:30 a.m.

I'm a bit smashed right now...we had too many margaritas at dinner. I got into a fight with Vanity (again!). She just can't shut up, so I told her to shut up or go home.

Good fucking night. Nice way to start a tour...

1 p.m.

Wow I just woke up. I feel great. Sleep–the great healer. I have to go to the radio station with Tommy in a while but first I'm going to go for a swim and lie in the sun for a bit.

I can't wait until Vanity gets the fuck outta here. She's so embarrassing, dancing around and lecturing us on shit. Who is she to tell us about anything? She's just a fucking crack head.

4:15 p.m.

Off to the radio station and then sound check. The whole fucking world is here for the first show tonight. Damn, I wish they'd give us a few shows to iron out the kinks. Plus this is a small gig, 9,000 or so. Ya, it's sold out, but even so...wish us luck!

See ya later, SIXX

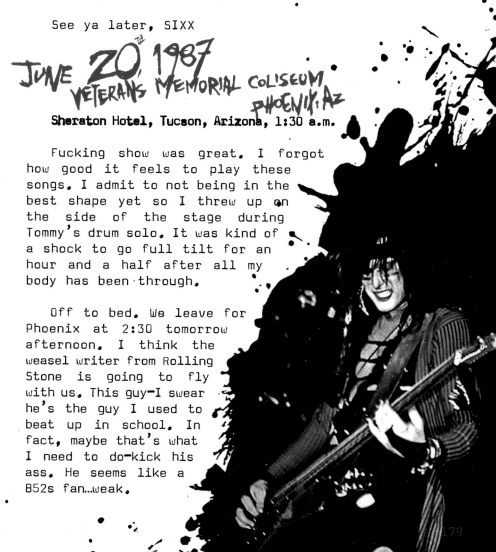

JUNE 20TH, 1987 VETERANS MEMORIAL COLISEUM PHOENIX, Az

Sheraton Hotel, Tucson, Arizona, 1:30 a.m.

Fucking show was great. I forgot how good it feels to play these songs. I admit to not being in the best shape yet so I threw up on the side of the stage during Tommy's drum solo. It was kind of a shock to go full tilt for an hour and a half after all my body has been through.

Off to bed. We leave for Phoenix at 2:30 tomorrow afternoon. I think the weasel writer from Rolling Stone is going to fly with us. This guy—I swear he's the guy I used to beat up in school. In fact, maybe that's what I need to do—kick his ass. He seems like a B52s fan...weak.

79

P.S. Good news—the bitch went back to her brothel…
or crack house.

VINCE NEIL: Nikki's fucked-up chick Vanity came out
to our show in Tucson. As usual, she started doing all
her crazy dancing right in front of us while we were trying to play. It was so bad that I told Nikki, "Dude, get
your fucking chick out of here!" She was driving everybody crazy. It was real fucking embarrassing.

ROSS HALFIN: Vanity was a dreadful, horrible thing.
She used to dance in the photo pit so everybody could
see her. All she'd do every night was dance like it was
her show. She'd just crouch down with her legs wide
open, like she was a pole dancer in a strip bar.

DOUG THALER: Vanity was the kind of chick who
would lecture you about how Coca-Cola would rot your
teeth and could strip the paint off a car, then she would
go home and get shit-faced on the other kind of coke. She
was always winding the band up when they needed to be
mellow. I'm sorry, but she was a real pain in the ass.

EVANGELIST DENISE MATTHEWS: Don't we just hate
it when others lie to us, but we don't feel the lie when we
are doing the lying? How could I point at anyone's
window and smash their glass when my own window
was already broken and I had lost all of my stones…or
better yet, my marbles? Firstly I had to glue myself back
together and then try to help others, but who can really
clean up but God? He makes sure we don't bleed to
death from all the shards of glass thrown at our feet
along the way.

NIKKI: We were all doing the best we could with the
tools we had. Unfortunately the tools we had were crack
pipes, syringes, coke straws and whisky bottles.

On the plane to Phoenix, 3:25 p.m.

I'm on the jet we have to use until ours is ready. The worm from Rolling Stone is with us! I'm gonna try and get him fucked up and slip him something...maybe I can enlighten him.

These writers always kiss up to you and then you get your throat slit when the magazine comes out. I say keep your friends close, keep your enemies closer... then you can see when their eyes turn brown.

Mars is hanging awfully close to Emi the background singer. Something is fishy. Mars always keeps to himself, but he seems just a bit smug and sneaky. The number one rule is nobody fucks the background singer—who would have thought Mick would be the first to try?

CHICKS = TROUBLE.

JUNE 21, 1987 DAY OFF

Clarion Inn, Phoenix, Arizona, 1:30 a.m.

Show was intense, even better than the first one. Danny Zelisko said he's seen us a zillion times and this is the best the band has ever been. We all ended up in the bathroom at the Coliseum doing tons of blow. There were loads of hot chicks and Vince as usual picked the best ones first and rolled out. Mick was hanging with that backing singer chick and me and Tommy did blow so long there were no chicks left when we came out of the john...lame. So I guess I'll take a Halcion, jerk off and go to bed...boring.

TIM LUZZI: The *Girls* tour may have pre-dated the arrival of crack cocaine but I remember some of Mötley used to make their own in the microwave in the dressing room. I didn't notice immediately, but after a few days I noticed the attention that the microwave was getting and began wondering why it was so damn important—especially seeing as the band's wives, girlfriends and hot chicks in the backstage holding area were getting so little attention by comparison.

NIKKI: Rule Number Two:

DONT GIVE A ROCKSTAR A MICROWAVE IN HIS DRESSING ROOM

It's kinda like giving matches to an arsonist.

Noon

```
Day off. I'm gonna lie in bed all day
and watch TV. Did I tell you MTV is ham-
  mering our video? The bad news is all
    these bands are coming out that are
     B and C rate Crüe copies. In the end
       the  record  companies  trying  to
       cash in will be the death of us if
       this  shit  doesn't  stop...I  feel
       bad for the fans.


       Rich Fisher always tries to plan
    something  on  our  day  off  and  I
     always say, It's a day off, leave
     me alone. I guess since we pay
        the  bill  it's  in  his  best
                     interest,  right?
                     I'm      really
                      gonna  try  to
                      be good today
                      and tonight.
```

4 p.m.

Just woke up again. I was just thinking about the time me and Tommy were tag-teaming this chick behind Kiss's drums while they were playing Rock 'n' Roll All Night here in Scottsdale. We thought it was just fun, then we found out it was the drummer's girlfriend (OUCH). Nice girl (I think her name was Bambi). Now there's one you want to take home to mom. Can you imagine? Hi Mom, this is my future ex-wife, Bambi...

It was also a nice way to get thrown off our first ever tour.

NIKKI: You know what was worse than getting thrown off the Kiss tour for bad behavior? Listening to Gene Simmons talk about himself all day and all night long. Sometimes I'd just sit there and say, "Uh-huh" and "Right" until he was done. For all his ego and bullshit I like Gene. But I can't like him as much as he likes himself. That would be impossible.

JUNE 22ND, 1987
TINGLEY COLISEUM
ALBUQUERQUE, NM

On our way to New Mexico, 12:50 p.m.

Right now I'm on our jet, we're sitting on the runway getting ready to take off. Holy fuck, it's insane. It's black...have you ever seen a black jet? I'm digging this. We have a stewardess (blonde), we each have our own assigned seat (leather). I already found a nice place to stash stuff for border crossings. The show is sold out...11,000 people.

183

Everyone is jacked up, so we're passing around a bottle of Jack with the stereo cranked. Tommy motioned me to the back of the plane and he slid me a bindle. That's my boy...

RANDOM SCRIBBLES

We are the future but the future looks bleak
I have no interest other than being uninterested
All these vampires masquerade as leaders
and prey on the minds of the weak
All I know is I don't care
And even if I cared I'd have no hope
to carry me to where I'd need to go

THINGS I HAVE TO DO:
1. SELL THE HEROIN HOUSE
2. DUMP VANITY

JUNE 23rd 1987 COUNTY COLISEUM EL PASO, TX

On the Mötley jet to El Paso, 1:30 a.m.

Good show but I'm fucking tired. I couldn't find any blow in this fucking town. I know Fred is holding...Doug and Doc are on him to keep me under control. If I'm tired and I'm doing my job, why can't I have a bump? They treat me like a kid.

It's fucking stupid. I'm gonna buy an 8-ball next time I score so I don't have to go through this drama.

We get into El Paso tonight around 2:30 or 3 so I guess I'll just be a good boy tonight. Boring. I hate it when people try to control me.

ROSS HALFIN: Nikki was never a mumbling, reclusive junkie–he always seemed to hold it together, but he would moan all the time. I'd ask him to do something in a photo session and he'd say, "Dude, I can't, I'm tired." Once I said to him, "It must be awful for you, having to stand against this wall backstage for two minutes so you can be on the cover of magazines. You could have a *real* job, like being a miner or working in Woolworth's." He yelled, "Fuck you!" which was what he always said to everything. But his general attitude–which made Mötley Crüe very successful–was "Fuck the world."

Nikki was never as bad as Vince. I arrived to shoot one session, and Nikki and Tommy said, "We've got to talk to you, there's a problem with Vince." It turned out that the previous time I'd shot them, Vince had told me to make him look thin–which wasn't always easy–and I recommended he wear a black T-shirt. That was two years earlier, and he was still brooding about it. That's how removed from reality Mötley Crüe was.

NIKKI: Ross Halfin was so fun to wind up. We'd just bitch and moan even if we didn't have anything to complain about. It was fun to make his job harder 'cause he took the bait every time. I was recently in Europe with Ross and I told him that for all these years I thought he was gay. He went on and on and on about it: Why? How could I? He said that he was married and has a son. After I let him go on a bit longer, I said, "Ross, two things: Even if you were, who the hell cares? I was just winding you up (again)."

That's Ross–the easiest wind-up in rock 'n' roll but a hell of a sweet guy (not that kind of sweet).

Hotel, El Paso, Texas, 3 p.m.

Weird to think I used to live here. I used to ride my bike down to Piggly Wiggly with my friends to look at the newest Hot Wheels and toys. They used to have popcorn at the door when you walk in so we decided we would get our popcorn bags half full and then go to the Hot Wheels section. We would bury the cars deep in our popcorn and walk out. Man, I fucking miss being a kid. It was a time of innocence. I wish I could go back, 'cause this life is hard.

Good news. Tommy met these dealers and they're gonna follow the tour thru Texas. We leave in the jet and they follow in their car...now that's door-to-door service!

EL PASO

Balcony in El Paso
Cigarette butts grace my balcony
And the remains of a dead pigeon seem somewhat poetic
The life form that scurries around below
Is a mixture of Tex-Mex and trailer park trash
I know you-'cause I used to live here, too
Guess that makes you just like me
Does that make you wonder about yourself?
Your secret's safe

                    I don't know why
            I'm here but I can't stay
                The more things change
        The more they stay the strange

                Sitting here on this plane
        Watchin' the empty faces crawl past me
        You know they all seem to have ingested
                The same melancholy pill
            Instead of warm, fuzzy and safe
            They seem cold and judgmental
    Little conversations come in and out of audio focus
        It's all slow motion but somehow moving at the
                        Speed of fear
        I feel such the animal, I'm always the animal
            My body's the cage-I'm locked in this cage
        My home is worn, it's torn, it's been abused
                            And I like it

                    I don't know why
            I'm here but I can't stay
                The more things change
        The more they stay the strange

                Here I sit in another hotel
                and it smells like someone else
            I lay in bed and I can taste the smell
        They smell of smoke, the drink, the stink
                And the stain on the floor
            I wonder was he with his wife
                Or another man's whore?
                Scratches upon the glass
            Tell of the drugs, and the radio
    Is still on to the music that made them dance
                I bet it was sweet
                            But me?
            Fuck man, I gotta get some sleep

JUNE 24ᵀᴹ, 1987 DAY OFF

Hotel, Austin, Texas, 2 p.m.

Mars is acting like a school kid around Emi. I mean it's cute and all but she's an employee. Onstage last night they were looking at each other all lovey-dovey... it made me wanna puke.

Chicks = trouble.

Tommy fucked this chick Robbin Crosby used to go out with (Tawny Kitaen). Now she's with the singer from Whitesnake and they wanna open up for us. Like I said...

Chicks = trouble.

Tawny used to shoot up with Robbin and after I met her she kept asking me to get her some dope. Like I said...

Chicks = trouble.

P.S. Speaking of trouble there's a club here that the bartender can hook me up. Think I'll get a bindle of china white.

DOUG THALER: I can understand why the other guys weren't happy when Mick started dating Emi Canyon. She was an employee, and when she got together with Mick, we suddenly had a situation where the guitar player in the band was being led around by the nose by an employee. Mick is a lovely guy, but he's one of those guys who gets totally dominated by every single female partner that he has. It's always the same story. All that ever changes is the girl's name.

JUNE 25TH 1987

Hotel, Austin, Texas, 5:15 a.m.

FRANK ERWIN CENTER
AUSTIN, TX

I just got back from Beale Street. Went to a few different clubs. Tommy, Vince and myself with Fred found an amazing strip club. The girls took us in the back and gave us lines and blow jobs free. Only in America. God bless Texas!

This lil girl named Ashlee gave me a number of a guy who sells packages of rigs for $5 a pop. He's dropping off a 12-pack...just nice to have around, never know if you're gonna need them (vitamin B? ha ha). The show is sold out and there's no sound check so I'm gonna have a little party in my room alone but I promise I'll be in bed by 7 a.m.

10:30 a.m.

Fuck, I did it again. I'm still up and I ended up in the hotel closet, freaking out. I took two Halcions about 30 minutes ago so I'm pretty mellow right now...but I was sure hotel security was coming to get me. I hate cocaine.

DANGEROUS IS
MY ANTICIPATION

189

6:45 p.m.

Just woke up. Rich said everyone was freaking out 'cause I wouldn't answer my door...fucking hell, I was just sleeping...damn, I wish everyone would just relax (I'm not gonna die). Got to go to the show right now then off to...somewhere. I need to look in the book...I have no idea.

Ross Halfin is here with some innocent-looking kid who has never left England before. I guess he might need some fucking-over Crüe-style.

Tim Luzzi

JASON BRYCE: I was sixteen in 1987 when I flew out from London with my dad's friend Ross Halfin to meet Mötley Crüe on the *Girls Girls Girls* tour. Ross was photographing them for an English magazine and invited me along as his unpaid assistant. My dad didn't want me to go because he thought Mötley Crüe would corrupt me, but Ross promised to look after me.

It was the first time I'd been anywhere, really, but I could tell this was a proper rock 'n' roll tour. Nikki was a full-on Jack-drinking, coke-snorting rocker, and as soon as he saw me, he started, "Dude, have some Jack! Have some krell!" Vince was quiet, but the rest of them were great.

On the third or fourth night I was there, we all went out for a Mexican meal. I was too young to legally drink but Nikki was pouring strawberry margaritas down my throat. There was this groupie with us, six feet tall in blonde hair and stockings, and Nikki told her, "If you want to hang out with the Crüe, you've got to sort my young mate out." So she came back to my room with me. She was...very talented.

Nikki was very moody. Before the shows he'd be really down and very solitary, just sitting on his own watching something depressing like *Sid and Nancy*. But after the show, if he wanted to party, he wouldn't leave you alone until you partied with him.

He seemed to be around at weird hours, like in the early hours when everybody else was asleep. One night he came to my room with Ross and a couple of girls. It was about four in the morning and they wouldn't give us any more alcohol on room service. So Nikki phoned down to reception and said, "Look, I'm Nikki Sixx, I need a bottle of JD now and I will give you a thousand bucks for it." They still wanted nothing to do with him. They just told him, "Sir, go to bed. You've had enough."

JUNE 26th, 1987
CONVENTION CENTER ARENA
On Mötley jet to Houston, 1 a.m.
SAN ANTONIO, TX

Tonight's show was killer but I really freaked out. Some fucking fans in the front had this big banner that said VANITY on it. That insane bitch has been talking to magazines, telling them we are getting married...she has NO RIGHT to do that. I have got to get rid of her!

MUSIC TO GET ON CD

1 Sweet-Give Us a Wink
2 Deep Purple-Come Taste the Band
3 Mott the Hoople-Greatest Hits
4 Bowie-Diamond Dogs
5 Queen-I, II and Sheer Heart Attack
6 Alice Cooper-Billion Dollar Babies
7 Sex Pistols-Never Mind the Bollocks
8 Iggy and the Stooges-Raw Power
9 AC/DC-Dirty Deeds
10 Lou Reed-Transformer

JUNE 27TH 1987 THE SUMMIT HOUSTON TX
Hotel, Houston, 3 p.m.

Checked my messages at home. David Crosby called—he said he would break my arms if I was getting high. I guess I won't be calling him back. My machine was completely full, so I just erased the rest of them without listening...there really isn't anyone I wanna talk to anyway.

The band is tight as hell, everything is on autopilot musically, the crowds have been insane, all the shows have been sold out. You'd think I would be happy all the time.

I'm reading Diary of a Rock Star by Ian Hunter. Maybe I'll release my diary as a book one day...yeah, right, can you imagine?

P.S. Doug called today and said everyone liked the idea for Wild Side to be the next vid. Radio is digging the track too. I think a live video is in order. Off to the venue now...

P.P.S. I told Slash when we were back in LA I'd try and get his band (Guns N' Roses) a support slot on the tour. It looks like it's gonna work out. I played the music to the guys and they liked it...there's no interest in them right now, but maybe this will help them (anything is better than Whitesnake). Slash is a good guy when he doesn't piss the bed...ha ha...

P.P.P.S. Maybe having these dealers follow us is a bad idea.

JUNE 28TH, 1987 DAY OFF
Hotel, Houston, 5 p.m.

Speaking of Houston...Doc was telling me how when the album was Number 2 we should have gone to Number 1. We had the Number 1 album in the country but for mysterious reasons (payola, anyone?) Whitney Houston was Number 1. That sucks. Girls should have been our first Number 1 album.

Fucked over by a black chick—it seems like a pattern is developing in my life.

Going down to T-Bone's room. The dealers have 2 oz of blow...they're giving it to us. Why not, it's a day off, right?

FRED SAUNDERS: On the *Girls* tour, every band member had their own very different approach to our days off. Vince would always be after pussy. Mick would be with Emi. Tommy would just be up for whatever was going on, and Nikki was kind of...shifty. He'd slide in and out of the picture periodically, but he was tough to deal with because of the mood swings brought on by the drugs.

Nikki could be very sensitive and emotional—he and I would sometimes have these big late-night talks where we'd both end up crying. On the other hand, he could also be a complete asshole—I couldn't possibly begin to remember how many times on the tour he punched me or told me to fuck off. And I always punched him back.

NIKKI: I guess that's why they call it liquid courage. Why else would you punch an ex–Hells Angel who is a fourth-degree black belt? But Fred had a huge heart to go with all his bravado. I used to have great talks with him late into the night and we both agreed...

Chicks = trouble.

Our next album, *Dr. Feelgood,* went to Number 1 but I still say it was our second Number 1 album.

JUNE 30th 1987 MYRIAD COLISEUM OKLAHOMA

Backstage, 7:30 p.m.

Backstage is the most boring place on Earth when you're trying to be good. In fact it's the most boring place on earth even when you're bad. I haven't written in a while. I seem to have nothing to write about (to you, anyway). I can never keep these diaries up on the road because everything just seems to become a massive blur. It's really the same thing day in and day out except the shows. To see the faces of those kids...I swear it's the only reason I'm alive...

Well, I better get ready for the show. Everybody is getting along really good...no drama yet. We're leaving after the show to Shreveport. In Houston I just played guitar in my room the whole time and wrote some cool riffs and ideas.

I'm glad we're out of Texas, it was a cocaine blizzard there. I was heading down a street I've seen before and know what was next for me. I've been taking a lot of Halcions that Rich Fisher turned me on to. Between these little pills and all the blow, it's like doing speedballs with the band's stamp of approval on it.

My newest trick is crushing up the Halcions and mixing them with blow in a vial—we call this concoction zombie dust.

TOMMY LEE: Halcion was like the '80s Xanax. You'd only need to take one and immediately it would be night-night–you would be fast out until late the next morning. Well, we would take four or five of them, then start drinking Jack–and then we'd leave the hotel and go out for the night. The next morning we would be exchanging stories–"Dude, do you remember what happened last night?" "I have no idea, but I pissed my bed!" "Hey, dude, so did I!" We would wake up and not have the first idea where we were. Those pills were bizarre–they were full-on blackout, and on that tour we were taking a fucking *lot* of them.

ROSS HALFIN: On the *Girls* tour, Nikki turned me on to doing coke all night. We'd still be wired at ten the next morning, so he taught me to drink Nyquil to knock me out. Normally people would take a spoonful if they had the flu. We would drink a bottle in one go then pass out.

INTERMISSION

Well, I don't know
about you, but I need to
take a deep breath for a minute. Maybe even a cold shower.

As Mick Mars says, "That scared me, and I'm fearless."

Maybe it's a good time to veer from the darkness
and lighten up just for a second. So let me take a
minute and make a couple points here before we move
on.

When I first placed my hands on these dusty old
diaries, scraps of paper and other assorted notes and
scribbles, all kinds of feelings came bubbling up—
mostly ones of complete shock and amazement that I was
able to make any music at all during this insane time.
I mean, music drives me (sometimes crazy) and songwriting is still the one place I can get lost in and
not wanna be found…it's my one and only drug and I'm
surely addicted to it. But we're not talking about
OD'ing on a double verse and a chorus.

I had totally lost perspective and music had mostly taken a backseat to the voices in my head and the demons in my closet. I was like a guy who throws the anchor off the side of the ship but forgot to attach it to anything. You're left floating aimlessly on the Sea of Stupidity. Your only hope is to be rescued, but unfortunately for you, you're in the middle of the ocean, and the search and rescue patrol is on vacation. At some point you have to ask yourself, Who is really to blame—yourself for being stupid or the rescuers for being unavailable? All I know is music was the sails I needed to reach land, but they had tears in them the size of the Himalayas.

So another question came up for me, probably the same one you've been asking yourself the whole time you've been reading this:

How is this fucker still alive?

JUST BECAUSE YOU'VE LIVED LONG DOESN'T MEAN YOU'VE LONG TO LIVE.

True, but...

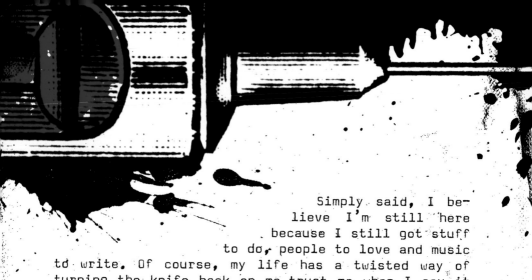

Simply said, I believe I'm still here because I still got stuff to do, people to love and music to write. Of course, my life has a twisted way of turning the knife back on me...trust me when I say it usually has a twist. And, to further my karma, it's usually one of humor.

I mean, I'll probably face my maker doing something so uncool like golfing or gardening. It would be too much for me to deal with to be sitting up there next to God, Bon Scott, Sid Vicious and Jimi Hendrix, and hear someone read my obituary from below:

NIKKI SIXX DIED TODAY...FUCKING GOLFING...

OK, enuff humor (you tend to make fun of death a lot after you've died and come back a few times...but more on that later). Let's not stray too far from the graveyard of my mind just yet.

What I can see clearly now is I was so busy running from my past that I didn't even see the headlights hinting that something disastrous was heading my way. A head-on collision was about to happen, yet I was too stubborn to take a hint, stubborn like a man who won't step back from a fight, only to find out his feet have been stuck firmly in concrete boots. Sometimes your choice is no choice at all...or so we think...

So back to the story at hand, one told by contradictions from loved ones, friends and foes who never knew they were signing the Rx on my prescription of the ultimate painkillers...the ones that numb the tornado in your head.

JULY
1987

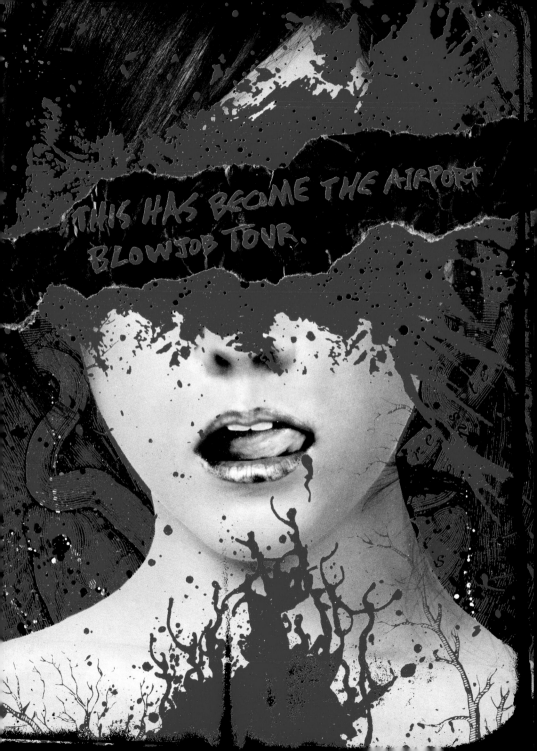

JULY 1st 1987
HIRSCH MEMORIAL COLISEUM
SHREVEPORT, LA

Backstage, 8 p.m.

This has become the airport blow job tour. After the gig when we get to the airport there's always a line of girls waiting...we've started taking them in the bathrooms of the private airports.

Oklahoma kicked ass. The show had that old school heavy metal energy. We almost had a riot before the doors opened but besides that all is normal.

Showtime. See ya...

JULY 2nd 1987
MISSISSIPPI COAST COLISEUM
BILOXI, MS

On the jet, 1:30 a.m.

We're sitting on the plane getting ready to take off for Biloxi. There is something about the fans in the South...they're insane. They're wilder and louder than the East and the West. That was a great show...what did I tell you about airports? As I sit here with a big smile on my face, the stewardess just brought me a bottle of white wine and a silver plate with one Halcion and four lines on it. I'm on my private jet and reading a review of how much we suck. It looks like everything is right on track...

TOMMY LEE: The *Girls Girls Girls* tour was absolute debauchery. It was fucking bananas. We started collecting bras, panties, shoes, dresses, skirts, naked Polaroids…everything. I remember walking on to one of our crew buses and it looked like it was fucking raining panties–there were literally thousands of pairs. It looked like a fucking bordello on wheels. They still exist somewhere: we put them all into road cases. Maybe we should open a museum?

NIKKI: The owner of the plane wouldn't let us hang them in the jet so we made the crew buses keep our "awards." It smelled like a fucking fish market in there. I hear they're at the Mötley warehouse…God help the poor bastard who opens that sealed road case.

Hotel, Biloxi, 5:30 p.m.

Just woke up. We stay here tonight. We all need a day off. Vince's voice is trashed, Tommy's hands are covered in cuts and scabs, my body is a wreck from throwing myself all over…and off…the stage, and Mars' back is killing him. He gets worse every year. I worry about him. I need to wash my leathers or even have a shower–it's been six days.

Off to the show…

NIKKI: The wear and tear of the road is something not usually seen by the fans firsthand. It comes up in photos–a line on your face here and there, or bags under your bloodshot eyes–but is easily hidden and always ignored. Showering was a luxury that myself, Mick and Tommy normally regarded as a nuisance, not a perk.

Reading back on this diary entry, I now realize the pain Mick Mars was in, but who would guess it would rear its head so violently in later years that he would suffer from a chronic degenerative bone disease called ankylosing spondylitis and would need a hip replacement operation? To put it lightly, he is a man of steel…all praise Mick Mars, the strongest man on earth.

JULY 3RD 1987 DAY-OFF
Hotel, Biloxi, 5:20 p.m.

I tossed and turned again all night. No drugs. I should have taken something to sleep but I'm trying to be good…

I just got the new Rolling Stone with us on the cover. Of course they had to take a swipe at us. The cover says:

HEAVY METAL: IT'S LOUD, IT'S UGLY, IT WON'T GO AWAY

I guess if I wanted critical acclaim I'd have picked music that doesn't ruffle any feathers…so maybe it's a compliment? Because we are loud, ugly and won't go away. Mostly 'cause they want us to.

NIKKI: When that issue of *Rolling Stone* came out, I was hugely offended. I really thought this would be the time we finally got the praise we deserved for our music. Looking back, I can't believe I took it so seriously.

I've been thinking a lot about Nona. She will have passed away a year ago next month. How life changes. She really was a mother to me. I only have good thoughts of her...she always had a smile and put food on the table. She was really into fashion so she would put patches on my clothes or make me bell-bottom pants when I started to emulate my rock 'n' roll heroes. In Jerome, Idaho, you might as well have a pink Mohawk as go into a store and ask for bell-bottoms...at least in the men's department of JC Penney...

Hell hath no fury like a small town boy with a dream.

RAISE YOUR HANDS TO ROCK

Sometimes I feel turned around
And upside down
And sometimes maybe I drink too much
But my heart's still in touch

I remember standing tall telling you
I'm gonna be a rock 'n' roll star
When someone said, Sit down boy
You already are

207

BOB MICHAELS: There was never a July Fourth that I didn't think of Nikki after one particular year–I think it was 1984. I went over to his house and he was stoned, and he fired a huge bottle rocket out of his garden. It set a forty-foot palm tree on fire and it fell onto a 1965 Mustang convertible that went up in flames. Nikki thought the whole thing was just absolutely hilarious.

JULY 5TH, 1987
MIDSOUTH COLISEUM MEMPHIS, TN

Hotel, 1:40 a.m.

Great show...sold out. We were jamming on Dancing on Glass and some guy threw a bindle onstage to me and motioned to his arm like he was shooting up. Nice. Anyway we're spending the night tonight. I have a great story about a girl, a banana and some leftover fireworks...but I'm tired. Off to bed...on my own.

I think the guys are going out to a strip club. I just know I'd get in trouble if I go. I'm gonna work on some music tomorrow and I don't want a hangover. Once I start, I can never stop...so I'll stop now...

DOC McGHEE: Nikki was actually more manageable than usual on the *Girls Girls Girls* tour. He wasn't as aggressive as he usually was. He didn't want to go out to clubs so much–I guess because he was sunk into his fucking heroin den. In a way I was almost grateful. When the other maniacs were doing their fucking crazy shit, I could think at least Nikki is in his room–he didn't kill anybody today.

JULY 6TH 1987 DAY OFF
Hotel, Memphis, 7 p.m.

Day off...nothing too exciting. Reading a book called Nigger by Dick Gregory. It's killer. It's about one of

the first black comedians and all the prejudice that
happened to him in the '50s and '60s. I can relate to
prejudice. When my mom was dating Richard Pryor people gave us so many looks and comments…a bit like the
ones I get in the hotel gift shop downstairs when I
still have my stage makeup on and my stinky sweaty
leathers. It's like I'm a leper to people in the
Midwest. Maybe I'm just a nigger?

NIKKI: I remember my mom dating Richard Pryor. He
was always nice to me. One of my most vivid memories
was living in a ninth-floor apartment in Hollywood. I
used to take Ceci down to the parking lot to play–we
didn't have a yard because we were right on Sunset
Boulevard. Mom hadn't been home in days, and we were
playing when Mom and Richard pulled up. They were
both smashed and my mom fell out of the car and
hugged me, and they both said hi, then went upstairs. I
stayed in the cement underground that was our playground. It didn't occur to me until years later what kind
of scars that sort of stuff left on my childhood…and it
never even came to my mind that Richard was black and
my mom was white. I've never cared about unimportant
shit like that.

DEANA RICHARDS: I was working as a croupier in
Lake Tahoe when I met Richard. I was working dealing
blackjack one night, and I looked up from the table and
into these eyes, and–BAM! I had never been out with a
black man in my life, and I didn't even notice that it was
a black man standing there. I just looked into those eyes
and that was it.

I saw him a few nights later and it hit me again, and then
a friend arranged for us to meet up. We met and went out
and ended up backstage at a show talking to Bill Cosby.
Then when Richard went back to Los Angeles, we used
to fly back and forth to see each other–we were deadly
serious about our relationship.

Richard was a very deep, intense man who was terribly hurt by the world. We used to go down to the beach a lot and he'd run through his routines and I'd suggest things he could change. He was always running around the beach with his arms up, yelling, "Will you let me be me?" He said I was the only person who had ever appreciated his soul. I certainly appreciated his spirit.

Nikki was about five then and Richard loved him–he thought Nikki was so cute, just "It." But this was the early '60s, and Richard and I would encounter racism. We'd go into restaurants and people would look at us really weird, and the waiters would refuse to serve us. Richard was very outspoken so he'd always say something and cause trouble, and then we would have to leave.

Eventually I moved to Los Angeles to be with Richard and left Nikki with my mother and sisters. I was going to send for him when I was settled, but when I got to LA, everything fell apart–Richard got arrested for beating up a hotel desk clerk and went to jail. Everything went to hell…and when I finally got Nikki back, it was hell on him too.

JULY 7TH 1987 MUNICIPAL AUDITORIUM, NASHVILLE, TN
On the jet, 2:30 p.m.

Every time I try to get Neglektra to do something exciting they always complain. They don't wanna spend the money…fucking lame. I used to think this was the cool label because they had Queen. Now I can see the truth…they probably fucked up Queen's career too…

When you're hot they act like they love you (they do love the money we make them)…but when you need

the support, there
is no love to be
found. Bob Krasnow is
so in the Stone Age.
Eventually we need to get rid
of this record company. All they do
is put our albums out...there's little or
no promotion and we still sell millions
of albums and sell out tours.

It's not just the label...it's management
too. They just don't know how to motivate the
label or threaten them. Imagine the damage we could do
if Elektra did more than throw it against the wall and
hope it sticks.

MY RECORD COMPANY THEORY

1. They're the bank for the music.
2. They distribute the music.
3. They print and press the music (and charge
back a huge %).
4. They should never own anybody's music just for
doing 1, 2 and 3.
5. You never see this happen in other businesses.

P.S. We do all the work, write all the music...they
loan us money...we have to pay it back, and they
own us? What the fuck is wrong with the
music business? No wonder they like us
fucked up on drugs. If we're out of
our heads, we won't see how they're
taking advantage...it's slavery.

P.P.S. See what happens when
I don't get fucked up? My brain
starts to work again.

IAN GITTINS: Mötley Crüe eventually regained control of the master tapes of their albums from Elektra Records. Both Nikki Sixx and the band's current manager, Allen Kovac, are legally bound from discussing the circumstances that led to this coup and the terms of the deal, but it is generally accepted that Elektra surrendered control of the masters in exchange for Mötley waiving royalty earnings that were due to them. As Mötley Crüe is still releasing new albums and touring massive arenas a decade later, it seems fair to surmise that Elektra may very well be deeply regretting that particular decision.

NIKKI: We had to sign a non-disclosure agreement so other artists couldn't find out how we did it. I can tell you this: Elektra chief executive Sylvia Rhone fell for it hook, line and sinker.

Rule Number Three: NEVER ALLOW EMOTIONS TO GET IN THE WAY OF BUSINESS

TOM ZUTAUT: As smart as McCartney, Jagger, Bono, Page and Plant may be, none of them own their masters that they signed away as kids to a record company. Nikki signed his masters away to Elektra as a young kid filled with hopes and dreams, yet as an adult he was shrewd enough to irritate then-head of Elektra Records, Sylvia Rhone, by behaving like a kid again to get her to give them back to him. Big music corporations rarely make mistakes like that, and it's no accident that it's Nikki who got his masters back. That's Sikki Nixx for you!

SYLVIA RHONE: Would I like to take part in this book? I don't think it would be appropriate.

JULY 8TH 1987
THE ARENA ST. LOUIS, MO
Hotel, St Louis, 4:30 p.m.

Need to go to the gym. Been having a few drinks (a half-bottle of Jack) every night but that's mostly it. I'm pretty proud of myself. But dear diary, I'm so bored. I can smell trouble lurking...is that why I agreed to let Vanity come to Minneapolis??

JULY 9TH 1987 DAY OFF
Hotel, St Louis, 10:55 p.m.

Another night in the same hotel. I met two girls in the lobby last night. We had a little ménage à trois. I was doing lines of blow off this one girl's ass...now THAT was fun. Fred came down to my room and said, Damn, Sixxdog, what are you doing? I said trying to beat the boredom, and he said, "It looks like you're doing a pretty good job." I love Fred. So I asked him if he wanted a bump and he said sure. I tapped out a bump on this other girl's ass and Fred snorted it, said, "Thanks" like it was an everyday thing and left.

God, do we lose sight of what's real out on the road, or what?

FRED SAUNDERS: We had laminates made for all that production staff on the *Girls* tour with special codes. We started doing it because the hotel lobbies were always swarming with kids so we couldn't say the band's names on our walkie-talkies: if we'd been overheard, there would have been a riot! So we gave everyone numbers:

1. Doc McGhee
2. Doug Thaler
3. Rich Fisher
4. Me
5. Vince
6. Nikki
7. Mick
00. Tommy

Then it spread to cover other things:

20. where are you?
100. krell
101. hotel
129. gig
268. tour bus
714. groupie
747. pig with lipstick

So we might say something like, What's your 20? Well, I'm with 6 who has a 747 and some 100 on the 268 on the way to 129. It stopped people eavesdropping and was a bit of fun as well. Sometimes the band would talk like that all the way from the gig back to the hotel…I mean, from the 129 to the 101.

JULY 10TH, 1987 KANSAS COLISEUM WICHITA, KS
Hotel, Wichita, 4:10 p.m.

What's with all the black girls chasing me down these days? Ever since Vanity started talking to the press, they're all coming on to me. It's like a fucking epidemic…

Tommy and Vince have been squabbling again. Those two can drive me and Mick crazy. But the band's sounding really good, and that's all that matters in the end...

7 p.m.

Whitesnake is supporting us now. They are so boring. I hate their new corporate music as well. David Coverdale was in Deep Purple so you'd think he was cool as fuck. But no, yesterday he told the crowd he had diarrhea...can you believe that shit? (joke!) And the fucked-up thing is he DOES have it. I walked into a bathroom after him and he told me not to go in the can 'cause he just sprayed water out his ass. Then he goes onstage and whines to the audience about it!

Every time I meet rock stars, I seem to lose faith...are there any left? Earth to Johnny Thunders, please wake up and put the Dolls back together...please.

That chick Tawny Kitaen that Tommy used to bang is out here with David Coverdale. I hope Tommy fucks her while Diarrhea Boy is onstage...

FRED SAUNDERS: What was Whitesnake like on the *Girls Girls Girls* tour? They were a joy to work with. They were just totally professional. Mr. David Coverdale is the Richard Burton of rock.

JULY 11ᵗʰ 1987
KEMPER ARENA KANSAS CITY, MO
Backstage, 7 p.m.

After the show last night we left for the airport at 1:30 a.m. Some days, when I sit in the plane looking over the skies, I wonder when this tour is gonna end.

I forgot—Vanity is coming in tomorrow—or is it tonight? I think she's been trying to stay off drugs so maybe it won't be a disaster—I guess she means well.

FRED SAUNDERS: Whenever Vanity came out to meet the tour, I wouldn't see her or Nikki apart from at the shows. I think she liked coke and heroin—well, certainly coke as much as Nikki did; they would just go and lock down behind the bed in their hotel room and do huge quantities of drugs.

JULY 12th, 1987
VETERANS MEMORIAL
AUDITORIUM
DES MOINES, IA
On the jet,
1 a.m.

We're flying into Minneapolis right now for a day off. The band sounded like shit tonight, everyone was drunk. Mick's on this Mars-ade kick...what is Mars-ade, you ask? Well, it's a lot of vodka and a splash of Gatorade (for coloring) so basically it's just vodka.

Hint: Never go to Mick's side of the stage for water. I gulped some down last night and just about puked...it was pure vodka. I think he's buffering his sorrow over that bitch he was with. I think a gun would cure his sorrow a lot better and faster. Shouldn't murder be legal for gold diggers?

MICK MARS: I was mostly drunk at all the shows on the *Girls Girls Girls* tour. I would drink straight vodka onstage, and sometimes Nikki would come to my side of the stage, think it was water and drink it. So on top of his habit, he'd get really drunk. We were all fucked up–I don't know how we got through a song, let alone the set. I'd fall off the stage quite a bit. We weren't the best sounding band, but somehow people seemed to keep coming and keep screaming.

JULY 13th 1987 DAY OFF
Hotel, Minneapolis, 6:10 p.m.

We're doing two shows at the Met Center. It's always a badass gig. 17,000 kids each night, sold out...nice...home of the Minnesota Vikings...

I'm so bored being off junk. At least I'm still able to get drunk every night, and zombie dust rules. It's my new best friend.

JULY 14th 1987
MET CENTER, MINNEAPOLIS, MN
Hotel, Minneapolis, 3 a.m.

. Tim is mad at me 'cause I made him drink Jack in front of the audience tonight. I got a little carried away and it got in his eyes and all over him. He's not digging that I make him dress like a priest.

Besides that the show kicked ass. I'm so tired of saying that...it's more exciting when we suck. God bless the Sex Pistols.

Vanity came in but stayed at the hotel...cool. She is a nice girl at heart but she just drives me nutz. After the sex, I wish she would turn into a bottle of Jack.

TIM LUZZI: *Girls Girls Girls* was the tour of hell so I guess they needed a priest. I would go onstage every night in a priest's robes and Nikki would grab my hair, tilt my head back and pretend to make me drink Jack Daniel's. He would hold his thumb over the bottle so I didn't actually have to drink, except for a few nights when he moved his thumb so loads of Jack cascaded down my throat. Maybe it was his revenge because I wouldn't take heroin with him.

EVANGELIST DENISE MATTHEWS: The earth has been known for vomiting itself up because of the sin and idolatry it produces. That is just what happened to my body. I had a demented, careless vision of my future and it wasn't very bright, but isn't that what the limelight is–the green slime underneath a filthy bathroom toilet seat?

NIKKI: I thought the Limelight was a club in NYC?

EVANGELIST DENISE MATTHEWS: Eventually it is idolatry, and that is what the Devil has led us to believe is the road to stardom, fortune, riches and the glamorous life, as if to fulfill our every desire. But then you wake up and find yourself lost and alone. We go from one person to the next looking for love and can't find it because we haven't healed our insides yet. We feel filthy inside and try our hardest to be pretty outside. Most people are walking around in a daze wishing they weren't alive.

JULY 15TH 1987
MET CENTER MINNEAPOLIS, MN

Backstage, 8:20 p.m.

After tonight's show we fly straight to Chicago.
I don't see any end to this tour...

JULY 16 1987
ROSEMONT HORIZON CHICAGO IL

Hotel, Chicago, 6 a.m.

Did a ton of cocaine tonight with Tommy and Fred
after the Met show and on the plane to here. Went
to an underground club in Chicago at 3 a.m....the
usual whores and hangers-on. I loved it, but now
the girls are gone, my ears are ringing and I'm
coked out of my mind watching the sun come up. So
I'm gonna rant...let me grab a couple Halcions and
a cocktail...then I gotta get some sleep.

Sometimes I feel like we're a dirt magnet. All
the lawsuits and accusations are just a way for
slimeballs to try and rape us for our money. People
think we're so fucking rich. If they really understood how much we spend on a tour like this (or
any other) they would be blown away.

Out of 100% of the money made, tours like
this bring in about 20-30% after all the costs
(this shit ain't cheap). Then we split it four
ways, and then there's that asshole Uncle Sam. So
out of $10 million we bring home say $3 million.
Split it four ways equals about $750,000, then tax
that...gives each guy about $400,000.

Now I'm not complaining but after 12 months on
the road that's about $30,000 a month. Then deduct
car, house, clothes and just living—you get the idea.

We're not fucking rich. There's not enough to give it away to little fucking assholes with made-up lies just to gouge us.

Why the rant? Because we're getting sued by some fucker who said he lost his hearing at our concert a while back. I bet he could hear just fine if I asked him if he wanted a check for $25k to go away.

Good night. Or good morning...

P.S. I left Vanity in Minneapolis—maybe she can hook up with Dozen Roses Boy. God, I'm an asshole.

4:30 p.m.

Just woke up. Another day, another show, another hotel...nothing on TV, nothing on my mind, nothing to write about...

Off to sound check. If it wasn't for these pages I call my friend, I would surely have no escape for the demons in my head.

JULY 17TH 1987 DAY OFF

Hotel, Chicago, 5:55 a.m.

Just got back from the show and then a transvestite bar where we all drank vodka shots, ate caviar and laughed our asses off at all the characters of the night. We had these twins with us who were making out with each other for our entertainment. Fans were outside the club for hours and the police came in at one point. When they did we had these silver trays with silver lids with lines of coke on them. I felt like it was going down but a cop just said they love the band and if any cops bust our balls while we're in Chicago just call them, and he gave us their numbers.

I almost asked if they wanted a line, but thought, Why push my luck?

Even with all that's gone good I feel the boredom of the road has started to set in and bigger and badder versions of Mötley hedonism are waiting in the shadows. It's lurking and whispering my name. Here's the sick part—I'm proud to say I'm just doing pills, blow and drinking (a lot)—no heroin. Good night, my sleeping pills are calling.—

9:20 p.m.

Damn it. Dark outside already and I just woke up. I unplugged the alarm clock so I can't see its fucking glow. Now the big dilemma...what the hell to order from room service?

JULY 18TH 1987, MARKET SQUARE ARENA INDIANAPOLIS, IN

Hotel, Chicago, 4 a.m.

Went to some strip club with the band. I asked the Whitesnake guys to come with us (saw them in the bar downstairs) but one of them...Vivian I think his name is...said he was gonna stay in and practice. What the fuck? There's too much world to destroy to be sitting in your room playing the same shit you played when you were 15. These guys put my ass to sleep. I can't wait for Guns N' Roses to come out with us. I gotta go, there's a redhead in my bed passed out, and I gotta kick her out.

Bored in Chicago, Sixx.

DOUG THALER: During the *Girls Girls Girls* tour, Whitesnake was actually bigger than Mötley Crüe. Mötley had a Number 2 album, but Whitesnake had a Number 1. They were originally only going to play a few early dates, but after I increased their fee from $4,000 per night to $10,000, they ended up staying with us right until the end of October–and I was glad they did.

On the jet, 2:30 p.m.

Sitting on the jet hungover. I guess I drank more than I thought last night. Vince and Fred said I was smashed. I think the zombie dust gives me the illusion I'm keeping it together. Oh well, beats junk...four aspirin, please.

We have a gig in Indy tonight then after the show we're leaving for my favorite rock city in the world...Detroit. Two sold-out shows...badass.

On the jet, 1 a.m.

Tonight we shot a live video for Wild Side. What would people think if they knew they were singing a raped and dismantled version of the Lord's Prayer...and knew how I came to write it? I wonder how Becky is now?

WAYNE ISHAM: When we came to shoot the "Wild Side" video, Nikki said what he always said to me: "I don't want the same old Bon Jovi shit." So we decided to do a really mental over-the-top live video.

I put cameras everywhere. Tommy had his revolving drum kit, so we put a camera on that. I wanted to put a camera on Nikki's bass but he wouldn't let me, so we put it on Mick's guitar instead. Then there was a huge Plexiglass ball with a camera in it that we threw into the crowd to get some crazy shots from there. Of course, being Mötley fans, they ended up breaking it.

The problem was Mötley had this thing called Double Bubble...they'd give you a bottle of Jack Daniel's before the show and shout "Double Bubble," which meant you had to drink straight from the bottle until the bubbles went up it–twice! So I was trying to work the main camera onstage, shit-faced, and Nikki came up behind me and bit me really hard on the arm. I suddenly had this searing pain and Nikki was standing in front of me, laughing his head off. He thought it was the funniest thing in the world.

JULY 19TH 1987, JOE LOUIS ARENA DETROIT, MI
Hotel, Detroit, 5:25 p.m.

Floating in depression. I can't seem to find a footing in life. I don't know why but some days I wish I was a kid back on the streets of Seattle, hanging out with other musicians who were bent on reinventing the music that drove us from insanity...Rob Hemphil, Rick Van Zandt and the others. School was a thing we did so we could do what it is we really want and need to do and that's to dream.

Now my dream is here and I don't have the tools to undo the damage done to me as a child.

Why am I so pissed?

Why do kids relate to me?

I got the second answer, but not the first. It's easy, 'cause I'm fucked up like them. Not by our own actions either...others broke us...not that it's hard to break a kid. Now us (the kids) are gonna break you.

Fuck everything...somebody get me a doctor.

JULY 20TH 1987
JOE LOUIS ARENA DETROIT, MI
Backstage, 11:45 p.m.

I love it when the band is on fire. Great show, second one sold out here. We slithered through the set like a sidewinder, fangs exposed yet somehow charming at times. I smiled all the while, what a Cheshire cat I must have looked like. Swigging whisky, reeling in contentment...moments like these must be savored...

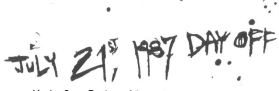

JULY 21ST, 1987 DAY OFF

Hotel, Detroit, 6 p.m.

I've been going from very up and happy to feeling completely depressed lately and I don't know why. No more or less drugs and booze than usual. Pills by the handful but nothing less than slightly out of control. I feel like something is gonna crash soon...it feels like impending doom.

I'll be at home this time next week. I don't know if that's good or bad...maybe both.

DOUG THALER: In some ways Nikki didn't seem so different on the *Girls Girls Girls* tour. The truth was that often you just couldn't tell if he was on a coke high, or a Jack Daniel's high, or whatever. All that we knew was that he was kind of shifty and we had to watch him like a hawk.

JULY 22ND, 1987 DAY OFF
Hotel, Detroit, 8:40 p.m.

Lay in bed all day watching TV. Nothing too exciting except that Doug called and told me Too Fast for Love has gone platinum...not bad for a lil punk rock record.

JULY 23RD, 1987
CINCINNATI GARDENS
CINCINNATI, OH
On jet to Cincinnati, 2 p.m.

Vince can never sleep alone. He has a different girl every night. I can't understand that, because I need to be alone. I'm always alone in a room full of people. I can never understand Vince holding hands with a girl that he's just met. It blows me away. It's not just getting laid-he has one flying in and one flying out every day. I've seen them pass in the hallway. He not only never gets caught, he has no remorse. Sometimes one is his old lady too.

Vince is a sex addict, but I guess me calling him an addict is the pot calling the kettle black.

FRED SAUNDERS: Vince Neil was very high-maintenance on the *Girls* tour. I think he thought he was Elvis Presley. When he got really drunk I would take all of his jewelry off him before he went out, because he was always getting robbed. The other thing he'd do was come in all the time boasting about exactly how many girls he'd slept with. Oh yes, he was a real piece of work all right.

JULY 24TH, 1987
THE COLISEUM RICHMOND, OH
Hotel, Cleveland, 2 p.m.

Woke up in Cleveland. These hotels are starting to look all the same. Another show tonight, I really need a day off. Thank God I'm home in three days. My hands are so bruised and cut up—my body is fucked up. I seem to do things to my body onstage that I don't feel until the adrenaline wears off—or the alcohol...

JULY 25TH 1987 DAY OFF
On the jet to Hebron, 4 p.m.

Sometimes I just run out of juice. I hit a wall and I can't move. It's not the hangovers or the half-life from the pills...it's something else. I don't know what it is, but the only way through it is to put your head down and drive into the end zone. It's like I have a chemical imbalance.

I was reading a story in the newspaper recently about low blood sugar and alcohol. I wonder if I have low blood sugar.

I can't wait to get tomorrow out of the fucking way and get home.

Anyway, I'm fucking bored and just rambling, so rather than bore you with my mundane scribbles, I'll just put down the pen and pick up the guitar. There's gotta be a song in there somewhere, just waiting to come out—I just gotta muster up the energy to pull it out…

MICK MARS: By this stage of the tour I couldn't tell if Nikki was high because I was normally high too. The shows were all pretty consistent: here comes the Jack Daniel's bottle, who can drink the most, how many bubbles can you do with it. I would line up shots of vodka one after the other then go back to my room and order champagne and wine—it was pretty fucked. But I don't think I ever realized quite how bad Nikki was getting.

JULY 26TH, 1987
BUCKEYE LAKE MUSIC CENTER HEBRON, OH
On the Mötley jet to LA, 2 a.m.

There were 40,000 kids tonight…what a great show. The band was firing on all cylinders. We were on top of it—40,000 kids all with their fists in the air, shouting at the top of their lungs. Some days you just nail it like a machine. The band was so tight and I could just feel the electricity from the crowd. This is a really nice way to end. Now we have four days off. Should get in about 8:30—I can't wait to sleep in my own bed. My clothes stink so bad. I need to change out my suitcase with new clothes.

FRED SAUNDERS: Buckeye Lake was a huge outdoor show with Whitesnake and Anthrax. We had a small disaster that day. When Mötley played "Smokin' in the Boys' Room," Vince was supposed to play a harmonica solo. Vince can't even play the harmonica but I can, so we'd cut Vince's mic off and he'd lip-synch and pretend to be playing, while the truth was that I was hidden at the side of the stage and playing into a mic. I used to watch him up there, posing and sucking in his cheeks. But at Buckeye Lake, I was practicing and the hidden mic was somehow on, so this "Smokin' in the Boys' Room" harp solo suddenly came blasting out of nowhere in the middle of a different song completely. Vince looked real pissed, as usual.

JULY 27TH 1987 AT HOME

Van Nuys, 9 p.m.

Home. Thank fuck. I washed my clothes, washed my car, checked my answering machine. I had 67 messages... erased them all. Went through the mail...I had a check for $650k sitting there. I keep telling the office to collect my mail and redirect it when I'm on tour. Come on, over half-a-million dollars sitting there in my mailbox on the street? That's some crazy shit...

JULY 28TH, 1987 AT HOME

Van Nuys, 10:20 p.m.

Slept all day.

I just wrote a new song called. A Is for Asshole.

A is for Asshole
B is for Being Me

JULY 29TH AT HOME, 1987

Van Nuys, midnight

I wish I missed someone as much as I miss smack.
It haunts me like a lover I never got to say goodbye
to.

Can't wait to get out of here. I feel like I'm hanging by a thread. I feel safer from junk on the road.
I've been fending off the wolves who have come knocking at my door. They all know I'm home…

God, please keep them away…

JULY 30TH 1987 AT HOME

Van Nuys, 6:40 p.m.

Today I'm laying in this bed and am so lonely—at
the top? I feel trapped in my own destiny. On days like
today, I understand suicide. I wonder if I will make
it all the way to the end of my life? I wonder if I
have the ability to love someone enough to make them
feel safe?

Days like these I hate to leave my house. I can
muster up a fake smile and be cordial, but deep inside
I feel nobody really likes me…and worse…nobody understands me.

I feel like I am completely alone on this planet.

NIKKI: In retrospect I can see now that depression was
not just knocking at my door but had clearly kicked it in
and made itself right at home in my head. Sometimes
things are so close that you just can't see them. I love the
word "accumulative"…emotional problems are so often
the end result of many things going on. It wasn't just the

drugs, the alcohol, the pills, the fame or the childhood. It was accumulative, and the list was growing and growing... and growing...

ORIGINAL SONG LYRIC

NOBODY KNOWS WHAT I'TS LIKE TO BE LONELY

I've got the power
I've got the power
I've got the power
But it still hurts
when you're all alone.

JULY 31ST 1987
CIVIC ARENA PITTSBURGH PA

On a flight from LAX to Cleveland, 11:45 a.m.

My time at home went so quick, so now it's another month on the road. I can't count the miles, or remember the hotels. I don't remember the cities and I can't see the end in sight. If it wasn't for the music and the fans this would be as close to Chinese water torture as you could get. Repetition...over and over and over...drip drip drip...

Ya I'm whining. I guess I'm just tired. This flight left LA at 9 a.m. We land in Cleveland at 4 then catch another flight to Pittsburgh where we land at 6, then we have a show...it's a good one. 16K, sold out. So I better get some sleep. I sorta forgot to go to sleep last night-I had some late-night visitors. Jason hasn't changed...

It's good to be outta LA.

AUGUST 1ST 1987 THE COLISEUM, RICHFIELD, OH

Hotel, Cleveland, 2:15 a.m.

I can't wait to sleep. I'm over-tired. My ears are ringing. I think I'm getting sick...or maybe my visit home is still in my system.

AUGUST 2, 1987 MEMORIAL AUDITORIUM, BUFFALO, NY

Noon

Wow, I just woke up...I really needed that sleep. Thank God the phone rang, we're supposed to be heading to the airport in an hour. It was a radio interview for our show tonight in Buffalo.

Here we go into New York. NY is almost as bad as LA for me. I'm not sure which is worse...the record company, the drug dealers or the girls. Maybe they're all the same person.

AUGUST 3RD 1987 DAY OFF

Hotel, Philadelphia, 4 p.m.

Why do I feel Mick has a gold digger on his hands? Mick Mars is the sweetest man alive, but he attracts dirt...he's like a dirt magnet.

CHICKS = TROUBLE.

AUGUST 4TH 1987
SPECTRUM, PHILADELPHIA, PA

Hotel, Philadelphia, 5 p.m.

Went down to the hotel bar last night, pretty sedate evening. Just had a few cocktails and met some fans. Kind of a nice evening. I feel good today, but I did get a call from Sacha-he said he wanted to see me. Of course he does...he's a heroin dealer.

I tell you, the East Coast is bad for me...here come the wolves.

I'm gonna change my rooming name so nobody can find me. How about some of these?

Anita Bath?

Al Coholic?

Seymour Pussy?

Or the best one of all...

Si Cotic

P.S. Now we're off to the first of two sold-out Spectrum shows. Woo-hoo... later.

AUGUST 5TH 1987

Hotel, Philadelphia, 4 p.m. SPECTRUM, PHILADELPHIA, PA

The crowd was so loud last night, insane. Philly really loves their rock 'n' roll.

I met this mulatto girl last night who was so beautiful that I couldn't believe it. She was really,
really nice. She came back to my room and hung out.
One thing led to another and afterwards when we were
laying there (I was thinking, This one's a keeper),
she said that she had a kid and she needs money for
rent and could I help her with her car payment...and
school for her kid. She was really pouring it on.

It went on forever...blah blah blah. Basically, would
I pay her for her services? So I kicked her out. Damn
it—maybe I'm the dirt magnet...

P.S. Another Philly show tonight...

RANDOM THOUGHT
IF YOU GO SHOPPING AT THE GARBAGE DUMP,
YOU'RE GONNA BRING HOME TRASH

ROSS HALFIN: Nikki went off with girls on the *Girls*
tour but they were never really his focus. He was far
more into the drugs. We'd get drunk and do lots of krell
and he'd want a girl, but essentially he was totally drug-
oriented. Often he'd end up staying in his room on his
own. We all knew that meant he had drugs and didn't
want to share them with anyone. Or he had a girl and
wanted to do her on drugs.

AUGUST 6TH 1987 DAY OFF
Hotel, Philadelphia, 3 p.m.

Me and Tommy stole the limo last night. It was funny
as hell. When we got back to the hotel and our driver
got out of the car to open the door for us, we locked

the doors, jumped over the seat and drove the car off. He was chasing us around the hotel parking lot and we accidentally crashed it through the hotel gate. The guy was so fucking pissed and then the hotel manager came out yelling, telling us to get the fuck out of his hotel. Fred Saunders had to talk him out of fucking calling the police. We said we were sorry (of course we're not) and didn't get kicked out the hotel. Maybe 'cause we've spent about $30,000 here so far.

FRED SAUNDERS: You know what? There was always shit like that going on with Nikki and Tommy. Especially Nikki. He had me at my wits' end. He had so many façades, and was so sporadic and unpredictable. There were countless management meetings called during the *Girls* tour just to try to figure out what to do with him. By the end of the tour I was hiring security guards at each hotel and just leaving two of them on his door permanently.

ROSS HALFIN: I always said that Tommy should have married Nikki because if they were gay they would be the ideal gay couple–made in Heaven. Tommy would do anything Nikki wanted him to. In fact, they all would.

Nikki was selfish, self-centered and a control freak, paranoid of what anybody else might do, but without him Mötley Crüe would never have been successful, It was his vision and you did what Nikki wanted.

NIKKI: There has been a lot said about control and I admit it: I was a control freak. But someone needs to be in control when everything is always outta control. I felt if I took my hands off the wheel we surely would have crashed. Even if I was drunk driving at least I was driving us somewhere…I was passionate, even when I was skidding outta control…

AUGUST 7TH 1987
CUMBERLAND COUNTY CIVIC CENTER
PORTLAND, ME

Philly airport, 2:30 p.m.

We're sitting on the Mötley jet getting ready to take off to Portland. Everybody is still cracking up about the limo.

I just remembered that Portland is where we started our Ozzy support tour in '84. What great memories. I miss Ozzy…I hope he's doing good…

Tommy just sat down next to me and said, Dude, I pissed my bed again last night. He's always fucking doing that. I said, Why don't you pee before you go to bed? And he said, I do, man, but I drink so fucking much!

That makes sense.

TOP FIVE TOUR ACTIVITIES

1. CRASHED LIMOS? 1
2. COCAINE? IT'S SNOWING
   8-BALLS
3. WHISKY? BY THE GALLON
4. WHORES? MORE THAN WE
   CAN TAKE ADVANTAGE OF
5. REPERCUSSIONS? NONE

GOD BLESS ROCK 'N' ROLL...

AUGUST 8TH, 1987 CIVIC CENTER, PROVIDENCE, RI
Four Seasons Hotel, Boston, 1 p.m.

After the show last night we flew into Boston (home
of Aerosmith and the Cars). We're hubbing out of here
for a few days. I love being able to get all settled
in and not having to pack up every day.

I sorta miss the bus sometimes. The lull of the
engine just rocks you to sleep, and the after-show
party always ends up as a wet spot on the floor somewhere in the back lounge. It's hard getting laid on a
road case, but beggars can't be choosers.

We're flying to Providence for a show and then back
here to sleep...if we do sleep.

TOM ZUTAUT: I went to one show on the *Girls Girls
Girls* tour with a girl whom I was on a second or third
date with, and took her backstage and introduced her to

Nikki. He asked me if I was serious about her, and when I replied that we were just getting to know each other, Nikki started telling her how hot she was.

As he bent her over what was a locker-room bench she complained that she was in the middle of her period. Nikki told her he wasn't scared by a little bit of blood and proceeded to have intercourse with her right there on the spot, in front of anybody who happened to be there. While I might have expected that sort of behavior from Vince, it was shocking to see Nikki behave like that.

At least he apologized to me afterwards and said he didn't know what made him do it. Maybe he didn't, but I certainly did–drugs, alcohol and too much fame and fortune. Only a narcissistic, strung-out asshole would grab his A&R man's date and do her backstage in front of an audience.

AUGUST 9TH 1987 DAY OFF

Four Seasons Hotel, Boston, 3 p.m.

I'm going back to bed. We have the whole floor of the hotel and it was completely insane last night...it was like a Four Seasons orgy. All the room doors were open and people were running up and down the hallway naked, bouncing from room to room. I finally had enuff at 5 a.m. I think Tommy and Vince saw the sun come up.

Sacha keeps calling the production office leaving me messages. I guess he has got an itinerary from Doc. If Doc really knew what Sacha does for money (besides driving a limo) he would have him shot. Considering Doc used to deal drugs, you would think he'd have a better nose for sniffing out dealers.

I haven't spoken to Vanity in a few weeks, and it's fucking wonderful. I wonder if she still thinks we're getting married?!

> **DOC McGHEE:** Sacha was a Russian who worked for me for quite a while as a limo driver out of New York. I knew he supplied blow to the Crüe guys sometimes, but that was no big deal—some days they would ask doormen or bellboys for blow! But I have to say I had no idea that Sacha was supplying Nikki Sixx with heroin.

> **NIKKI:** It's no big deal to supply cocaine to the band. I think this comes under the heading of "Keep them fucked up and keep them out on the road."

AUGUST 10TH, 1987 CENTRUM, WORCESTER, MA

Four Seasons Hotel, Boston, 12:30 p.m.

Just ordered some room service. Got to catch the plane to Worcester for two sold-out shows. We will come back to the hotel after...

OK, time for me to bitch right now...

I love playing our music but I can't take the monotony of playing the same set every night. When we're playing more than one night in a city (like tonight) or when the cities are real close, I know a lot of the same fans see the same show. I just wish we could have no set list; the band could know 30 or 40 songs, and we could just call them out as we go along. We could have our opening and closing songs but otherwise fill it in as we go. But the bands feel more comfortable with a set list. It's such a great show, but another night of feeling frustration at playing the same set in the same order for me.

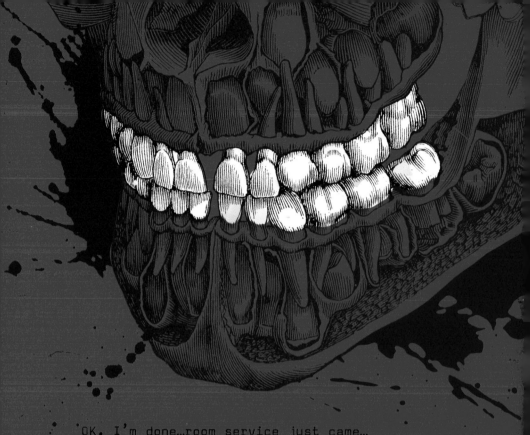

OK, I'm done...room service just came...

AUGUST 11ᵀᴴ 1987
Four Seasons Hotel, Boston, around noon DAY OFF

Another great show for us last night. Going back
for another in an hour or so. Nothing new to report
except that after Worcester we're going to NY and
I'm nervous.

If I believed there was a God, I'd ask him for
strength right now...

AUGUST 12th, 1987 DAY OFF

Parker Meridian Hotel, New York, 4 p.m.

I've been thinking about when I was in rehab and how hard it was for me to face my addiction. I couldn't handle their force-fed God-driven system but what gave me strength was talking to the other junkies. I always have people coming up and talking to me about drugs, how they can't get off and how they have lost hope. I try to help in my own way...

If I could ever get myself straight I know I could help others. But you can't help anybody unless you help yourself...

Going over to Scores for dinner in an hour with T-Bone and Vince.

Midnight

Just got back from dinner. Guess who our limo driver was? Right...Sacha...fuck! When I saw him I knew I was dead in the water...so I ask him if he has any, and then he asks me why I haven't called him back. It's like he's punishing me for not answering his calls. All these dealers are on a power trip, like that fuck Jason.

In the end, when I was in the bathroom taking a piss, he handed me a bindle of Persian smack. I asked him, How much? He said, Oh you can pay me later. Fuck...so now I sit here looking at this shit, knowing I shouldn't, but I already did a couple of bumps in the bathroom and I have this girl coming over.

Heroin is great for sex. You can't cum.

At least I'm not shooting it. I'll call down to room service and get some tinfoil and just chase the dragon.

AUGUST 13, 1987
MEADOWLANDS ARENA
EAST RUTHERFORD, NJ
Parker Meridian Hotel, New York, 7 a.m.

The girl just left. She brought some blow and I kept going in the bathroom and chasing the dragon. I had to kick her out. All these bimbos are the same. I wonder how they can even tie their shoes, they're so stupid. Sometimes I think I should just buy a blow-up party doll. Same level of intelligence, plastic and full of air...

The problem is, I'd probably fall in love.

I have to go to bed. I have a show today.

5 p.m.

I just woke up. I feel like hell. Too sick to try to clean up.

The only way out is the hair of the dog...or is it hair of the dragon?

7 p.m.

Off to the Meadowlands-am I demented? I forgot Vanity said she's coming to NY and I said OK. I'm sick to my stomach in more ways than one...

245

Parker Meridian Hotel, New York, 1 p.m.

Vanity came in just in time for the show last night. The first hour or so it's nice to see her, then I start to get this uneasy feeling like she's gonna say something and embarrass me. It's like the same movie over and over again. I need to stop this. She's not a bad person, I know she can't help it…she had a fucked-up childhood like me and it's her struggle with God and cocaine that is driving her insane. But I need to just end this. We don't belong together.

I'm gonna hide these diaries 'cause if she found them she would lose what's left of her mind. Also I'd better hide my lil bindle of Sacha special blend and the packet of fresh rigs he gave me at the show last night. Or better still, take them with me.

P.S. We have a gig in Troy tonight, I think I'll leave her here. I'll be back about 2 or 3 a.m.

NIKKI: I had good reason to be nervous about New York City. In 1985 Mötley played Madison Square Garden. After the show we all went back to the hotel, and as soon as everybody was in their rooms I jumped in a cab and went to Alphabet City with a couple of thousand dollars in my pocket.

I found a shooting gallery, went in, scored some dope and went back to the hotel. It was pure china white. Eddie from Twisted Sister was hanging out with me, and there was a girl with us. Eddie was high on coke and he wouldn't shut up. I wanted to fuck the girl but I couldn't get him out of the room, so I asked him if he wanted a bump. When he said yes, I gave him a big line of smack and told him it was coke. He snorted it and passed out.

I fucked the chick, then when she passed out I went to the bathroom and started shooting coke and china white. In no time I was freaking out. When I came out of the bathroom and saw this girl passed out on the bed and a guy unconscious on the couch, I lost my mind. I thought people were coming to get me, so I threw all my drugs out the window.

A couple hours later I came down and realized I'd just got fucked up and gone to that psychotic place again. So at eight or nine in the morning I ran down to the street. People were walking past on their way to work, and there I was in just my leather pants, no socks or shoes or shirt, makeup all over my face and hair all matted and gross, looking for my drugs. Amazingly, I found them–so, of course, I went back upstairs and did it all again.

When Eddie and the girl woke up, they found me in the bathroom puking my brains out. I wasn't addicted to heroin at that time, so it really fucked me up. At the show the next day I was so fucking ill, so I told every-body I had the flu. I have no idea if they believed me. So yes, New York and I had a little history.

AUGUST 15TH 1987 CIVIC CENTER, PROVIDENCE, RI

Parker Meridian Hotel, New York, 4 a.m.

Just got back from the show. Drunk. No sign of Vanity.

Hmm.

11:30 a.m.

I'm laying here in bed and can hear Vanity in the other room talking a mile a minute on the phone. I have no idea when she got in. It's probably better not to ask.

Heather is out here and so is Sharise with Vince. I've always liked Sharise but I sorta feel sorry for her. Vince really can treat her like shit...not that I'm an angel.

Of course, fucking Mick has fucking Emi.

It's strange when Heather comes out to join Tommy on tour. I always feel like I'm her albatross. I know she doesn't even understand me. She grew up in Westlake, she was a cheerleader, the most popular girl in school, her dad was a doctor. She was the kind of human that was my fucking enemy as a kid! I don't think she understands this dark animal called Mötley Crüe but she loves Tommy as Tommy and that's all that matters.

Off to Providence tonight...I'm gonna leave Vanity here again. Sacha gave me some china white last night in the limo. I can only shoot for a couple more days or I'm gonna be hooked again.

NIKKI: As the years pass, I think Heather Locklear is the one girl Tommy let get away. She had everything as a kid that I never had, so in the end, maybe I was jealous. She has proven to have class and always takes the higher road, and ironically that is exactly what I believe Tommy desires.

TOMMY LEE: If somebody's girl came out to join the tour, we'd leave them alone for a few days, then as soon as they'd gone, we'd reconvene and crank up the fucking madness machine—"Yay! The girls are gone!" It wasn't really a question of the girls are gone, let's get some fucking pussy, although there was an element of that. It was more about now they're gone, we can fucking party! We can stay up all night and be weird.

AUGUST 16TH 1987 DAY OFF

Parker Meridian Hotel, New York, 4 p.m.

The show was shitty last night. I played like shit. I can feel the tension in the band…maybe it's because the girls are out here. Everyone is acting like a bunch of bitches. I came back to the room and Vanity wasn't here, so I shot up. I overdid it…fucking OD'd.

When Vanity came in I was passed out in the bedroom with a needle laying next to me. When I came to she was just screaming at the top of her lungs. She was freebased out her mind and I'm sure it freaked her out, but she wouldn't stop screaming. She kept shouting about the Devil. THAT wasn't much fucking help.

I had Fred calm her down and put her in some other room. She told Fred I was shooting up and I lied and said I was just drunk. He didn't believe me, but he went along with it.

I sorta feel dope sick today. I can't get hooked on the road. I'm just gonna take some sleeping pills and get through today. I'm outta junk and that's fine by me.

P.S. Axl called me today and told me Slash is strung out and wants me to help him…talk about bad timing…

EVANGELIST DENISE MATTHEWS: Do I believe in the Devil? Well, the Devil believes in the Devil, and plays the greatest con game of hide-and-seek. He has most believing that he doesn't exist; that's how he wins them over. I think the greatest deceit is that there is a party going on in Hell, and the Devil is throwing it and he thinks you're special because it's your Death Day.

We go backwards when we should be going forwards, and forwards when we should be going upright. Satan is the principality and power of the airwaves. Ultimately he is stealing our prayer life and we romance his witchcraft, not to mention our children's tiny innocent eyes. Sin breeds sin and it is nothing for us to enjoy. Yes, I had much to repent for.

NIKKI: Huh?

AUGUST 17TH 1987 CIVIC CENTER, HARTFORD, CT
On the jet, 2:30 p.m.

Sitting on the Mötley jet waiting to take off for Hartford. Everybody is in good spirits...both Hartford shows are sold out.

I never saw a chick shop as much as Emi...fucking hell. I see her in the hotel lobby with carts full of clothes, then she just sends them home. Mick's gonna need a bigger house just for her fucking shoes.

We're taking off now. I'm feeling a bit sick still, but I'm gonna be all right...I stopped just in time, I almost got hooked again...almost.

AUGUST 18TH, 1987 CIVIC CENTER, HARTFORD, CT
Parker Meridian Hotel, New York, 1 p.m.

Wake-up call just woke me. I've gotta leave for the Mötley jet in 30 minutes. We have another Hartford show tonight...then back here. I'm really sick of this hotel...it stinks in here. I won't let housekeeping in for fear of what they might find. I can't wait to break the news to Vanity that we're finished.

AUGUST 19TH 1987 DAY OFF
Parker Meridian Hotel, New York, 2 p.m.

Spoke to my grandfather today. I miss him. He's been fishing and hunting a lot lately. We always end up talking about Nona. I know he's lonely.

We're a lot alike.

AUGUST 20TH, 1987 MADISON SQUARE GARDEN NEW YORK, NY
Backstage, 7 p.m.

Backstage at the Garden among all the hangers-on, groupies, assorted business people, record company pigs, promoters, radio people, girlfriends, wives and managers. It's the hottest ticket in town. It's like a movie back here. I smirk and nod as people talk to me. Mostly I'm uninterested but I do see a few friends and people I respect.

I was actually looking for Bob Timmons, hoping he might be here. I want to talk to him about trying to get clean when the tour is over. I have this feeling I'm gonna die if I don't stop...at some point I'm gonna run out of luck.

Time to get ready to go onstage.

ALL OF MY HEROES ARE DEAD

Today my radio won't play
You-you died and left me here this way
I guess you lived your life
Like a loaded shotgun
You thought that your choice
Was no choice at all
I wanted to be just like you

All of my heroes are dead now
Left me here
In this wasted ghost town
All of my heroes

Yeah-your exit had such charm
And you-you ran a fortune
Through your arm
You lived your life like
A Molotov cocktail
Always set to explode
Behind the veil
I wanted to be just like you

AUGUST 21ST 1987 BROOME COUNTY VETERAN'S MEMORIAL ARENA BINGHAMTON, NY

Parker Meridian Hotel, 2:40 p.m.

Last night's show was one of the best we've ever played. New York can be a hard audience to win over, but we got them…tore the place up. Great night, and we all celebrated together. Lots of whisky, champagne and lines for all, nothing but smiles on everybody's faces…

I even found myself not fighting with Vanity. I guess knowing I'm done with her drama has made me more forgiving. I didn't see Bob, but I still didn't do any dope. Going to Doug's house in the Poconos in a couple of days…gonna BBQ and hang out.

I'm going shopping before tonight's show. I need some new T-shirts and boots.

AUGUST 22ND, 1987 NASSAU COLISEUM, LONG ISLAND, NY

Parker Meridian Hotel, 1:15 p.m.

We're leaving this hotel in a couple of hours. This fucking room is like a tomb. I've OD'd in here, fought in here, fucked in here (a few different chicks) and I need to get out. There's room service trays all over the room, blood on the sheets and the towels are black from hair dye. I bet they're gonna charge me some stupid destruction fee, and to be honest I didn't (really) destroy the place. I mean the TV and furniture is all intact, ha ha.

I think we're gonna have a killer show tonight. Off to Nassau Coliseum then off to the Poconos, staying on some lake up there by Doug's house.

AUGUST 23rd 1987 DAY OFF
Poconos, midnight

We all went to Doug and Jeanne's house for a BBQ.
A nice mellow night. Doug's kids were running around.
No drugs, just a few beers. We play Pocono Downs
tomorrow. Vanity is getting a car down to NY to catch
a plane back to LA. I'll tell her on the phone when
she gets there that it's over. I have a feeling she
won't care. It's the best for both of us.

I'm gonna start cutting the bad people out of my
life. I hope she does the same. One would be me.
Goodnight.

DOUG THALER: During the *Girls* tour, my wife Jeanne and
I were living in Pennsylvania, and I would commute to Los
Angeles each week. Mötley came out to our house the
day before their show at Pocono Downs racetrack–I
remember it was a beautiful Sunday evening.
We even did some boating. Nikki was OK
that day, but that was how he was back
then, really in-and-out: he'd do something really shitty and look wasted,
then the next day he would somehow pull it all together and be part
of the group again.

AUGUST 24th 1987
POCONO DOWNS RACETRACK,
WILKES-BARRE, PENNSYLVANIA
Backstage, 6:40 p.m.

Everything smells like horse-
shit. I guess it would, right? It
is a horse track. It reminds me
of growing up in Idaho.

I just told Fred I was done with Vanity. He said that's probably for the best...I'm sure the guys will be relieved too. I wish her well.

P.S. This place is huge. It looks like about 30,000 people. The weird thing is, there's a racetrack around our stage...ha ha ha...

AUGUST 25TH 1987 WAR MEMORIAL, ROCHESTER, NY

Backstage, 7 p.m.

Some kids broke into Vince's room and stole his wallet and clothes. He had $5k in his wallet—he's fucking pissed (I don't blame him...).

11:20 p.m.

Vince is such an asshole sometimes. I'm sitting here backstage waiting for him to return from the hospital. In fact, so are the fans...waiting...nice. Tonight he was making a sandwich and he reached for the mustard to put on it. There was only Grey Poupon (my fave) which he hates, so he threw the mustard jar against the wall. It exploded and flew back and cut his hand wide open. He's now at the hospital and we're still waiting to play the fucking show. Nice move, bro...can we say spoiled brat?

VINCE NEIL: Fuck, the mustard jar incident was pure *Spinal Tap*. It was me being a fucking idiot. I don't like Dijon mustard but catering always had it backstage—they never had yellow mustard, even though I had been asking them for weeks to change the rider. So when I saw Dijon mustard yet again, I was pissed and I took the jar and threw it against the wall.

The glass smashed, bounced right back and sliced my finger almost right off: it was just hanging by the skin. I severed the nerves, the artery, the tendons; blood was spurting out of it. We were about to go onstage but they had to rush me to the hospital because I was going to bleed to death, and a week later I had an eight-hour surgery to re-attach the finger. It was just a temper tantrum–me being Prince Vince.

FRED SAUNDERS: I couldn't believe it at the upstate New York show when I saw Vince Neil pouting and throwing this fucking mustard at the wall. It bounced back and sliced his hand right open. Vince said, "Well, I guess that the tour's over," and Nikki said, "Bullshit–there are two hundred people on this tour." The tour continued, and for weeks Vince had to wear these gloves that looked like boxing gloves. Like I said, what a piece of work.

Hotel, 2:15 a.m.

Bored...going to sleep. This is a ghost town. There's nothing on TV or the radio, no clubs...no room service. Even the bar is closed. This is surreal at best. I think I must have died in NY and this is Nikki Sixx's hell. Bad time to have quit sniffing glue...

But at least I don't have a cast on my arm from a mustard jar, ha ha...

2:30 p.m.

OK, it's official...I have cabin fever.

We woke up early and came here to the beautiful Utica (exactly). We have a show tonight here. Poconos to Utica is like going from the pot to the frying pan for me. I mean, I'm the first to admit the countryside is so pretty here. It's green and the air is clean. Everybody looks like they're taken from a Norman Rockwell painting or from the cover of a postcard. Dogs are running around wagging their tails as a squirrel scampers up a tree with his newest trophy (an unopened acorn). I looked up at a cloud as it was slowly drifting by changing shapes from a heart to a smiley face. To top it off, this ice cream truck just drove by playing a nursery rhyme song out of tune. There are a trail of kids running down the street after it, yelling and screaming, "Ice cream, ice cream!"

God save me…I'm in hell.

P.S. The good news today is I finally spilled the beans on the phone to Vanity. She just said OK…no emotion at all. I guess she really didn't care-cool.

AUGUST 27th 1987 DAY OFF

Hotel, Landover, Maryland, 2:15 p.m.

Got in late from the show in Utica last night. Pretty good show considering the squirrels and ice cream trucks. I just woke up. Need to order some coffee and breakfast. What am I gonna do today, diary?

I'm so bored. I smell trouble. Thank God for Halcions I slept so good.

Hotel, 2 a.m.

Now that was fun! I just went and broke into house-keeping and picked up 20 or so garbage pails. Then I collected loads of chairs. Everybody was asleep or doing stuff in their rooms. I balanced the chairs against the room doors all along my corridor, filled the buckets with all kinds of shit-piss, water, beer, basically anything I could find-and put them on the chairs...

I sprayed hairspray on every one's door, set it on fire, knocked the door and ran. I had my system down pat...hairspray, light, knock, hairspray, light, knock, etc etc. So then when everybody opened their door, their door was on fire and then this bucket fell on them and soaked them!...ha ha ha...

Fred Saunders was fuckin' some chick, so he came to the door with a big fucking hard-on and the bucket fell on his dick. He ran down to my room and said, Sixx, fuckin' come out, I'm gonna kick your fucking ass! I said, Fuck you, dude! and he kicked the hinges off my door. But as usual, he didn't do anything 'cause he saw how much fun I'd had.

I love Fred, I hope he can get it back up...I'm sure I'll hear about it tomorrow.

Backstage, Capital Center, 11:55 p.m.

Band was tight as hell tonight, everything was right in the pocket. Damn, I love it when all pistons are firing...great crowd.

Not a lot to do here. Gonna go look for a club or something with Fred and Tommy. I'm sure Fred has a little ace in the hole. If not, I know some of the truck drivers said they were getting a shipment of krell in.

P.S. I just got a blow job from this girl who started crying and thanked me afterwards. What the fuck?

FRED SAUNDERS: Ace in the Hole was like our tour catchphrase. A friend of mine gave me a gift of an 1888 silver dollar coin that he had machine-drilled hollow so it would hold a gram of coke. I'd carry it around. You just had to twist it to open it and there was the coke. If we were out in a club, Nikki and Tommy or Vince would ask me for Ace in the Hole if they wanted a little jolt.

Sometimes we would get to the hotel in a new city, check in, and Nikki and Tommy would start ringing my room right away and pester me for Ace in the Hole. I'd say to them, "Come on guys, we've got a job to do"—there would often be interviews or an in-store sign-ing. But those guys wouldn't quit hound-ing me.

AUGUST 29th 1987, CAPITAL CENTER, LANDOVER, MD
Hotel, 3:10 p.m.

Just woke up. I sat in the room with Tommy and Fred and did coke all night, talking, listening to music, drinking. Right now I feel like shit. I'm so tired and hungover. I still feel drunk.

259

AUGUST 30TH 1987
HAMPTON COLISEUM, HAMPTON, VA
On the jet, 1 a.m.

The band sucked so bad tonight. Everyone was hungover.
How can we kick ass last night and suck tonight? I
wonder if any of the fans that saw both Landover shows
thought they saw two different bands.

Mars was knee-deep in Mars-ade and Vince lost his
voice halfway through the set. I know for sure I was
just sucking ass as well. We never suck like Aerosmith
did in their drug days—I mean, we don't forget our own
songs or anything. We just lose the groove and lag or
pull the music. We're more metal and Aerosmith is more
groove-oriented, so when we suck it just sounds like
the engine is outta time. It feels...whatever...

Hotel, Hampton, Virginia, 5 p.m.

I need to stop.

I don't care about our shows some days—just how am
I gonna find some drugs? Coke, pills,
heroin, I don't give a fuck. Just
gimme something, anything...I feel like
I'm dying and I don't know why.

AUGUST 31ST 1987
DAY OFF

We have six shows in the
next eight days before we get
any time off.

I'm depressed...this tour
seems to be going on forever.

NIKKI: I used to look at the tour dates and think, When is this going to end? And when it does, what do I have to go home to? It was a very confusing time. I resented that management just put us on the road and left us there. Tommy and Vince were both married—it must have been hard for them to keep things together. I was different. I felt detached from everything.

We knew we needed a break or something was going to break. We asked for time off and Doc always said no. I was so immature and fucked up that I didn't know he was actually breaking the band up, little by little. In the end, 15 percent of nothing is nothing, so our manage-ment was killing the goose that laid the fucking golden egg.

DOC McGHEE: I always had a real problem with this line of argument of Sixx's. Sure, the tours were too long for them, but only because of the way they behaved on them! Don't forget, these were guys in their twenties who were only being asked to work two hours per day. What about all the guys who get up at 5 a.m. to lay bricks and only get two weeks off a year? If Mötley Crüe was burned out on the road it was purely because they had stupid fucking drug habits. It's not rocket sci-ence.

SEPTEMBER 1ˢᵗ 1987

COLISEUM, RICHMOND, VA

Backstage, 7:55 p.m.

Just got a massage. My body is torn up, my hands are cut up and bruised, all part of trying to break your bass at every turn of a chorus. I have my bass strings so high so I don't fret them out. Mick says playing my bass is like playing a telephone pole with high-tension live wires on.

On that note—time to crack the whisky and go make a mess of the youth of Richmond's minds.

SEPTEMBER 2ᴺᴰ 1987

CIVIC CENTER, ROANOKE, VA

Hotel, Roanoke, Virginia, 2:30 p.m.

Flew in after the Richmond show last night. I wanted to raise some hell but it was too late and there's nothing to do in Roanoke. I called Fred but he said everybody had gone to bed. He told me to come down to his room for an Ace in the Hole. He chopped out a couple lines for me and we were hanging out listening to Merle Haggard but I guess I was just too fucking tired to keep going. I came down to my room to look in the phone book for hookers...and I just woke up. I still had my clothes on...even coke isn't working lately.

Amazing what sleep does for you. I just put on Diamond Dogs by David Bowie, one of the greatest albums ever recorded.

Gonna order breakfast...bye.

We had the last couple days off. It's been very uneventful so I haven't written. I've been sleeping a lot...weird. We're taking a chopper into the gig in an hour—big show. Sold out. I don't know who's playing with us. I guess it doesn't matter 'cause everybody is there to see us anyway.

P.S. Mick is like a fucking puppet to this bitch. Why does he always let these chicks lead him around by the nose? And if she mentions God one more time I'm gonna stab her in the face with her crucifix.

DOC McGHEE: Mick was the closest thing to being a punching bag in Mötley Crüe. He was the easiest to pick on because he was the quietest and he never fought back. Mick's just a really good kid who wants to be happy and he's never been happy. When Nikki and Tommy got loaded they were pretty mean, gnarly guys and as soon as Mick and Emi got together they just fucking beat at them nonstop. You know what sums their relationship up? The time that Tommy was running naked down the hallways of a hotel in Ohio and the police arrived, went to the room next door and arrested Mick for it.

SEPTEMBER 6ᵀᴴ 1987
DANE COUNTY COLISEUM, MADISON, WI

Hotel, 4 p.m.

Touring with the same band for support gets so boring after a while. I guess if it was a band I really loved and not fucking Whitesnake, it wouldn't be so bad. This is actually worse than when we toured with Iron Maiden...I remember being backstage listening to them and thinking all their songs sounded like the theme from Bonanza, with the gallop and all. I really can't wait for Slash and the guys to come out.

My fave support so far was Cheap Trick. I am and always will be the hugest Cheap Trick fan...and they are the greatest guys ever. We've got a show tonight...maybe I'll go late so I don't have to hear Whitesnake. The sad part is, I love Rudy Sarzo to death—maybe he should play in Mötley and I should go to the nuthouse.

> **RICK NIELSEN:** Mötley Crüe and Cheap Trick toured together in Europe and America. We used to be real bad together. The guys in Cheap Trick were never heroin addicts but we'd drink and party hard. I would see Nikki stumbling around sometimes, but I didn't know exactly what was causing it. I knew when drink was involved, though, because I was normally there drinking it with him.

SEPTEMBER 7ᵀᴴ 1987
LA CROSSE CENTER, LA CROSSE, WI

Hotel, 3 p.m.

Another show tonight but I'm ready to go home and make music. I'm over drugs and I know they're over me.

I woke up at 9 a.m. for some odd reason. I am playing Sweet's Desolation Boulevard nonstop...great songwriting. They were always sold to the world as a pop band but like the Raspberries they were a metal band at heart. We could all learn a lot about hooks from those guys.

I'm on a mission to take the band to a new level musically. I think we've just scratched the surface. Me and Tommy are having a lot of talks about what's next...I'm excited. I want a Number 1 album that knocks the world on its ear.

SEPTEMBER 8th 1987

FIVE SEASONS CENTER, CEDAR RAPIDS, IA
Hotel, 5 p.m.

I wrote a cool song today. All I have to do is listen to Whitesnake to know what NOT to do.

We fly back home to LA after the show tonight. Thank fuck...But what will happen? I have changed my phone number at home and have had a 10 foot security gate and fence installed around the house while I've been away. I'm determined...

I'm a digital anti-Christ analog poltergeist
Like a cannibal watch me beat my meat
Shoot my gun right between the sheets

Like a criminal I'm on the take
I rattle nerves like a rattlesnake
Anti-trust public enemy
Steal your fruit and I shake your tree
You just love to hate me

All the preachers say
All the teachers say
All the speeches say
I'm so whoreable

Van Nuys, 11 a.m.

It's great to sleep in my own bed again. To say I've decked out my pad is an understatement. Ralph Lauren, crushed velvet comforters, burled walnut antiques, gargoyles, Persian carpets… everything from the 1800s. God, I love this place, except for the memories…but maybe they can fade.

The gate and fence around the house looks so medieval… I love it. Jon Roberts really set me up nicely.

I just called the office to get my new phone number and spoke to Karen Dumont. I told her Vanity had really trashed my house while I was gone, she didn't clean up after herself at all. Karen told me she was looking for a place and would be interested in housesitting when I'm back on tour. I told her I would think about it, but between me and you, she would be doing me a favor. I'm always worried about some crazies breaking into my house while I'm gone.

5 p.m.

Just got off the phone with Robbin. He's coming over to pick me up in his new Ferrari and we're gonna catch a movie. I drove my Harley today. The battery was dead so I jumped it down Valley Vista and headed up and down Ventura Boulevard. Went to an antique store and bought an insane antique silverwear set in a walnut case. Wow…they just don't make things like they used to.

KAREN DUMONT: I used to work in PolyGram's New York office and moved to the LA bureau in 1986. When I moved to Los Angeles I was told not to even *talk* to Mötley Crüe, because they were trouble. But they'd sometimes drop by the office, Nikki more than the rest of the band, and eventually we became friends.

Nikki asked me to stay in his house during the *Girls* tour because he was going out with Vanity and he was afraid she wasn't taking very good care of his place. He asked me if I would go over and stay there, to keep an eye on the place and on her. Vanity was very unreliable and a lot of people hated her, but actually I thought she was OK.

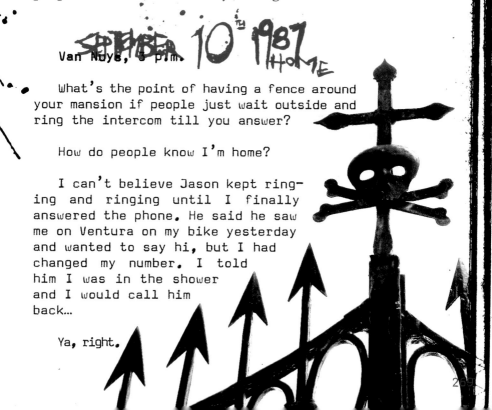

SEPTEMBER 10th 1987
Van Nuys, 3 p.m. HOME

What's the point of having a fence around your mansion if people just wait outside and ring the intercom till you answer?

How do people know I'm home?

I can't believe Jason kept ring-ing and ringing until I finally answered the phone. He said he saw me on Ventura on my bike yesterday and wanted to say hi, but I had changed my number. I told him I was in the shower and I would call him back...

Ya, right.

SEPTEMBER 11TH 1987 HOME
Van Nuys, 2 p.m.

I can't fucking believe it. You will never believe this one. I came home from the store today and walked into the house and Vanity jumped from outta nowhere. She scared the fuck out of me. Her eyes were popping outta her head. She was screaming, If you hate me so much, hit me! She was trying to scratch my eyes and face. I kept backing up until I was in a corner.

As she said for the 100th time, Hit me, hit me, hit me if you hate me, I knocked her out cold.

She hit the wood floor with a thump. I dragged her by her hair to the front door, opened it and pulled her onto the front steps. I looked down the driveway and there was a limo parked at the end. The driver got out and said, Is everything OK? I said, Is this trash yours? He said yes and I said, Then get it off my property. I pushed the button to open the gate and kicked her down the front steps...

Fucking psycho bitch! I just got off the phone to the cops and told them she broke into my house and was trying to gouge out my eyes so I had to defend myself. They're on their way over now. I'm gonna file a report and get a restraining order.

FUCKING HELL!

5:40 p.m.

I had torn up Jason's number but now the fucker has left it in my mailbox-I feel like they're all out to get me.

10 p.m.

Sitting here alone listening to music. I'm still shaken from the Vanity shit.

Guess I'll take my bike out for a spin...I wonder what the guys are doing.

TOMMY LEE: I used to go over to Nikki's house quite a lot when he was dating Vanity. It wasn't always pretty. I remember one time when I was there they had a huge fight, and he flushed a three- or four-karat diamond ring down the toilet.

NIKKI: Wow, I forgot about that. I'm glad Tommy brought that up...I need to call the insurance company.

EVANGELIST DENISE MATTHEWS: What killed my relationship with Nikki? I believe the fame and possessive search for fortune, love and the exaltation of a dead Vanity, full of narcotics, is what broke me. My Bible says the woman that lives for pleasure shall die in it. It seemed to me that no matter where I turned as Vanity, it was leading me to death. And though you rent your face with painting and make yourself beautiful, God said, "Yet I will make your lovers hate you." He did just that...and it couldn't have ended any other way.

Van Nuys, 11:45 p.m.

Just returned from dinner with Bob. We went to a snotty lil French restaurant on Ventura Boulevard. We talked cars most of the time and split a nice bottle of wine, and that's all. I'm feeling like I can control this. Maybe I can just not overdo it. Maybe I'm not as bad as I think I am...I've been pretty sane lately.

Today was mellow. I went to the mall and just walked around. I had a baseball hat and a sweater on... nobody noticed me. I was listening to Prince today...a lot...and Thompson Twins...how gay is that? Better put on some Hell Bent for Leather to redeem myself...

I haven't even taken sleeping pills to sleep. Gonna go light some candles and crawl in bed with a Roald Dahl book...

BOB MICHAELS: Nikki and I used to go to a French restaurant over on Ventura Boulevard. The only reason we used to go was that it had vodkas at the bar that had been frozen for a month so we'd see how wasted we could get on martinis. The meals would always end with us pulling out of the driveway, which was a major traffic intersection, and doing multiple doughnuts in the road with the steering wheel jammed to the left and the accelerator right down. We couldn't see where we were going and it was a miracle we didn't crash. It never occurred to us that we would. Nikki had always got away with so much that he felt untouchable.

Van Nuys, 6:30 p.m.

Dear Diary, I'm such a loser. I'm a dreg and a liar. I feel like backwash. I feel shame...I got high last night. No, not just high-I lost my mind again. I ended up in the closet shooting coke...I've been doing

so good. I'm so confused. It didn't start off so bad.
I thought I could control it...

P.S. I just woke up and I'm too sick to even eat. I'm
going back to bed. Maybe if I just hide under the covers
and go to sleep, this will all have been a nightmare...

Why do I take everything too far? I make myself
sick...literally.

SEPTEMBER 14TH, 1987 HOME

Van Nuys, 2 p.m.

I just got a call from the office. Karen said Sacha
called for me—he's in LA and wanted to know if I need
a limo (a code word for junk?).

Why not?

P.S. I guess nobody knows what Sacha really does
for money.

7 p.m.

Sacha came over—he actually does have his limos
here. He moved his business here...he says NY is too
crazy. I told him I am basically clean but have
chipped, and shot coke, and now I feel bad. We talked
about control. He said if I wanted him to help me control it, he would. I agree with him—if I didn't do the
coke, I would be really OK. It's then, and only then,
that I end up in the closet.

Sacha is actually a nice guy. Jason is such a fucking egomaniac—how can a dealer have a big ego? He's
always holding out on the gear or his connection if I
want to buy quantity. Where Sacha gave me Abdul his
direct dealer's number, 'cause he's still got to go
back to NY and bring some clothes and furniture back
here. He doesn't deal coke any more, he says people
get too weird on it. Tell me about it...

273

So I got some Mexican tar that I'm just gonna smoke until I go back out on the road. If I just do it once a day, it's like having a beer in the afternoon.

I called Jason and told him I was gonna report him to the police if he ever came here again. He freaked out. So now I have no real connection to coke (Thank God)...I feel pretty fucking safe right now.

Gonna go chase the dragon, write some music and go out for a bike ride...end of a day in the life...

DON'T LAUGH (YOU MIGHT BE NEXT)

I've been dreamin'
In black and white so long
You know I didn't always hit the shit
But my livin' days are way past gone
I've been thinkin'
Of where I went all wrong
I been livin' in this hole so long
I feel like it's where I belong

Don't laugh—you might be next
Like you got nothin'
You wouldn't like to forget

I've been thinkin'
On why I went so far
I just been chasin' this dragon
All around the block
And I ain't got no car
So now you're sayin'
It's a weakness in my soul
Yeah before you write me off so quick
You better look around at the people
That you know

Don't laugh—you might be next

SEPTEMBER 15TH 1987 HOME
Van Nuys, 5 p.m.

I was checking the mail a few hours ago and Vanity pulled up in a limo. The first words out of her mouth were how sorry she was. She looked better than I've seen her in a while. I told her to come in. It was nice. I gave her my new number and told her we could be friends. It's better to be this way than that way.

10 p.m.

Vanity just called and said she wanted to come over and watch a movie. What the hell—what can it hurt?

SEPTEMBER 16TH 1987 HOME
7 a.m.

Vanity just left to go score some blow. She came over last night and we were drinking and she asked if I wanted a bump. God, it sounded so good—so we did lines all night until we ran out. I told her I have some money in the safe and she took my Jeep and went to get some more. I know I said I wouldn't but I'm not shooting or basing it. I'll just go till noon or so and sleep it off…gate just rang, be back…

Cool, the liquor store just dropped off some Cristal—I need a drink bad. I'm pretty wired. I ran out of everything. Nothing is worse than running out. I'm gonna call Abdul for a little tar drop-off.

Noon

Abdul dropped off a quarter-gram but Vanity is nowhere to be found. Fucking bitch! I think she stole my money. I'm going to bed…fuck, I'm pissed…and to think I was having fun.

Vanity just called, she's coming over. She said she had to wait for the stuff and didn't have my new number with her. She said she was sorry…am I a sucker or what?

I'm glad I have a place to write this down…otherwise it would just be me and the voices in my head…

SEPTEMBER 17TH 1987 HOME

Van Nuys, 5 p.m.

Just off the phone with Karen. Told her I was leaving tomorrow and asked her to watch the house. I'm leaving the key under the gargoyle at the front door. I haven't been to sleep yet but I think I held it together pretty good. I know if I told her the truth she wouldn't watch the house, and I can't trust Vanity not to come here and go whacko. I hid all my drug paraphernalia in the safe behind my mirror in the bedroom. Nobody knows it's there. I had the bricks torn out and the safe installed last year.

I got new sheets for the guest bed—I went in there and it smelled like cat pee…thanks Slash! Not a very nice way for Karen to start her stay. I'm just hoping it's not the mattress. Maybe I can spray something on it.

I can't believe I did freebase with Vanity all night. It ended as always…I threw her out at about 8 a.m. She was getting crazy and telling me about God. Also, I forgot I bought Whisky and sent him to obedience camp! He's getting dropped off here in two days…I hope Karen doesn't mind. I'm going back to bed until tomorrow morning.

KAREN DUMONT: When I moved into Nikki's house my only condition was that he didn't do drugs while I was there because I couldn't handle that. I didn't know what I would do if he was going off his head. Doc and Doug were pleased when I moved in because they thought Nikki liked me and they hoped I might be a good influence on him. I remember the day that I moved in the spare bed smelled of piss and Nikki said Slash had pissed on it. He didn't want to buy another bed so I used to sleep on a couch in the den.

EVANGELIST DENISE MATTHEWS: Nikki and I could not have made our relationship right without Jesus and so it was not meant to be. Otherwise it surely would have been. We both needed all of those experiences just to get to the next step. Most of us are used as stepping-stones for each of us to climb to the next level. Some are used to make us fall down and go "Boom!" Just as long as we get up and keep climbing…

SEPTEMBER 15TH 1987 DAY OFF

Leaving home in limo, 8 a.m.

I feel so drained right now. I'm in the limo…I don't wanna ever come back to this life. I'm so excited to leave for tour. I didn't have time to pack this morning so I'm taking the same dirty clothes I came home with back on tour.

Why is it that every time I get a foothold, I slip and fall back into the muck? I'm surrounded by derelicts...they search me out, they hunt me, they find me and try and kill me. I hate drugs but I can't stop. When we're done with this tour in Dec I wanna go into rehab in Jan (I need to tell Bob Timmons to book me a room for Jan 2). I'm selling the house and moving away...today I actually prayed to God.

I can't believe I did freebase again.

I can't believe I did Vanity again.

I can't believe that I thought I could just chip junk.

I hope I'm not gonna be dope sick.

I can't believe I'm considering AA/NA/CA.

I can't believe I'm considering rehab.

I can't believe I prayed to God.

NIKKI: The armor was starting to crack. I can see from my diary entries that I was looking for a way out of the quicksand. Maybe I was finally hoping someone was going to throw me a rope. For the first time I think I was actually willing to grab it. Seeing these entries now, I was screaming for help. I just don't think I was screaming loud enough.

LA SUCKS

Drive down the freeway with your head in a bag
You should be told you're not alone being had
Sniff some paint, sniff some glue
Look at the effect this city's having on you
I understand your teenage angst
I understand trying to kill the past
Maybe we should all move far away
Maybe it can all be blamed on LA
Don't tell me about me
and I won't tell you about you
If you need a therapist,
try suicide or go to the zoo
This city's built on drag queens, clichés and sins
Rumors and back-stabbings at the Café Le Trend
If you live in this town
you're a sucker and a clown
Bullshitters by the ounce, liars by the pound
There's always a fool with a vial full of dreams
There's always a bum falling apart at the seams
Gold lamé high heels a Rodeo Drive bitch
Some desperate old groupie
trying to get herself hitched
Worn and torn it's ripping apart
Another 6.5 will be too much for my heart
Riots and floods and shootings oh my...
I wonder if I'll ever get out of this city
alive?
Ya-LA sucks

Backstage, about midnight

First show back...man, it's great to be back on tour. It was so good to see the guys. No matter how bad it gets between us, at least I know they really care about me. They don't want anything from me. They're not trying to kill me (that I know of-ha ha)...

Tonight's show felt like a three-hour set. I was dripping toxic waste after one song...all the blow and booze and gear was just pouring out of me. I didn't even have one drink onstage...

God, I hate LA...or I guess I hate the people I attract in LA...

SEPTEMBER 20ᵀᴴ 1987
Hotel, noon

MARKET SQUARE ARENA,
INDIANAPOLIS, IN

I can't believe we're back in Indy just two months
after we played here. Doc's greed is showing. There
are so many Mötley fans out there but he just goes
where the easy money is and doesn't help us build new
fans in new cities (or countries). Between you and
me, I think we need a new manager. This guy doesn't
like us—he just likes our money. He's never here or in
the office. He's acting more like a record company
every day...he does lil of the work and takes all of the
credit. He just throws it all against the wall and if
it sticks, cool—if not, he blames us.

ALLEN KOVAC: I have managed Mötley Crüe since the
late '90s, and while I don't want to criticize their previous
management, I do have the impression that they were
just following the money. The trick is to maximize what
you do in a city, instead of going to it multiple times. The
advisers Mötley had back then didn't explain the amount
of work they had to bear, mentally and physically. They
didn't consider that when artists get tired they are likely
to take sleeping pills, or self-medicate with alcohol.
Mötley Crüe was abused by the system—their record label
and representatives didn't explain how things worked—
they just wanted them to stay on the treadmill.

SEPTEMBER 22ᴺᴰ 1987 DAY OFF
Hotel, Tulsa, Oklahoma, 2:20 p.m.

Rich Fisher decided to rent a helicopter and everybody
is flying over to a restaurant to have a big dinner.
I said I would go, but I know I won't. I can't face
being social. I'd rather stay here. I feel so uncomfortable in my skin. It's been creeping up on me for
a few years—the bigger we get, the sadder I feel...

P.S. Just called Bob Timmons...got his answer machine.

BOB TIMMONS: Nikki would call me sporadically during the *Girls* tour asking for help but would never take it. He used to cover up his depression with anger–he felt that since now he was successful people wanted to be around him but they liked the fame, not him, so he self-medicated his pain through his drug use. Mötley Crüe lived in an unreal world–I remember on an earlier tour being backstage with them and David Lee Roth coming in and throwing an ounce of cocaine on the table and saying, "Hey, guys, there you go!" That was their attitude: We are rock stars, so this is what we do.

SEPTEMBER 23RD, 1987
TULSA CONVENTION CENTER, TULSA, OK
Hotel, Tulsa, 5 p.m.

I feel fragile and tormented and uncomfortable in my skin. What happened when the heroin left is that the comfort left. I'm drinking more than I have in past tours to try to replace the comfort that smack gave me. I hate to admit it, but maybe I'm not even who I think I am. I'm feeling fragile and weak, and I'm supposed to be on top of the world. Now I've started chipping again.

Bob Timmons called back but I wouldn't talk to him.

SEPTEMBER 24TH, 1987
LLOYD NOBLE CENTER, NORMAN, OK
On the jet, 1 a.m.

Tonight's show was hard work. We're sitting ready to take off for Dallas. Fred is pissed at me (even though he won't admit it) 'cause before the show was started tonight, I hid in a road case by the side

of the stage as the intro to The Stripper was
playing. Fred was running around freaking out
'cause he couldn't find me. He was turning over
cases and screaming to cut the intro tape...ha ha ha...I
jumped out just in time to start the show. When I
looked over at the side of the stage he was as white
as a ghost. I smirked and he just shook his head...

FRED SAUNDERS: Nikki was always doing shit like that. The bigger Mötley Crüe got, the cockier he got. He would always be dragging his feet and delaying things just because he could. Before the shows the band would have what we called PCPs–pre-concert piddles–and Tommy, Vince and Mick would find a bathroom, but Nikki would just whip out his dick and piss wherever he was, in a corridor or on the side of the stage. He was quite the charmer.

SEPTEMBER 25 1987

Hotel, Dallas, 1:45 p.m.
REUNION ARENA, DALLAS;

Excited for the show tonight and tomorrow.
I love Texas. I'm going to be good...maybe go
to the gym and write some music. Off to the
sound check...see you after the show...I'm not going
out.

DALLAS = TROUBLE.

SEPTEMBER 26, 1987

REUNION ARENA, DALLAS, TX
Hotel, 4:30 p.m.

Last night was insane. It was another great
show...as always, Dallas kicks ass. We stomped thru
the set like a mechanical Godzilla (or Crüezilla).
Then off to the best strip clubs in town. We had
girls piled on us...blondes, brunettes, red-
heads. $100 bills were everywhere. I must
have spent $5k on my own. I'm sure we dropped
$25k last night between us...goddamn fun.

As the night went on and the drinks flowed I sorta lost my memory. I was trying to savor my zombie dust but I think it got the best of me. Mick and Emi went back to their room (of course) but Donna McDaniels came out with all of us. When I woke up there were panties on my lamp and her shoes at the end of the bed. I remember her coming back to my room for a bump but that's all I remember.

God I hope I didn't fuck her. Can you imagine if I did the very thing I am busting Mick's balls for? CHICKS = TROUBLE.

Off to the show...I'm so hungover...

Backstage, 7:30 p.m.

Everybody is busting my chops, laughing and asking if I fucked Donna. Oh Lord. I saw her and she just gave me a hug, and said she had fun last night. But she didn't ask for her panties or shoes—what does that mean?

Time to get on the war paint. We're spending the night in Dallas tonight. I'm coming straight to my room after the show.

11:45 p.m.

I pulled a runner tonight—straight off stage and into the limo then escorted right to my room. I'm watching a documentary on Hitler, Eva Braun and their drug use...OK I get the hint.

Hotel, Dallas, 3:35 a.m.

Just had a knock on the door. I looked thru the peephole and saw two fucking gorgeous blondes. They said,
"Hey Nikki!" and I said, "You have the wrong room." They
started laughing and said, "Come on Nikki, open the
door, we know it's you!" I said again, "You have the
wrong room," and one of them said, "Oh no we don't, we
were here last night with you and I left my shoes."

So I opened the door and said I was sick. They
said, "Oh, well we thought you might wanna do a repeat
of last night. We had a blast!" I said I did too, gave
them the shoes and panties and told them if I wasn't
sick I'd love to hang out. One of them said, "Thanks,
but these aren't my panties…" and her girlfriend said
they weren't hers either. Oh Lord.

2:20 p.m.

Flying out to Denver soon. Robbin Crosby is coming
out for a few days to visit then my grandfather is
coming to Salt Lake.

Hotel, Denver, 10:45 p.m.

Just got into the hotel. Nice hotel, there's a full
spa downstairs, I'm gonna take advantage of it. I
asked Rich to get a doctor out…I need my monthly
penicillin shot to ward off any drip that's brewing.

Robbin gets here tomorrow morning. We have adjoining
rooms just like the old days when we were roommates.
Fuck, we had fun back then! Ratt was just starting to
get going and Mötley was on the way. We nicknamed him
King 'cause he's so big. Nobody could kick his ass but
I always tried, ha ha. We used to go to this café
right by our house every day 'cause we didn't have a
refrigerator and talk for hours. I love him. He's
been struggling with dope, but he says he's clean now…
just drinking.

TODAY'S PLAYLIST WAS

Aerosmith—Get Your Wings
Aerosmith—Draw The Line
Aerosmith—first album
Aerosmith—Rocks

Goodnight.

NIKKI: Aerosmith was touring the *Permanent Vacation* album at the same time that we were touring *Girls Girls Girls.* We would sometimes land at the same airport but we never really saw each other, just each other's planes. One night Steven and Joe left a note on the window of our plane, like a ticket you get on the window of a car when you park in the red zone. It told us that if we weren't careful, the way we were going, we would crash and burn the way they did. We all snickered at it, but it's interesting that I was too ashamed to write it in my diary...because I knew they were right.

P.S. I've never known which is funnier—Aerosmith writing "Dude Looks Like a Lady" about Vince, or Dire Straits writing "Money for Nothing (and Chicks for Free)" about Mötley.

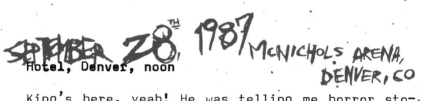

SEPTEMBER 28TH, 1987 / McNICHOLS ARENA,
Hotel, Denver, noon   DENVER, CO

    King's here, yeah! He was telling me horror sto-
ries about his band. He pretty much hates them.
Blotzer is a fucking asshole all the time these days
and Percy thinks he's such a rock star (Dude, you're
in Ratt, you're not Steven Tyler or Jagger). I guess
all bands are the same.

It's so weird to see King has put on so much weight. He must have gained 50 lbs. I guess he really isn't doing drugs. Every time I quit drugs, I start to get fat. I always say I'm not sure which is worse—being a drug addict or being fat.

On that note—time to order some food...

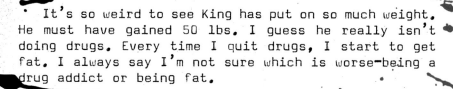

SEPTEMBER 29TH 1987
McNICHOLS ARENA, DENVER, CO
Hotel, Denver, 4:45 a.m.

The night's show was really good. King said he was blown away at how tight we were. There were Denver's finest girls there (what is it about strippers and rock stars, anyway?) so we brought them back with us to the hotel. We rented another room under the name Justin Case and piled them all in there. Tommy and Vince came over (Tommy brought his blaster, I brought the music) and we had room service bring eight bottles of champagne, two bottles of Jack and a bunch of food. We all hung out, turned up the music, and the girls danced for us, then everyone picked their girls and headed back to their rooms. Now the girls are gone...I'm going to bed...fun day.

Safe and sane—three Mötleys and one Ratt.

P.S. King thought Whitesnake was great. He said I'm just a fucking punk and I don't like them 'cause they can really play. I punched him in the neck and he knocked me against the wall (it fucking hurt) and then we both started laughing.

FRED SAUNDERS: Nikki and Robbin had a special camaraderie. They were both pretty big guys–Robbin was six-foot-four–and when Mötley and Ratt were both starting out they used to work the Hollywood club circuit together. They were also drug buddies and were always sneaking off together. They were competitive but Nikki was a lot stronger-minded and could normally persuade Robbin to do whatever he wanted. Robbin was quite depressive and Nikki thrived on that sort of thing: If he saw a weakness in a person he would sense blood and be all over them like a shark in the water.

NIKKI: I miss Robbin and I often think of him. We did heroin together the first time with King's friend Smog Vomit from a band called Tex and the Horseheads. When I finally got away from junk, Robbin went even further down than I did. He lost it all and ended up homeless, divorced and bankrupt. Eventually he got AIDS from sharing needles with squatters in LA and I was gonna lose one of my best friends in the world. It wasn't AIDS that took Robbin from me (or any of us for that matter)–it was heroin. He had changed so much that I had to cut him out of my life.

I let him stay at my house in 1990 with the understanding that there were to be no drugs in my home. I had young children and I was clean and sober. One day when he was out of the house, I went into the guest room and saw he had a crumpled brown paper bag in there. It looked all too familiar to me so I opened it and there were needles and spoons and the usual stuff we use to kill ourselves. I had to ask him to leave. That was a sad day for both of us. I remember crying as he drove away. I never saw him again.

A few weeks later he called and asked to borrow $10,000 so he could get out of debt and back on his feet. I told him I loved him and he was one of my best friends in the world, but being a former junkie myself, I knew where the money would go and I felt I would be killing him rather than saving him. I told him if he would get ninety days sober, I would give him the money in a heartbeat. He told me to fuck off and hung up on me. It broke my heart because I knew he didn't mean it. I was so heartbroken I couldn't even go to his funeral. I still feel guilty to this day, like maybe I could have done more.

ROSS HALFIN: Robbin wasn't as mentally strong as Nikki and couldn't handle smack like Nikki did. I remember once walking down the street in LA and Robbin was literally sitting on the street begging. It was boiling hot but he was sheet white and his feet were all blue and blistered. Robbin eventually caught HIV from needles and died of AIDS.

11:40 a.m.

Just got off the phone with Doug. I told him Doc is on his last legs with the band. He told me I'm over-reacting and we got into a bit of a fight. Doug is such a nuts-and-bolts manager, the day-to-day guy, but Doc holds us all back (including Doug). He never follows up on any of our ideas or visions. He's here to massage the label and get our ideas to become real but he's so busy bragging, spending money and playing golf that he can't see the future. Well I can see the future very clearly and it doesn't involve him. I give him six months...if that. I need a manager who is into technology and marketing...maybe one doesn't exist? I want more from a manager.

People think I'm a control freak but I just want the best for us. I want us to be the biggest band in the world and to break all the rules. I feel if I don't push we won't ever do anything different from every other fucking band.

OK. Enough from me...gonna go jump on King's bed and wake his lazy ass up (and then run...)

ALLEN KOVAC: I first met Nikki in 1985 when he was dating Lita Ford and he was an angry punk who didn't care what anybody's opinion was. But I liked him—underneath it all was a person whose eyes and smile showed he had character and who wanted to understand the business side as well as grow as an artist. I wanted to manage Mötley Crüe—which I eventually did—largely because both Nikki and Tommy had a real exuberance and wanted to learn.

On the jet, 2:30 a.m.

King just looked at me and said, Wow, this doesn't suck...ha ha...I had the waitress bring him a line on a silver platter with his own bottle of champagne. Fresh tacos and chips for everyone except Vince, who had his usual tuna sandwich. The show was cool tonight but the altitude just kills you here. It doesn't matter how good shape you're in. Mick asked King to jam with us in Salt Lake...that will be fun. Tom's coming in tomorrow...we should be there in about an hour. Today I'm happy.

Hotel, Salt Lake City, 12:30 p.m.

Tom is coming in today to hang. I'll have my grandfather and King with me. Sorta like the dad and brother I never had. The girls in Salt Lake are so beautiful. This is a town of suppressed people raised with a religious iron fist and sexual repression. So need I tell you, Diary, of the fucking debauchery that comes from the mixture of Mötley Crüe and Mormon girls?

After the show I'm flying back to LA on the Mötley jet and I don't know why. I need a girl-friend—a nice normal girl...where is she? Maybe I'll find her tonight...

291

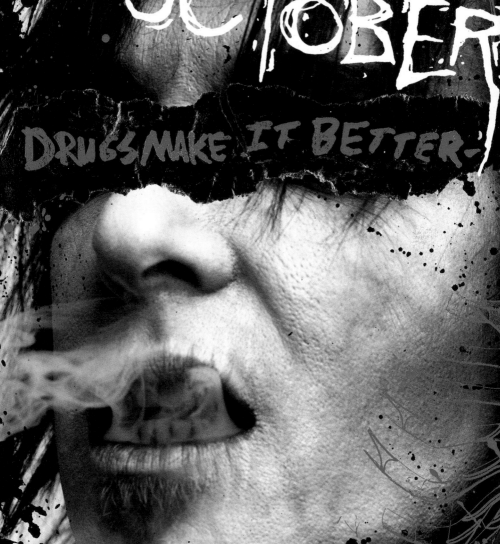

OCTOBER

DRUGS MAKE IT BETTER-

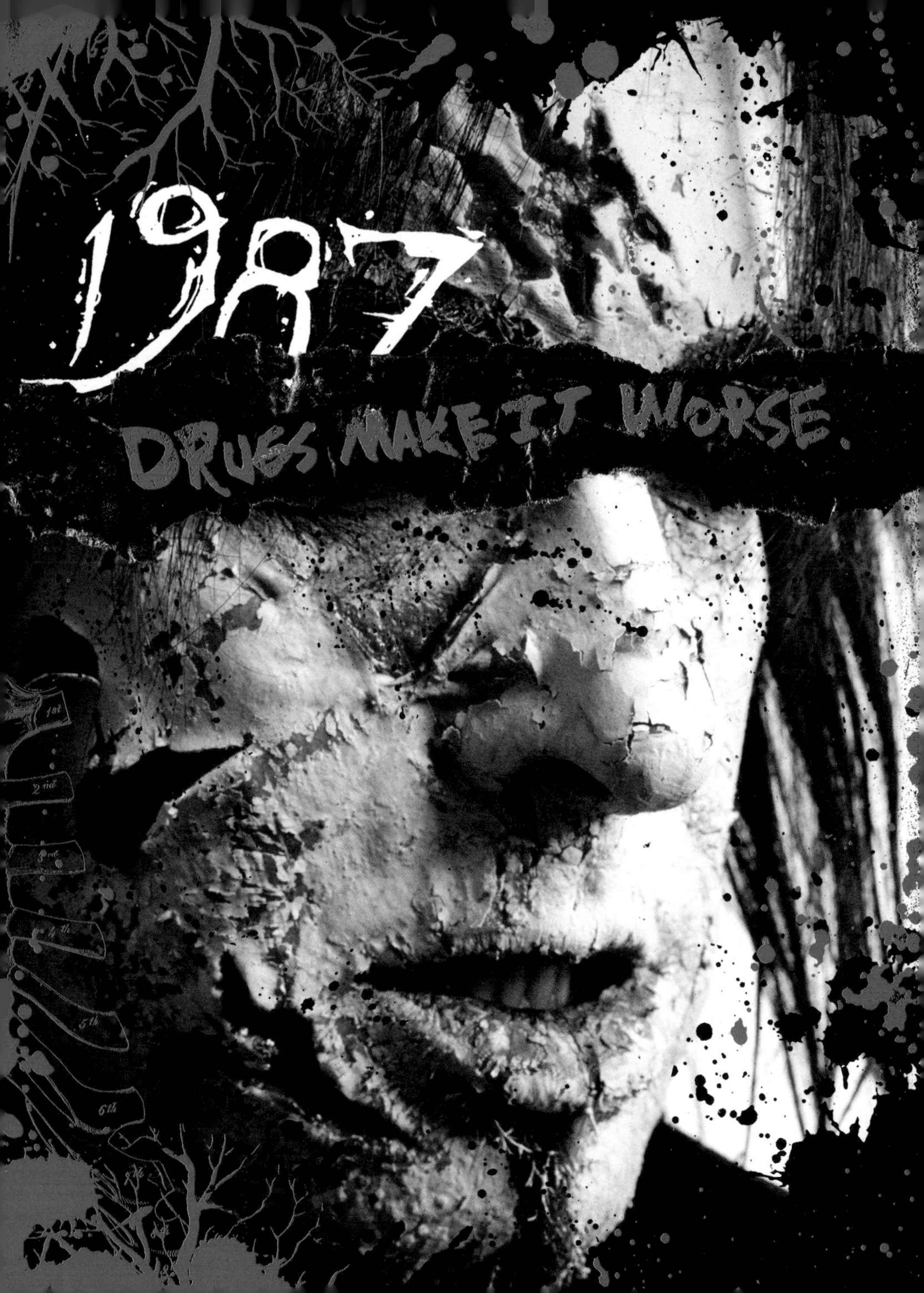
1987
DRUGS MAKE IT WORSE.

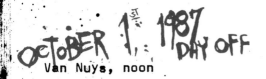

OCTOBER 1ˢᵗ, 1987 DAY OFF

Van Nuys, noon

Home sweet home…just woke up. Flew in from Salt Lake last night…Robbin flew with us and Tom stayed then drove back home. The flight was smooth and the sky so gorgeous. Our pilot would tip the plane to the left and you could see the stars so clear that we even saw a shooting star. Then he would tip to the right and you could see the arc of the Earth with spotted lights from little suburbs as we were getting close to LA. It feels like an electric tomb…I sometimes wonder if I will ever get out of here alive…

Karen has gone to stay with a friend while I'm back home—says she feels weird being here while I'm here as well but I wish she would stick around. It might stop me from going crazy.

1:30 p.m.

Abdul has a friend who sells rock. I had an oz cooked up and brought over—it will be here in a while.

I'm depressed, and I don't know why. I can't get outta this place in my head. I can't shake it off. Drugs make it better—drugs make it worse. Every time I'm gonna stop I get the itch…

3:45 p.m.

Oh my God—as soon as I got the rock and hit the pipe I thought my heart was gonna jump outta my chest. The whole house started shaking, rolling and shit was falling off the walls. It threw me on the ground and I realized we were having a fucking earthquake.

. I didn't know what to do so I ran outside, pipe in hand, and the door locked itself behind me. I was naked and had to run around the back of the house and break the window to get in. Then the alarm went off, and the security company called. Days like this I wish I didn't get out of bed…

5 p.m.

Flushed the coke in case there is another quake. I don't think my heart can take it. I took a few pills and I'm starting to get tired. We have a show in San Diego and I don't want any chance to get more coke. I'm gonna go play my guitar and lay in bed till I fall out.

IAN GITTINS: The Los Angeles earthquake of October 1, 1987, measured 5.9 on the Richter scale. It killed eight people, injured scores more, and left 2,200 people homeless and more than 10,000 buildings badly damaged. However, Nikki Sixx was by far the most infamous Los Angeleno to react to the quake by running out of his house butt-naked and waving a crack pipe.

OCTOBER 2ND, 1987
SPORTS ARENA, SAN DIEGO, CA

Van Nuys, 10 a.m.

Wow I just woke up. I slept 16 hours straight. I'm starving, I don't think I ate yesterday at all. I'm gonna jump on my bike and go grab some Mexican food down the street before I have to leave for San Diego.

I had a dream I was a kid laughing and playing with my father. I was so happy and then he just faded away right before my eyes. I was alone in the middle of the street looking for him frantically...that's the feeling I feel inside a lot.

12:30 p.m.

I'm gonna drive down to San Diego with Robbin. He's on his way over now. After being in his Ferrari I'm thinking about getting one...not that I'll ever be home to drive it.

OCTOBER 3RD, 1987
DAY OFF

Van Nuys, 1:10 p.m.

I have the next few days off. Had a pretty good show in San Diego, a lot of people from LA came down. It's easier to say hi and hang out in San Diego rather than LA...the Forum is always a zoo. Someone said the record company was there but the band didn't want to talk to them. Fuck them.

Gonna go to a movie with Bob. I need a normal night out...I'm over being me. Even writing in this diary is boring me 'cause it's all about me.

OCTOBER 4TH 1987
DAY OFF

Van Nuys, 10:30 a.m.

Went to a movie last night with Bob and came home and played guitar til about 1 a.m. No visitors, no phone calls, perfect night...wrote some really cool songs...

Noon

Gonna go get the car and jeep washed. It's so pretty outside, I might lie in the sun. Riki might come over, and Pete...spoke to Slash, he's as excited as I am to have Guns tour with us.

THE STRUGGLE FOR NORMALITY
NORMALLY ISN'T SUCH A STRUGGLE.

POWER TO THE MUSIC

Who said music's dead in the streets?
Don't know what they're talking about
They gotta put a bullet in my head.
If they want to keep me down.

OCTOBER 6TH 1987, LOS ANGELES, CA
GRAND WESTERN FORUM, 10:15 a.m.

Sitting outside drinking coffee and playing guitar... what a nice day here in LA. Today I'm happy. Days like today, I reflect a lot...it seems like a lifetime ago when this was just a dream. Yesterday was another safe and sane day. My problem is when I'm not doing drugs and drinking I'm actually happier til the boredom kicks in. Then there's this lil demon in my head that says, Come on, just one, and I lose all control...

This road has an end. I just don't know where it is.

2 p.m.

I'm gonna ride my Harley to the Forum. I'm gonna go early and go up by the beach. It doesn't get much better than riding your bike up the coast to the first of two sold-out hometown shows. I've got Memory Motel by the Stones running thru my mind, over and over...

3:30 p.m.

I'm sitting here on the side of the road looking out over the ocean. I'm glad I brought my diary along. It's too beautiful not to stop and take it all in and even try to write it down.

I know she's out there, my soul mate. Of course, they say that if you're looking, you'll never find whatever it is you're looking for. For now, I'm just looking out over these rolling waves and being re-minded how small I am.

Better go or I'll miss my own show...ha ha...

7:30 p.m.

Backstage...I just got out of the back of a cop car. I was riding my bike and as soon as I pull up to the show this cop pulled me over. I told him I was play-ing a show and he said he didn't care, I was speeding and he wanted to see my license. I told him I don't have one and he said I was going to jail. I said if I wasn't onstage in about an hour there would be a riot and he said again he didn't care. So I told him to fuck off and he arrested me...

Doc came out and talked the cop out of it and I had to apologize. How demoralizing to apologize to that fuckhead, but I bit my tongue and said sorry. I'm sure he wanted to kick my ass like the cops did outside the Whisky years ago…

Gotta get ready…time for a shot of JD then kick LA's ass—today and tomorrow.…

OCTOBER 7TH 1987
GRAND WESTERN FORUM, LOS ANGELES, CA

No entry

OCTOBER 8TH 1987
LONG BEACH ARENA, LONG BEACH, CA

11:45 a.m.

Yesterday was a nightmare…probably the worst day of my life next to Nona dying.

Vanity showed up at my house after the first Forum show with a baseball of base. I stayed up all night and day until show time the next day…they had to send a car to get me and when I got to the Forum yesterday for our second show I was so frazzled I couldn't even talk. I hid in the dressing room fearing my heart would explode till it was time to go on. I had to snort about a 1/4 gram to get onstage. I truly thought I was gonna die onstage last night—what is wrong with me? Why can't I say no to drugs? They haunt me…or hunt me…

P.S. I should be the happiest man in the world. My dreams have come true. I need to quit—this is killing me. Vanity is killing me. Drugs are killing me…or am I already dead? I won't make another year. I know it.

NIKKI: This was the beginning of the end. I knew I was either gonna die or get sober. I knew how to die. By then I'd had many secret overdoses and seizures so I understood where the line was and I was just inches from crossing it. The dying could be easy...it was the living that I didn't know if I could do.

POSSIBLE T-SHIRT SLOGANS:

REHAB IS FOR QUITTERS

or

WHY DO YOU THINK THEY CALL IT DOPE?

OCTOBER 9TH 1987 DAY OFF
Van Nuys, 7 p.m.

I've just been hiding all day under my sheets. I won't answer the phone. No TV, no music, just me and my .357 on my bedside table...it seems to be talking to me in a whisper. I know it seems dramatic, but you're not inside my head. I feel like I need to check into a nuthouse...I know it's only a matter of time till I die. The question isn't how anymore. It's when.

OCTOBER 10TH, 1987 OAKLAND STADIUM, OAKLAND, CA
Van Nuys, 4 p.m.

I haven't been to sleep in over 48 hours. I don't think I can make the show. I can't even write...my hands are shaking so bad. I keep hearing voices every time I hit the pipe then I come down and nobody is there. I'm losing it. I need some dope to come down and nobody is around...all I have is coke. No booze, nothing...not even one fucking pill. I'm just not gonna answer the door or phone. I can't do it. I'm too paranoid...I can't face people. Fuck...what am I gonna do? There's a sold-out stadium waiting and I'm dying here and nobody really gives a fuck. Neither do I. I wish I could die. I'm gonna go take a hot shower and lay in bed, maybe I'll fall asleep...ya right...I'm soooo fucked...

TAKE ME TO THE TOP

Take me to the top and throw me off

OCTOBER 11, 1987 DAY OFF

Van Nuys, 2:30 p.m.

Yesterday was about as low as I've gone. I hadn't slept in days and was so based out I missed the Mötley Jet. Actually I didn't miss shit-I just never showed up. Doc had a jet sent for me to take me to Oakland Stadium. I was out of my mind-I was so fucking coked out, I felt like I was gonna have a heart attack.

When I got there, there was a band meeting and they all asked me if I had been shooting up...they wanted to see my arms. Thank God I was freebasing...no traces except the insanity. I finally made it onstage and went home right after the show. Everyone is pissed at me and you know what? Fuck them! I'm sick of this fucking band! On top of that bullshit my stomach has really been killing me lately. There are little traces of blood again every time I take a shit. This always happens when I'm drinking too much or I up the drugs. I guess after a while that shit tears my guts open. Problem is I haven't been drinking as much as doing drugs...maybe my insides are coming out?

TOMMY LEE: Oakland Stadium was the point we all realized Nikki's shit was getting *really* bad. When he didn't make the flight we all started freaking out and saying, "Fuck, we're playing a stadium tonight–this isn't just an arena or a club!" Dude, that would have been the worst no-show of all.

Sixx had to get a later flight and when he turned up he just looked like shit–a lovely shade of gray. We asked to see his arms and of course they were a mess. But we never thought of going as far as asking Nikki to leave the band. The truth was we were *all* fucking around with shit, so we were in no position to bust his balls about it.

VINCE NEIL: Playing Oakland Stadium was a real big prestigious deal and there was Nikki, fucking it all up for us. There were a lot of people depending on us, and when he didn't show I thought it just wasn't going to happen. I was just glad we got through the show, but I have no idea how Nikki managed to do it.

`Van Nuys, 4 p.m.`

```
    I forgot to write down another of my stupid lil
mishaps. The other night I fell and smashed the back
of my head on the fireplace in the bedroom and I probably
only remember 'cause my head is still pounding.
My stomach and my
head are
killing me.
```

I feel like I'm slowly rotting away both physically and mentally. I was playing guitar last night and could barely make a chord I was so fucked up; Painkillers, whisky and cocaine…what a lovely life, right?

Karen came back today. I opened the door to her and it was all I could do to say hi, then I just came straight back to my room. She must see how sick I am.

KAREN DUMONT: I was only ever in the house a few days when Nikki was there and he hid things very well, but occasionally I'd see him really the worse for wear. He'd been foolish enough to tell me what he liked to do–close his bedroom door, go into his walk-in closet and get ripped. He was so paranoid that all the doors had to be closed, so I insisted his bedroom door always had to be open, and if it wasn't I'd bang on it and shout until he opened it. It used to scare me that Nikki had a gun.

OCTOBER 13, 1987 MEMORIAL COLISEUM, PORTLAND, OR
Hotel, 4:30 p.m.

I'm getting a weird vibe from the band. Either nobody wants to be around me or they're trying to punish me for Oakland and you know what? It's really pissing me off…we've all fucked up in this band. Vince killed someone, Tommy has fucked up a thousand times, Mick has fucked up too, and nobody has ever complained when we're all doing coke and junk all night. So I missed the jet? Fuck, I made the show! Now I'm the rock 'n' roll nigger of the band. Fuck them!

Maybe I should quit the band. Then they'd be fucked with no songs.

OCTOBER 14 1987
DAY ONE

Hotel, Tacoma, 2:45 p.m.

People...everywhere...there seems to be nowhere to hide, not even on the inside.

OCTOBER 15, 1987
TACOMA DOME, TACOMA, WA
Backstage, 6 p.m.

I can be such an asshole sometimes. My mom and my sister came to the hotel yesterday and I had been up all night and day and was freaking out of my mind. I was in the middle of staring out the peephole looking for people who were spying on me when my mom and sis knocked on the door and said, Hi Nikki it's us, we're here to see you. I don't know why but I completely lost my mind, calling them every name in the book and to fuck off, etc etc. Between me and you I don't know if it was the drugs talking or the shame of being so high on coke and I didn't want them to see me. My mom is coming to the show tonight. I'll try to make good.

On the jet, midnight

I'm drunk...sitting on the jet leaving for Canada. My mom came to the show and after she started in on me about the hotel I lost it again. I had her thrown out of the building...called her a whore in front of everybody...I think in moments of confrontation it all hits me how I was abandoned by her and my father and it comes out in all sorts of evil ways. My sister had no part in it but somehow I have linked them together in my mind. I know I made a lot of people uncomfortable tonight with all my screaming and breaking things but I can't help how I act. I wish I could part with all this anger...

CECI COMER: My mother and I went down to meet Nikki in Tacoma. I had both of my boys with me–Jake was two years old and Caleb was just a baby. I had to pay for parking in the hotel garage and it was all the money I had. First there was a bunch of crap in the lobby–Nikki told me via the front desk to wait for ten minutes, which turned into an hour. When I finally got permission to go up to his room I knocked on the door and Nikki asked, "Who is it?" I got pissed because he ought to know it was me, but I said, "Hey, it's Ceci, I've got the boys with me, you coming out?" He just yelled, really loud in a raspy voice, "Go away!" I was totally crushed and saw red. I went back home completely raw, just thinking, What an asshole. I felt scorned.

DEANA RICHARDS: Oh my God, this was so painful...We got to the desk and asked for Nikki. They told us which room he was in so we called, but he didn't answer. So we went up to the room and kept knocking on the door. We could hear him in there, but he wouldn't come to the door. He told us to go away. It was horrible. The whole day was like a horrible blur to me, just so awful.

It was like another night years earlier, when Mötley Crüe was just getting big, and Nikki invited me and Ceci to a show at the Paramount Theatre in Seattle. I was so glad and so excited to see him, after all those years. Ceci and I went backstage to talk to Nikki, and I put my hand on his back, and he just angrily shook it off and went out of the room.

He went into the rest room with Ceci, and when I followed them in, he was taking cocaine. It just broke my heart. I asked him, "Nikki, what are you doing?" And he said, "I know exactly why you have come here—you want something from me. You want my money." It shocked me so much, because it was the last thing on my mind. So I left...and then I didn't see or hear from Nikki for a very, very long time.

NIKKI: Believing that I had been abandoned by my father and later my mother had left me holding a garbage truck full of feelings and all that garbage had begun to stink. I didn't know how toxic it actually was at the time. When we think of storing stuff away you usually think some day you may need it, but with feelings it's different. You store it away and forget about it, then one day—like a serial killer keeps all the dead bodies in his garage—something starts to stink. They say a dog is the first one to smell his own shit. I think a drug addict is the last.

ON WITH THE SHOW

Frankie died just the other night
Some say it was suicide

OCTOBER 16TH 1987,
PACIFIC COLISEUM, VANCOUVER, B.C., CANADA
Vancouver, 7:30 p.m.

Sitting backstage yesterday after the Seattle family massacre in Tacoma I was having a few drinks with some girlies and it seems they have some connection to fresh packs of needles so I told them to join me in my room after the show. I snuck an oz and 2 grams of Persian into Canada with me but I told them to bring an 8-ball 'cause I don't wanna run out. I'm not gonna let them know I have any dope. Fuck that...bad news travels fast. Gotta put some Mott the Hoople on the boom box and get into going onstage. My body is so tired I feel like I could just lay down and die.

Tonight should be fun. One girl's name is Mouse. I don't know the other's...or care.

OCTOBER 17TH 1987
Hotel, 3:50 p.m. DAY OFF

Stood in front of the mirror today and all I could see was death. I have lost so much weight and my skin is yellow if not gray. My eyes are sunk into the back of my head and my smile has disappeared. I dress it up with leather and cover it with being defensive just to get through this hell...ain't fame great? Anybody want some? 'Cause you can have mine...I hate it.

NORTHLANDS COLISEUM, OCTOBER 18TH 1987 EDMONTON, ALBERTA CANADA
Backstage, 6:05 p.m.

Sitting here reading my own diaries...I'm really making myself sick. These drugs haunt me. These pages are an ongoing bitchfest. I'm smart enough to know these drugs and alcohol are killing me and my music, so why can't I get ahold of this?

I dreamt my whole life of making music and I have every reason to be happy yet I can't be. How do I get out of this downward spiral? I can't find a way out of this hole. I would like to say to myself, If you're in a hole, put down the shovel, but I can't. I'm so addicted, it's all I think about, but I know there's more. Is it the fact that I've never mourned not having a father? There is a reason and I'm sure it's right in front of my face. I'm too proud to ask for help but that's what I need.

I have to get a grip. I have to quit. I feel like I'm rotting. In the mornings when I wake I can smell death on me. It's right around the corner and unless I get out I'm not gonna make it. How do I stop? Do I have to go to rehab? Is there even a reason to live? It's insane that I ask myself that but I sometimes wonder if anyone would miss me if I died…would anybody even show up to my funeral?

I shot up a lot of coke last night with Tommy…I mean a lot. My fucking arms look like pincushions. Have a show then off to Calgary. Mouse and Laurie (is that her name?) are following us…

TOMMY LEE: I think the time I finally figured out that Sixx and I were fucking crazy and had gone insane was in Canada when we ran out of heroin and cocaine, and sat up all night shooting up Jack Daniel's. Afterwards, I just thought, What the fuck was *that* all about? It didn't even occur to us that we could always just drink the JD. Bro, let me tell you, there was something seriously wrong with us.

THERE IS NO HERO IN HEROIN.

OCTOBER 19TH 1987
OLYMPIC SADDLEDOME, CALGARY, ALBERTA, CANADA
Calgary, 6:30 p.m.

After yesterday's show we flew here and I ended
up shooting up all night by myself. I tried shooting up Halcions too—whatever works. I got about
two hours sleep. I gotta play a show. I'm gonna
order a few drinks and get out of here. I never
even unpacked...

OCTOBER 20TH, 1987 DAY OFF
Hotel, 5:20 p.m.

Just woke up. I pulled another solo all-
nighter. I'm actually out of coke. Those chicks
Mouse and Laurie have been with Tommy and I know
they got rigs and dope but I said I wasn't doing
anything and have holed up in my room. I feel so
bored. Playing guitar is boring...listening to
music is boring...fucking is boring...I'm boring.

Doug Thaler asked me if I would consider rehab.
At least he cares. I'm tired of touring and tired
of drugs but I can't seem to get off either.

AA saying:

SICK AND TIRED OF BEING SICK AND TIRED

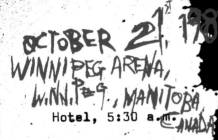

OCTOBER 21st, 1987
WINNIPEG ARENA,
WINNIPEG, MANITOBA, CANADA
Hotel, 5:30 a.m.

Tonight's show was really tight. It felt magical. Then afterwards Tommy and Fred came back to my room and we sat drinking and doing lines. Zombie dust was involved as well. I snuck outside and set fire to a door with lighter fluid and hair spray—I thought it was Rich Fisher's room. It set the fire alarms off and security came running up but Fred managed to turn it around so it was their fucking fault. Tommy and I were listening behind the door and pissing ourselves laughing.

Then an hour ago Doug called and told me I could have burned the hotel down and there was some Chinese family in the room who are really freaked out. Shit! I was just fucking around. It's not like I really did catch the hotel on fire! Fucking bullshit! Now everybody is pissed at me (again). Can't anyone take a joke round here?

P.S. I'm gonna slow down. You wouldn't believe the blood. Off to Toronto now...

FRED SAUNDERS: Nikki, Tommy and I were sitting in Nikki's room and he went to the bathroom—or so we thought. Instead he'd gone outside, got lighter fluid and poured it all over a room door and doorjamb. He lit it, banged on the door and ran off, so by the time the guy opened the door it was fully ablaze. There was a young Chinese guy with his son in there—it could have killed them. Hotel security came up and I started yelling at them that what the hell kind of hotel was this? I had a band to look after and didn't need somebody sneaking around trying to set fire to their rooms! They apologized to me. Nikki was hidden in his room, just sniggering.

OCTOBER 22ND, 1987 DAY OFF
Hotel, Toronto, 7:15 p.m.

Fucking hell, I need a day off. My hands are fucked up and cut up, as is my body from throwing myself around onstage. I have a pulled hamstring and my ankle is sprained—who said rock 'n' roll isn't physical? Hahaha...Tonight me and T are going to a club and then gonna go and do radio around midnight.

Breakfast is here...gotta go. SIXX

Hotel, 5:30 a.m.

Drunk—me and Tommy had a blast tonight. We beat the fuck outta some jackass who mouthed off to Tommy. His name was Axl. At first I thought we beat up Slash's singer but it was some other guy. Then we went upstairs to this radio station...the DJ Joey was fucking cool but I think we got him fired. We had too much fun...oh well...

JOEY SCOLERI: In 1987 I was a twenty-year-old DJ with a metal show on Q107 in Toronto. I called myself Joey Vendetta. The show ran every Friday from midnight to 2 A.M. and I was excited by the chance to talk to Mötley Crüe on the program.

I was expecting to interview Vince and Mick and no offense to them but Nikki and Tommy were the guys you wanted to talk to. Tommy was banging Heather Locklear and Nikki was banging everybody else. So I was thrilled when Nikki and Tommy walked in the studio, although I think they couldn't believe this young kid was the DJ. They had loads of people with them. Everybody was pretty wrecked–I remember Tommy had just had a fight in the club downstairs with some dude who had dissed Heather.

We started the show and I said, "Hi, I'm Joey Vendetta, Nikki and Tommy from Mötley Crüe are here, and we'll be talking to them after this." I put on a track from *Girls Girls Girls* and as soon as it started, Nikki handed me a bottle of Jack. It didn't take much to make me want to chug it–I was a twenty-year-old being handed a bottle of Jack by Nikki Sixx, so I chugged half of it in one shot! I was hammered inside two minutes and I just thought, I'm fucked.

Then Nikki asked me if I'd ever had cocaine. I said no and he said, "Well, you're starting tonight." He took out a bag and it wasn't just a gram–you'd have needed a shovel to move it. He scooped some up with his little fingernail and put it under my nose, and I sniffed some up each nostril.

I didn't know then that, when you're drinking, cocaine helps to level you out, but in thirty seconds I went from Mr. Drunk to Mr. Super-Confident. When the record ended I started gabbling like Wolfman Jack on acid, talking 100 mph. I started interviewing Nikki and Tommy and every other word was "fuck" or "bitch"–we were talking like we were sitting in a bar somewhere, rather than on air.

Nikki said, "Can we smoke this?" And so we were smoking hashish during the interview. Everybody could hear us going *pssssch* while we were talking—it wasn't too hard to figure out what was going on. Then Nikki got the blow out again, so the listeners could hear us smoking *and* snorting away.

Suddenly Nikki said, "Let's play a game—Guess What We're Doing? We can give away tickets to our shows!" He grabbed a mic on a boom stand, pulled it towards his crotch and turned to face a metal wastepaper bin in the corner. He whipped his dick out and started pissing in it—there was no plastic bag in there so it was really loud. People were phoning in and asking, "Are you running water?" And Nikki started screaming, "No, I'm pissing in a wastebasket!"

Then Tommy said, "Guess What I'm Doing, Toronto?" and pulled his cock out and started banging it against the desk. I said, "Um, there's no need to do that," but Tommy was saying, "Dude, just listen to the noise it makes!" Meanwhile, people were calling in, saying, "Is he banging his cock against the desk?"

I decided to put people on the air, which was an incredibly stupid move. Our program director always told us to try to make the listener the star. Obviously because I was drunk and high I didn't do any pre-screening whatsoever, so the first call went like this:

> Caller: Hello, I'm Megan.
>
> Nikki: Hi, Megan, how old are you?
>
> Caller: I'm twelve.
>
> Nikki: Oh good, I like twelve-year-olds. You get to hear the bones crack when you put it in...

She just giggled. Thankfully she had no idea what he was talking about. When Nikki and Tommy and all their hangers-on left, I felt exhausted, like a hooker who'd been fucked by everybody. As I cleaned up all the beer cans and Jack bottles I realized that I might be fired on Monday, but I figured even if I was, I'd be a legend regardless.

On Monday I got called in to see my program director. He told me to hold up my index finger on my right hand, which I did, and he asked me, "What does it do?" I said I don't know, and he said, "It hits the OFF button on the microphones. You're supposed to be the one in charge–now get out!"

Mötley Crüe invited me to their dressing room at their Toronto gig, and Nikki and Tommy said it was the most fun they'd ever had on a radio interview. We got on really well. I wasn't tight with Vince or Mick. Mick always seemed a real bummer, but now that I know how ill he was, and what he had to put up with from those retards Nikki and Tommy, I totally understand why.

OCTOBER 23ᴿᴰ 1987/DAY OFF...
Hotel, Toronto, 4 p.m.

Wow two days off in a row. I have such a hangover...some kid in this band last night told me and Tommy he kicked in the doors of the venue here when we were sound checking on the Theatre of Pain tour...I remember that. All the fans came rushing in...ha ha ha...Then after we spoke for a bit he went onstage with his band VO5. You should have seen these guys' hair! It was to the ceiling! But the little fucker could sing his balls off. He told me, You just watch, I'm gonna be a star someday...

I told him, Be careful what you wish for...

NIKKI: Well, that kid got his dream–he later joined Skid Row and became Sebastian Bach. I always like that kind of story. How often do we get to see someone get exactly what they wish for?

OCTOBER 24TH 1987
CIVIC CENTER, OTTAWA, ONTARIO, CANADA
Backstage, Ottawa, 4:30 p.m.

Don't really feel like writing. Nothing new really going on. I'm doing pretty good–my track marks are healing. I got a little addicted up here in Canada, but I kicked it with sleeping pills…nothing new to me.

Tonight is gonna be a good show but tomorrow is Maple Leaf Gardens–how fucking cool is that? Sold out–I wish Nona could have seen this…

OCTOBER 26th 1987 DAY OFF
Hotel, Toronto, 3:30 p.m.

Last night's Maple Leaf Gardens show was insane…we were so good. We were all looking at each other with big smiles, it felt like the old days.

Another night in this hotel. Right now, I need two things…to get outta this hotel and to get outta this hotel. We've been here it seems like a week. I've basically moved in…I've duct-taped the drapes shut, no housekeeping allowed in again. I have scarves on top of all the lamps. Room service trays are every-where you look and I have my NY Dolls poster above the bed. It's really quite nice in here, but time to go. The band wants to go visit the local strip club tonight–it's always like shooting fish in a barrel.

P.S. I still haven't called home once. There's really no reason to. I'm sure Karen is doing fine...as long as the ghosts don't come crawling out of my closet.

POISON APPLES

Took a Greyhound Bus down to Heartattack and Vine
with a fistful of dreams and dimes.
So far out didn't know that I was in,
had a taste for a life of slime.
When push came to shove, the music was the drug
and the band always got to play.
Sex, smack, rock, roll, mainline, overdose.
Man, we lived it night and day.

We loved our Mott the Hoople,
it kept us all so enraged.
And you love us and you hate us and you love us.
'Cause we're so fuckin' beautiful!

OCTOBER 27TH 1987
THE FORUM, MONTREAL, QUEBEC, CANADA
Hotel, Toronto, 1 p.m.

Just got room service. Need to start to pack up my room 'cause they're coming for luggage at 1:30. Then we take the jet to Montreal and after the show we fly to NYC. In the afternoon we fly to Bermuda 'cause we're doing an MTV contest there called Mötley Crüise to nowhere.

ROSS HALFIN: When Nikki fucked girls on the Girls tour, he did it pretty quietly because he wanted to get them off on their own to his room and do it with his drugs. The only exception was Montreal. There was a girl backstage after the show who was up for a gang bang and forty-three of us did her. Tommy went first, Vince went second, I was third because, for some reason I forget now, Nikki wanted to be nice to me, then Nikki went fourth. The only person who didn't want to was Mick.

That girl was OK, oddly enough, but there was also a repulsive Hells Angel girl with a shaved vagina there. She had bad teeth, horrible tattoos and a bullet belt, and I still have a picture of the tour manager, Rich Fisher, going down on her while Nikki watched, laughing. The fact that she was so awful appealed to Nikki: he always liked doing the worst thing imaginable. And normally he did it.

NIKKI: To me, ugly has always been beautiful and beauty usually turns out to be very ugly. When I was younger I always hated my face. It was too sweet and innocent—no armor to protect the exposed nerves. That's one of the reasons I distorted it through makeup and theatrics later in life. When I take photographs I'm attracted to documenting the darker, truer side of life or fantasy.

Girls? Back then, the sooner it was over, the sooner I could go off the deep end. What they looked like only interested me if they stood out from the crowd. A fucked-up biker chick was more interesting to me than a model—who they were was what interested me. Broken people attract broken people. I was like a guy getting ready to jump off a building without a net. The sooner I got the sex over with, the sooner I could hit the pavement…and kill the pain.

OCTOBER 28TH 1987 DAY OFF
Hotel, Bermuda, 8 p.m.

Just got into the hotel. Man, it's dead here. The bar isn't even open. Doc is here—he keeps looking at me like he's expecting my head to spin around and spit green pea soup on him at any moment. When I say something, he laughs, but it's a nervous laugh, like a person waiting on impending doom. Maybe it's good—managers need to live in fear. I'm gonna watch TV…I know…weird! I snagged a sleeping pill from Fred so I can sleep.

The last few days I've been eating like a horse. I guess my body needs some nutrition. I put it through the ringer in Canada.

DOC McGHEE: The Mötley Crüise was a competition and the idea was that the winners had no idea where they were going. So we took them to the Bermuda Triangle. MTV was involved, and on the first day I got a call from an MTV guy saying two of the competition winners were being held in customs. It was two guys–the customs officers had opened their luggage and found flying gear, girls' outfits and dildos in there. I had to go down to customs to get them out.

That evening we had a welcome cocktail party and the two guys turned up in full drag. Tommy didn't realize and thought one of them was gorgeous–he told me, "Dude, she's fucking smoking!" When I explained they were two guys, Mötley didn't really want to be around them. Bizarrely, it turned out that one of them designed costumes for Mötley and just happened to have won the competition.

DOUG THALER: When Mötley came back from Bermuda they told me all about these two wild cross-dressing kids who were on the cruise. I later went on to manage one of those wild cross-dressers in a band called the Toilet Boys. By then he was going by the name of Miss Guy.

OCTOBER 29TH 1987 DAY OFF
Hotel, Bermuda, 2 p.m.

Me, Tommy and Fred got Vespas and rode around the island this morning. We wore our helmets backwards and acted like kamikaze pilots. I haven't laughed so hard in a long time. We took some pictures...I can't wait to get them developed. OK, I gotta take a shower (it's been over a week) and go to this boat for some contest or other.

We fly home tomorrow. Gonna shoot a video for You're All I Need with Wayne. I promise not to let Sikki rear his ugly head. I can't wait to see my dog that I've hardly met.

DOC McGHEE: We all sailed out to an island for a limbo contest. I thought, I can never ask Mötley Crüe to limbo, they will fry my ass, but Vince is so fucking twisted in the head that he *wanted* to limbo. The contest was for couples only, and when Vince and Tommy went up to the gay guy in charge, who was called the King of Limbo, he said they couldn't do it. He had no idea who Mötley Crüe was. Vince started going crazy and yelling that it was his fucking party so he could do what he wanted, but the King still wouldn't let them. Then the King started to limbo under a twelve-inch bar and Vince was so pissed off that he started throwing bits of chicken at him. He hit him in the face and the King of Limbo stormed off so then I had MTV and an angry crowd on my back. Great. Just great.

Spent today filming the video for You're All I Need with Wayne. I wonder if I should send Nicole a copy?

I told management I need to change my room name when the tour starts back up to Sharon Needles. They didn't like that very much so of course that's gonna be my new name. Rather fitting if you ask me.

Random Unused Lyric

Nothing to share except these needles

WAYNE ISHAM: Before the video for "You're All I Need" we had a long talk over what we wanted to do. We'd seen this news story about a guy who killed his girlfriend, which Nikki related to events in his own life—he kept saying there was a personal angle, but I never really understood what he was talking about. Plus he always loved the Sid and Nancy idea, so we wanted a video about a self-destructive relationship.

The video started with the police putting a girl's body in an ambulance and arresting her boyfriend, then it went back to tell their story. There is a lot of yelling and screaming but no actual violence—not that that stopped MTV from banning it, as usual. They said it was too literal and implied violence.

It was a typical ballsy Crüe thing to do—they just loved to step up and do stuff other bands wouldn't touch. Originally the band wasn't even in the video, but the record label made us add some band footage, which we shot in my studio. I wish I could say I looked into Nikki's eyes and saw the mental state he was in back then…but I didn't.

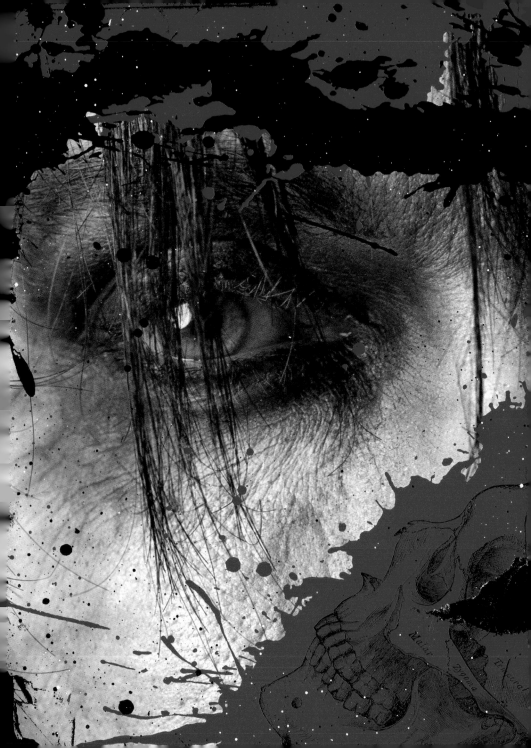

NOVEMBER 1ˢᵗ 1987 DAY OFF
Van Nuys, noon

I'm reading On the Road by Kerouac again. I feel so connected to writers like Kerouac, Allen Ginsberg and William Burroughs. I hear people say they wish they were old enough to have lived thru the '60s and other people say they should have been around in the 1920s. This was a time when I would have loved to be alive. Their ability to shock society with their words and fillet the law with their freedom leaves me envious.

I'm drug-free (today) and feel sooo alive. It's good to be home. So far the cockroaches of my life haven't discovered I'm home yet. I'll be outta here before they come to feed on my weakness. Karen seems amazed that I'm lucid. That makes two of us. Maybe I'm beating this thing little by little...

P.S. I love these lines from the book I'm reading. To me this describes Mötley to a T:

Here's to the crazy ones. The misfits. The rebels. The troublemakers. The round heads in the square holes. The ones who see things differently...

KAREN DUMONT: Whatever he did, Nikki managed to put a good front on for me. He was stronger than anyone I know at making things look OK. The fact that he functioned so well while doing massive amounts of drugs shows how good he was at keeping things together.

There were times that he looked really rough, but I naïvely just put it down to him being a lazy slob. He'd laugh at me telling him off, but he was never nasty to me and I never realized how badly he was doing. I had always thought being messed up brought the nasty side out of people. Vince was more like that–he was scary.

NOVEMBER 2ND, 1987 DAY OFF.
Van Nuys, 3 p.m.

Home sweet home. I had breakfast this morning with Karen. I actually cooked...I think she was just being kind 'cause I could hardly eat the eggs, they were like rubber. I told her about the new video being based on the movie Taxi Driver. She said she didn't know if MTV would have the balls to play it. That's fine by me. It's becoming so boring, a bubblegum channel, and there are all these cheeseball bands coming out and just ruining everything.

I honestly don't think anyone understands what Mötley is or they wouldn't try to copy us. We're a train wreck, a bastard child between punk rock and heavy metal, and some people somehow think it's cute. If only they knew. We would rather slit your throat than be part of this...so I hope MTV DOESN'T play it.

I went to the dog park with Whisky. Wow, there are a lot of hot girls there! Maybe I should have showered a week ago when I said I would...they probably thought I was a homeless guy. That's better for me.

CHICKS = TROUBLE...and meeting a chick
in a dog park is a perfect setup for disaster.

P.S. Today's my last day home. Gotta go back on the road tomorrow.

RODEO
Laughing like gypsies, show to show
Livin' my life like a rolling stone
This is how my story unfolds
Traveling man, never at home
Can't find love so I sleep alone
This whisky river has a long way to flow
All that I know is life on this road

Van Nuys, 8 a.m.

Limo's here. I have a noon commercial flight to New Orleans where our jet will take us to Mobile. I never unpacked (again). Maybe I'll just throw these clothes away and buy new ones on the road...there are holes in most of them anyway.

On the jet, 5 p.m.

Sitting here on the jet waiting to take off. I think Vince must have pulled an all-nighter...he looks a little tattered around the edges. Me? Yes, it's usually me that's tattered, or better yet shattered. It's amazing what a few days without a hangover will do for your disposition. I'm feeling creative, which for me means life. I struggle between creativeness and being somewhere between slump and completely dry.

Backstage, Mobile, 7 p.m.

Just got to the gig. I'm so tired I couldn't sleep on the plane much. I've been thinking about my mother and father a lot. The last few days it seems, when I don't do drugs, that's what I do. I guess maybe the drugs are a part of me killing the pain, but for once thank God I didn't do anything the last few days. It's nice to not have been still up when the limo showed up.

I'm gonna go over and see Slash and the guys... they join the tour tonight. Now the bad news for them—Tom Zutaut told me they were a younger, crazier Mötley. Does that sound like a challenge or what?

SLASH: We were really excited to go on the road with Mötley. We had a lot in common—we were both from LA and were total hell-raisers. We had toured Canada with the Cult and played with Iron Maiden and Alice Cooper, but Mötley Crüe was cool and they were at their peak. It was a chance to hang out with a bunch of guys who had been around a lot longer and test the water to see if we were crazier than them.

LIVIN' IN THE KNOW

TV says 10 dead for Christmas,
stalker on the loose
Another freeway shooting,
and I'll be hangin' by a noose.
I can't seem to shake it, I can't bend the spell.
Special thanks to Mom and Dad for bringing me to hell

NOVEMBER 4TH 1987 CIVIC CENTER, ALBANY, GA
Backstage, 6:10 p.m.

Spent the night in Mobile last night. So good to see Slash. Guns N' Roses was awesome last night but our fans can be so brutal. They just stood there for the most part and stared—they just don't want to see anybody but us. Maybe some day we will do "An Evening with..." but Doug says that is suicide. Anyway I think they're gonna be huge but what do I know? I thought the same about the Ramones...

Last night I drank very little (half a bottle of Jack) but I can feel the demons in my head knocking and I don't wanna let them in (or out).

327

NOVEMBER 5nd 1987 DAY OFF
Hotel, New Orleans, 1:30 p.m.

Today I've decided to write my mother a
letter...probably with no real intention of mailing it.

Dear Mother,

I'll start off this letter by asking how you are—with no real interest
in an answer. I'm just trying to be polite—a good son, so to speak.
If I were honest, I would ask you something with a sharper edge to it.
Maybe something not so simple, maybe something we both could relate
to, rather than how's the weather? and is work treating you well? Oh
hell, we've never been ones for hiding our disdain for each other. I mean,
you showed yours by abandoning me years ago. But why don't I get to
the point—did you ever miss me when you shipped me off to
Grandma's? Was I even in your thoughts? Did you cry like I did once
your car turned the corner and sped away? I'll tell you—I used to
love you, even though I didn't know you. That's the innocence of a child,
so I don't regret it. Nona and Tom always gave me love unconditionally
but as a boy I pined for my mother. I'd lie in bed at night wondering
if you were out buying me presents that very day. Waiting for
your phone call (that never came) and in my heart I knew you were
always planning for my return. I knew it was just a matter of time
and you would save me. I really thought you loved me, but I was
wrong. You weren't out buying me anything but a fucked-up childhood
and you weren't planning anything except how to ruin my innocent
life. Let me ask you an honest question—how did it feel when I did
the same to you? Does it burn when my name is mentioned on the
radio? Do you feel like your guts were torn out, or do you still feel
the same? It would be sad if you still felt the same, because my plan
of ripping your heart out would have failed. I think I've done a good
job so far but we're not done...not until you're dead, and only
then, will we be even. I guess life just doesn't always work out—but
you started this. I hope you die with a broken heart. Isn't life grand?

Love, Your Son (?)

DEANA RICHARDS: Tom always told me that eventually he would tell Nikki the truth of what happened when he was a child–that Nona and my sisters had taken Nikki away from me when I always wanted him back. I always prayed that Tom would tell him that, because I wanted Nikki to know the truth more than anything else in the world. But Tom never did.

One time in 2001 Tom had gone out to join Nikki on tour and they were passing through Seattle. I went to the airport to meet Tom for an hour and asked why he still hadn't told Nikki the truth, but Tom just said, "He won't listen." I asked him, "What do you mean he won't listen? Nona has been dead long enough now for you to tell Nikki the truth, and I think you're dragging your feet."

I looked at Tom and said, "I should have been strong enough to fight you guys. You could never have taken Nikki away from me if I had been strong enough to fight you." And he looked at me and said, "Yes, we could have!" He had a look on his face, and venom in his voice, and I suddenly realized he'd been part of the plan all along.

My daughter Ceci has literally saved my life, because there have been a few times that I thought I just couldn't go through the pain anymore and I wanted to end it all. Because Nikki and I were separated all those years, but I never, ever wanted it.

TOM REESE: Bullshit! I never said that to Deana. She is just on a big guilt trip. She twists the truth and she tells lies as she has done all her life. I've told Nikki the truth many times. Deana was so full-on on drugs for so many years that I don't know how many brains she's got left, really. I've told her before, the way that she goes through life..but I'm not going to get into this anymore. I'm seventy-eight years old and I just don't need it.

CECI COMER: There are so many things that Nikki doesn't know about the life my mom and I had back then. She always acted like everything was OK but often it wasn't. She had a stroke in the '80s and got really sick one winter, and we ran out of food and oil in the house we were renting. I ate ketchup on toasted bread and woke up with frozen hair so many times that year. Mom always loved Nikki and wanted him with us, but we had some hard, hard times.

I think Mom and Nikki's relationship is too common and very sad. It takes the focus off the right things and keeps them in a dark place. By now all the stories are so convoluted and everyone seems to suffer from selective memory. But I do know this–whatever happened back then, Mom always wanted Nikki by her side. She's never really given up. No mother does. The bottom line is that he wants and needs his mother and she wants and needs her son.

NOVEMBER 6th 1987
Backstage, 7:45 p.m. CAJUN DOME, LAFAYETTE, LA

Guns is onstage right now but the weirdest thing happened a few minutes ago. The band walked in and we had a line of coke about six feet long. I asked the Guns guys if they wanted a bump and they all just looked weird at each other. Finally Tommy said, Come on, you guys are supposed to out-Mötley us! So Axl bent down and did the smallest little bump and then coughed, then said they had to go onstage. When they walked out, we all looked at each other and then started busting up. Vince said, Fine, more for us, then we did the coke ourselves with Fred, Hawk and some of the road crew.

I gotta call Zutaut...fuck, it wasn't that much blow anyway...

SLASH: Axl was never really a drug guy but Guns N' Roses was a full-on heroin band and you can't do that on the road so we were pretty clean on tour. Coke was never my drug of choice either. Our drug thing was more like a-day-in-the-life, a personal internal crisis that we didn't want to be known, whereas Mötley was hell-bent on being the band with the most excessive, outrageous public persona. Mötley pushed the envelope to be the most alcohol- and coke-consuming band going. That was their whole image.

NIKKI: They say be careful what you wish for…but we were never careful.

NOVEMBER 7TH 1987, LAKEFRONT ARENA, NEW ORLEANS, LA
Backstage, 5 p.m.

Tonight's show is gonna crush, the crowd is going crazy out in the parking lot. They're already ripped, shouting Crüe! Crüe! Crüe! You can feel it when it's on edge…rock 'n' roll! Impending chaos is good…

Gonna go out tonight for a bit.

NOVEMBER 8TH, 1989. MISSISSIPPI COLISEUM, JACKSON, MS.

On the jet, 4:20 p.m.

We just landed—I'm hungover like a motherfucker.

Heather is here so Tommy hung out with her last night. Mick was with fucking Emi. Vince did the same thing as always—a strip club. So I took Slash out to some cool bars in the French Quarter of New Orleans after the gig. We got fucking smashed. I took him to the Dungeon but they wouldn't let us in. Slash asked why and Fred explained that I had cut the bra off a girl in the club the last time I was there. Unfortunately for me it was the owner's girlfriend.

P.S. I scored a balloon of Persian—no needles, just chasing the dragon. It's so easy in New Orleans. I bought it right in front of everybody and nobody even saw it go down, not even Fred. I can spot a junkie a mile away...and obviously they can spot me.

NIKKI: When Mötley toured with Ozzy in 1984, we had a date in New Orleans in Mardi Gras. Ozzy Osbourne and Mötley Crüe in New Orleans on Mardi Gras = bad move! Our management was very nervous, and so was Sharon Osbourne. Ozzy went out with Vince and they got into all sorts of trouble. Tommy and I took Ozzy's guitarist Jake E. Lee out to the Dungeon Club. As always I had a knife, and there was this girl in the club in a top that was basically exposing everything but there was just enough material there to piss me off. So I took my knife out, grabbed the top and cut it off. Her boobs came flying out and I said, "Now the party's started!" All of a sudden this shadow appeared above me—the club security guard. She was his girl-friend. Then security took me and Tommy and Jake and threw us into the street and started hitting us with these baseball bats with spikes on them. We were all cut up and beat up and we ran off. When we showed up years later at the Dungeon, they told us we were banned. I said that was a long time ago and they said, "Not in *our* minds."

FRED SAUNDERS: We spent hours driving around the French Quarter of New Orleans trying to find a friend of Nikki's to score some heroin. I said that I wasn't going to let him do it so he fired me. Nikki was always firing me left, right and center. Then we tried to go to the Dungeon Club and they refused to let us in, which, frankly, I was neither surprised nor bothered about.

NOVEMBER 9TH 1987 DAY OFF
Marriott Hotel, Huntsville, Alabama, Room 432, 4:30 p.m.

We played Huntsville a year or two ago and some kid claimed we had shot shattered glass into the audience and blinded him. Doc says he is suing us—the kid says we had cannons onstage (uh, that's AC/DC) and shot glass outta them. I even heard we might have shot pieces of metal too...what the fuck? I hope that kid doesn't come to see us tonight.

Oh yeah, he's fucking blind, so he won't.

333

NOVEMBER 10TH 1987
Hotel, noon VAN BRAUN CIVIC CENTER, HUNTSVILLE, AL

Fuck, I just got a call from Rich. Me and Slash were drunk and wrestling in the bar last night and I guess he landed on his neck. He's pretty messed up. He's gonna have to wear a neck brace to support his neck. Fuck, I feel bad...it's always fun until someone gets hurt...

P.S. I'm still wondering if that blind kid's gonna show up to see the show.

> SLASH: Nikki and I had been in the bar for hours drinking shots and we started wrestling. Nikki is a pretty big guy and he fell on top of me. The next morning I woke up with four dislocated vertebrae in Tommy's drum tech Spider's bed. I had to see doctors and have acupuncture for the next three weeks of the tour. And all the time I was onstage, I had to keep my top hat on and not move an inch.

NOVEMBER 11TH 1987
Hotel, 3:10 a.m. ~~JEFFERSON~~ CIVIC CENTER, BIRMINGHAM, AL

Battling everything. I feel like I'm at war with everything and everyone. I don't understand...why don't I feel anything but anger? The only time I don't feel is when I'm numb. It's just not working like it used to. I'm tired of writing about it, but this is my only way to vent. I'm so fucking tired, and I don't know why. Why is it that the word why is always on the tip of my tongue-WHY?

Why was I treated like I was as a kid-like I was just in the way?

Why did my mom always want to be with someone
other than me?

Why did my dad leave me?

Why do I have no belief or trust
in a God?

Why am I here?

Why can't I stop doing drugs?

Why can't I find love?

Why, why, why...

FATHER

All these years, an angry child
Broken, shattered, torn inside
I feel old, I feel dead
Barely hangin' by a thread

Father, where were you?

To my father, how could you run?
You walked away, abandoned your son
Broke my heart, left me dying
So fucked up, where I came from

What's a father without a son?
It's like a bullet without a gun

CECI COMER: My own father has always questioned whether I am his child or not, and has made it clear over the years that he was more important to himself than I was. It's different with Nikki's dad because Nikki never had the chance to be slapped in the face like that. He's just had to guess.

He may be better off that his dad wasn't around like mine, but the pain eats at you that you don't know the real truth—your own truth. I know Nikki wonders what it would have been like to have a dad, but it's the coulda-woulda-shoulda syndrome that is so hard to deal with because ultimately you will never know.

2:15 p.m.

Someone was just banging on the door over and over until I just screamed fuck off. Then Fred called and said it's time for bags. I guess we're leaving at 2:30. Fucking pills and smack...so what do I do? Roll over and start writing. You're my only friend and I feel I need to talk to you. I can't seem to find my smile, I can't seem to find my passion, I can't seem to find myself...I'm drowning.

I'm not sure which is worse, my addiction which haunts me or my gradual slide into insanity. I can't even get into words what I feel—I know I don't know, and that's a crazy fucking feeling. I'm gonna try and pull myself up by the bootstraps and suck it up, but to be honest the decay is starting to show.

Backstage, 6:30 p.m.

Just got to the gig late because of me. I think I'm in Alabama. I ran straight into Duff, he was standing there in boxer shorts, no shirt and cowboy boots. I said, Hey Duff, nice look, and he said some girl stole all his clothes when he was passed out last night. Now that's fucking funny. OK, I need a drink.

P.S. Hey what has 48 legs and 12 teeth? The front row in Alabama...

NOVEMBER 12TH 1987 DAY OFF

Marriott Hotel, Savannah, Georgia, 4 p.m.

I called home and checked my answering machine. I had two calls. One was a wrong number and one was some girl (don't know who) saying, Hey Nikki, fuck off.

That pretty much sums up my life back home.

SAVANNAH CIVIC CENTER; NOVEMBER 13TH 1987 SAVANNAH, GA

Hotel, 2:40 p.m.

Just woke up. My eyes are crusted over. Nice look. Been nose deep in Animal Farm by George Orwell for the zillionth time. I just love this book. It's something so parallel to rock 'n' roll. After all we are sorta the animals taking over society, never really thinking out what the end will be—and if we do, it's tainted. Great book.

337

Last night me and Tommy filled the elevator with all the furniture from our rooms and then Tommy ran and phoned Slash and Duff and told them to meet us in the lobby. We waited and then jumped in the elevator and pushed Lobby. When the doors opened they were waiting. We were just kicking back and everybody started laughing, so we all just rode up and down the elevator drinking and doing lines until the hotel said they were gonna throw us out.

Ah, rock 'n' roll...

TOMMY LEE: One night Slash was drinking with me and Nikki and trying to keep up with us shot-for-shot on the Jack Daniel's. We were sitting at the bar for hours drinking, then suddenly Slash put his head underneath the bar and puked everywhere. He was starting to go down so we took him to his room, where he immediately passed out. We set him on the bed and took a Polaroid photo of Slash lying on his back passed out, and Nikki put his balls sac on his chin. That picture became Slash's tour laminate: lying unconscious, with Nikki's nuts sitting on his chin.

NOVEMBER 14th, 1987 COLISEUM, COLUMBIA, SC

Hotel, 4:30 p.m.

I look back on my diaries and half the time I don't even write down when the dealers show up...it seems too redundant. But I said I would try to capture every moment, good or bad, in my diaries, so here goes.

It's been snowing again. I haven't been sleeping more than an hour or two for a few nights. I'm starting to hide in my room again. I feel like I might be getting back to my old habits and it's like a car skidding out of control, there's nothing I can do about it. I don't want to do the drugs but it's all I think about. If I don't do it (well, I can't not do it)...I found a few old rigs in my suitcase and shot up my last bit of junk, after snorting tons of coke last night...so I'm outta junk. Wish I'd found the rigs when I had some blow—a speedball would have been nice. I'm so sick.

DOC McGHEE: People ask why we never confronted Nikki about his addictions, but we'd always try to talk to him and it just did no good—it got ugly really quickly. Artists die on the road and fans say if the other band members really loved them, why didn't they help them instead of letting them die on their own in a hotel room? They probably tried loads of times to intervene but eventually, when somebody is obnoxious all the time, you get numb to it.

NOVEMBER 15TH 1987
GREENSBORO COLISEUM, GREENSBORO, NC

Backstage, 7 p.m.

Bored. Can't wait to get onstage to have something to fucking do.

NOVEMBER 16TH 1987 DAY OFF

Hotel, Knoxville, 5:30 a.m.

Got into Knoxville two hours ago on the jet. Went down to Tommy's room, did some lines and listened to music. We ran out and went down to Fred's room for an Ace in the Hole but he just had a tiny bit. Fuck! I have a day off tomorrow and I'm in the mood to get high. Now I'm fading...goodnight.

FRED SAUNDERS: I had a little trick that I would sometimes play when Nikki was hounding me for coke late at night. He would ring my room saying, "Dude, Ace in the Hole," and before he turned up I'd crush up a sleeping tablet, make it into a line and give it to him to snort. We'd start talking and within five minutes he'd be yawning and saying he was tired. Then I'd walk him back down to his room and put him to bed. I don't think he ever figured out I was doing that.

3:25 p.m.

Great show last night in Greensboro. I really felt like I was in one of the world's greatest bands for an hour-and-a-half. I felt there were no soured decaying souls up there. We punished the audience with volume and it hasn't been that tight in a long time. After the show was different. We were trying to get some blow—it was the weirdest thing I've ever seen! It's like we mention it and the airwaves go quiet. Nobody will respond or they say they're busy and will get back to us. I think someone's been telling the crew and staff not to give us drugs.

Midnight

Sitting here alone staring around this room wondering what the hell I'm supposed to do when I'm not onstage or on drugs.

I have moments of complete lucidity and I ask a lot of questions, and they hurt, 'cause I don't have most of the answers.

SLASH: I was amazed on that tour how Mötley Crüe always had this whole intricate system going of people with walkie-talkies looking for blow. They always seemed to know where the nearest blow was, but to be honest, trying to stuff as much coke as I could into my face seemed pretty boring to me. Had it been a dope thing, it would have been a lot darker and more dramatic.

KNOXVILLE COLISEUM, KNOXVILLE, TN NOVEMBER 17TH 1987
Hotel, 1:40 p.m.

Some nights when I lay my head down all I hear is ringing, and it's getting worse every year. I never really mention this, I guess it's just become normal to me, but lately I hear it when I wake up too if it's quiet. I guess as long as it goes away when I'm done touring it's OK.

NOVEMBER 18TH 1987 JEFFERSON CIVIC CENTER, BIRMINGHAM, AL
Hotel, Knoxville, 3:15 a.m.

Show was good, sold out as usual. Drugs yes, alcohol yes, groupies yes, depression yes. Some girl asked me for an autograph and I asked her why. She said 'cause she admires me. I said maybe she should see a shrink then! She started crying and I started laughing.

Fuck this. I don't wanna be a star.

I don't understand anything anymore. Bob Timmons keeps calling asking me to consider rehab. I ask him if there's one that won't preach God to me like the last one. He just sighs and has that nervous laugh. Nobody understands me...nobody.

I'm lonely...I don't know how to live and I can't seem to die.

Backstage, 6:15 p.m.

Just flew in to the gig. No hotel until we get to Atlanta. I feel like my skin is rotting off me. I smell like shit and my shit has more and more traces of blood in it. I can't explain how I feel other than I feel like I'm about to burst into tears at any moment. I walk around in circles in my room night after night...I can't seem to find a path. What the fuck is happening to me? I can't wait to get this show over so I can hide. You know, I don't know how much more I can take. I'm calling Bob and asking him for a number of a psychiatrist. I'm crying out for help on the inside and pretending I'm OK on the outside. But I know it's not a good façade at all.

TOMMY LEE: Nikki was never that stumble-around-fall-down guy who gets told to get his act together. He would just go to his room and get high alone. We all sort of did it. After months of being on tour with the same three guys, when it was travel-eat-sleep-fuck together, we just wanted to go to our rooms after the shows sometimes and not see each other. I'd sit in my room and do a couple of grams of fucking cocaine by myself. The guys would phone my room and say, "What are you doing?" and I'd say, "Nothing–'bye!" Then a couple of hours later I'd be calling them: "Hey, dude, you got any blow?" We were just all apart, playing these games in our own little worlds.

NOVEMBER 19TH 1987 DAY OFF
Ritz Carlton Hotel, Atlanta, Georgia, 8 p.m.

Did a lot of nothing today. Played guitar a little, read, nobody to call really except the office...Doc is MIA again. I guess he's on vacation somewhere. It kills me to think of him laying on a beach somewhere with a drink in his fat little hand watching the sun go down and being able to enjoy some of this fucking money we make for him while Doug and the band are just slaves to the grind.

Spoke to Slash at his hotel, told him to meet me here around 9 or so and we'd go out...maybe hit a strip club. I asked him to invite the guys but only Duff and Steven ever show up. I'm really trying to get outta this funk. I talked to Bob Timmons and asked him if there is a drug for depression. He told me yes, but getting sober would cure a lot of this feeling. I have to admit as I sit here with a whisky in my hand and a plate of half-eaten eggs...it's scary but intriguing. I know when I'm losing my mind on drugs I would do anything to stop, but when the drugs wear off and the head clears I feel the need to try and control it one more time. But now something else is eroding me and I don't know what it is.

Bob said he could find me a psychiatrist in LA who deals with addiction, but I said this is deeper than that. My wounds are bursting at the seams and the original pain is filled with pus. Is it childhood issues or am I just losing my sanity?

343

NOVEMBER 20TH 1987.

THE OMNI, ATLANTA, GA.

Ritz Carlton Hotel, Atlanta, Georgia, 5 a.m.

I'm drunk and in a great mood. Slash and me sat at the hotel bar and got smashed. He threw up spaghetti all over the bar, and then ordered another drink. I always wanted a little brother, I think I just found him...goodnight.

TOM ZUTAUT: From one glass of whisky to the next fix of junk, Nikki and Slash were both on the same train at the same time, skipping from one party to the next, looking for the most fun to be had by all in their wildest rock 'n' roll fantasies. Slash was also very social, fun to be with, kind and considerate, and appreciative that Nikki gave Guns the shot on the Crüe tour. He was also always the last one to leave the bar, so it wasn't hard for Nikki to find him when he wanted to have fun or get high.

Axl was different. He was very serious about working hard to move G N' R to the next level and was not happy about the excessive partying his band was falling into. What Nikki didn't know at the time was that Geffen was about to give up on *Appetite for Destruction* at around the 200,000 mark and tell Guns to make their next record. Instead, the Mötley tour kept the G N' R night train on full-speed overdrive and tipped the scales in favor of Geffen continuing to promote *Appetite*. It ended up selling more than 20 million.

4:20 p.m.

Got a sold-out show here tonight then another show back here in a few days. Fucking weird routing. Writing some music, poetry, reading...nothing much on TV. My life is all about the rock 'n' roll grind of hotel-gig-hotel-gig-hotel-gig...the repetition just wears you down. Then add a few hangovers, a pill or 10, a bindle or two...and oh God, don't forget the girls who can barely count to 10 and the hangers-on who say they're your friends...

It seems like a never-ending cycle, so I get a lot of pleasure out of fucking with room service people. I'll answer the door naked or have my knife out, only wearing cowboy boots, and ask them which city we're in (still having my makeup on from last night's gig)...it's fun to watch people trying to act like nothing is wrong. Sometimes I get a call from Rich or Fred and they say, Siiiixxxxxxxx, you're scaring the people in the hotel again! OK, off to the gig...

Backstage, 7:45 p.m.

Just got off the massage table here in the dressing room. We were having a few drinks and Doc just came in and said Axl got arrested for jumping into the audience. Slash is up there singing a Stones song and it's not going well. Guess I'd better get ready...I think the crowd is probably getting unruly.

11 p.m.

Slash wants to go out 'cause he's pissed off at Axl, so I'm taking him to a killer strip club. I guess they need to wait for their singer to get bailed out tomorrow. I don't think I'll offer Slash any junk 'cause I know he used to have a problem...one of us slipping back is bad enough.

DOC McGHEE: Axl Rose was onstage in Atlanta when he saw one of the security guards, who turned out to be an off-duty cop, pushing their fans around. Axl jumped off the stage and started fighting the guard, so security grabbed him and took him backstage. So Slash sang a few songs, and Guns' drum technician sang "Honky Tonk Woman"–four times, not terribly well. I told security, "Look, let Axl finish the show then shoot him for all I care,"

345

but they called the police. I said to Axl, be nice to the cops and they'll let you go. Then a cop walked in and asked him for his full name, and Axl said, "Fuck you!" That was it–he was arrested and in the cells for the night.

NOVEMBER 21ST 1987 UTC ARENA, CHATTANOOGA, TN

Hotel, Atlanta, noon

We're leaving for Chattanooga in a few hours. I'm so hungover and I don't remember much. I woke up with some black girl at 6 a.m., don't have a clue where or who the fuck she is. I kicked her out. I think I broke into Doc's room and sawed his bed in half last night but I'll have to wait and see—maybe I just dreamt it.

I need coffee. There's a line on my bedside table but I think I could puke if I did it. I think I remember something about zombie dust.

Backstage, Chattanooga, 6:40 p.m.

Fuck I feel like dog shit. I can't wait to fly back to Atlanta and go to bed. I puked in the bathroom on the plane twice. I guess I did saw Doc's bed in half...my memory is clearing. I also tried to throw Fred's bed out of his window (that's why I have my black eye) and Mick tried to jump out of the window...he was fucking outta his mind. Doc told me we all had our dicks out on the bar and poured Jack on them and lit them on fire too. What the fuck, I have no pubes left. Gotta do a show. I can hear Guns up there playing, so I guess everything is back to normal.

DOC McGHEE: Nikki and Tommy cut my bed in half with a knife so that when I got in it, it collapsed. Two days later they got a pellet gun, put a load of records at the end of the hallway and lay shooting at them. By the time security came, the hallway was littered with pellets and shattered vinyl.

One time in Switzerland they bought what they thought was a pellet gun but it fired flares. They got it back to Vince's room, Vince fired it, and this flare shot out and bounced off the wall. They all ran to my room to tell me, but of course when we got back to Vince's room, the door had closed behind them. So I went down to reception to get a spare key and there was this guy with the whole hotel's room keys on a huge chain on his neck who said, "Sure, I'll come and let you in." I said, "Nah, just give me the key"–I was almost wrestling him to try to get it off him. In the elevator to the room I was telling him what a great hotel it was, and as soon as he opened the room door, smoke poured all down the hallway, the sprinklers came on and the bed was on fire. So we got kicked out of that hotel.

Spent a million dollars on amphetamines
Crashed a lot of cars
Fucked all the stupid stars in Hollywood
Because I could

NOVEMBER 22ND 1987 THE OMNI, ATLANTA, GA
Hotel, 1:10 p.m.

Fuck, I went straight to bed last night. I slept 12 hours straight. Wow…I felt like shit yesterday. I have no idea how I got so fucked up, but I did. Doc still can't figure out how I got in his room and cut his bed in half. We do it to Rich Fisher all the time—go in his room and steal his pills. I think I might go down and take a steam in the gym and get a massage. I feel fucking great today. So is this what sobriety would feel like? Hmm…

347

11 p.m.

Wow, just offstage. A while ago I was standing in the hospitality room and this black chick came up to me with her son, mom and dad, and introduced me to everybody: "This is Nikki, blah blah blah." I had no idea who the hell she was but I went along with it. I asked if anybody wanted a drink and went to my dressing room to get some beers for them. I pulled Fred aside and asked him who the chick with the kid was. He said that was the girl from the strip club I was with the other night.

What the fuck? OK, so I guess I was fucked up, but why did she bring her kid and mom and dad? What the hell did I say? All of a sudden I came down with a really bad stomach ache and had to excuse myself. I was polite but I couldn't get out of there fast enough. So I'm sitting in my dressing room hiding until they leave...what the fuck?

CHICKS = TROUBLE.

Off to the Mötley jet...going to Orlando...

NOVEMBER 23RD, 1987 DAY OFF
On the jet, 2:45 a.m.

Tommy and Vince are fucking smashed and bickering. Mick is looking sick of it all and I'm just staring out the window into this darkness. If we don't get off the road, we're gonna break up...trust me on this one.

Stouffers Hotel, Room 1267, Orlando, Florida, 11 p.m.

Just back from the bar. I tried to talk to Tommy about how I'm feeling and I just don't think he understands. He's happy all the time...makes me feel even crazier. Maybe I'll try Mick...

11:15 p.m.

Went to Mick's room to talk to him but Emi was there so I left.

3 a.m.

I just took a handful of pills. If I'm lucky maybe I won't wake up...goodnight.

NIKKI: A few years later I was put on an antidepressant and my life turned around in three days. It was an experimental drug at the time, now known as Prozac. I had been off tour for months and had only left my house a few times. I was finally off drugs but the depression was getting worse. In 1987 I knew something was wrong but I didn't know what.

MICK MARS: Did I know how depressed Nikki was then? Not really. Not at all. I didn't really pay attention except when he was bullying me and Emi. I just did my gig, did what I was supposed to do and I was normally drunk anyway. I didn't really care. The band was self-destructing so I just thought, Fuck it.

I'm feeling rotten today
I guess
I forgot I am shot
I'm not OK
So long to pain,
So long to games
So long say goodbye
Someone tell me why,
I'm feeling cold inside
Do I wanna, do I wanna die?
Someone tell me why,
It's building up inside
Do I wanna die and
Kiss it all goodbye?

I'm a sinking ship
On a sea of bliss, I'm not OK
I'm blind to this
Is this just a test
To help me see?

NOVEMBER 24, 1981. LAKELAND CIVIC CENTER, LAKELAND, FL
Backstage, 6:45 p.m.

We took a chopper to the gig here. Izzy just came
into the dressing room (miracle) and introduced us to
his girlfriend. Oh my God-can I say Bruce Dickinson
all over again? It's this chick Suzette that I fucked
in a reh room in Hollywood when she was 17. Then I
used to buy drugs from her later. She would come over
and I'd tie her up and treat her like a farm animal.
She's cute as long as she doesn't talk. I used to gag
her so I wouldn't have to hear her coke babble. Life
is weird and getting weirder all the time.

When she came in with Izzy I acted like I never met her. Then when Izzy left, Tommy said, Sixx, dude, that's the chick from the Whisky A Go-Go bathroom floor, remember that? Oh fuck, I forgot about that, too.

We chopper back to the hotel after the gig—we have another show here tomorrow. Guns is at the same hotel as well as our road crew. Tim needs to lighten up. I have him dressed as a priest onstage and he looks like a broke-dick dog over it. Maybe I need to get him drunk. He loves me, I know, he's always looking worried, like he's my Jewish auntie or something. Tim, I'm not gonna die...I'm not that fucking lucky.

P.S. Finished reading Animal Farm and I'm starting in on Queer by Burroughs again.

NIKKI: Suzette made me think of Bruce Dickinson because Dickinson used to hate me because I fucked his wife. I would just like to point out in my defense that a) I had no idea she was his wife, and b) it wasn't my fault that she climbed in my hotel window in England, asked me to fuck her, then afterwards said, "Thank you" and climbed out again.

ROSS HALFIN: Bruce Dickinson actually wrote the song "Tattooed Millionaire" about Sixx. He hated Nikki because he was fucking Dickinson's wife at the time. Then again, so were Vince and Tommy, come to think of it...

NOVEMBER 25TH 1987 CIVIC CENTER, LAKELAND, FL
Hotel, 4:20 p.m.

I just woke up. I was up till noon doing blow. We hired a big conference room and just fuckin' went crazy...Slash, Tommy, Steven, Duff, some crew guys, a bunch of whores and cases and cases of booze. We have a dealer here who just gives the shit to us. He gave us each an 8-ball and we did our best to do it all. It was insane...we piled it all up on the table. I'd never seen so much coke. Me and Tommy were trying to figure out how to cook it up so we could freebase it but we didn't have all the needed supplies. We tried our damnedest and ended up smoking it wet outta a glass ashtray. My fingers are fucking blistered. I got about two grams sitting here on the table next to me. I should just flush the shit but the guy will just bring more so I might as well do a line and go to the chopper...fuck, I need a drink...my hands are shaking.

P.S. Suzette came to my room before the party and wanted to fuck me. Tommy was in here with me doing a bump and I told her to leave. She got all crazy and I threw her out the door and she slammed into the wall and started crying.

CHICKS = TROUBLE.

NOVEMBER 26TH 1987
JACKSONVILLE COLISEUM, JACKSONVILLE, FL
Backstage, 7:30 p.m.

Here at the gig. The show last night was loose and
    tired. The fans didn't know. Guns is getting
    better, the crowd is digging them more and
    more, I have a good feeling for them. If the label
    will support them they have a shot. They're not
    like the other bands who came after us...they're
    more like us.

On to more exciting news... I don't feel so
depressed (probably 'cause the drugs are keeping me
    from feeling) but I have been having bad side
    aches like my liver is going south. I don't
    understand why I get traces of blood when I
    shit. I wanna get a doctor out to one of these
    gigs and ask, but I know what he's gonna say.

        I can't figure Vince out lately. He seems
    to be slipping away. When I talk to him it's
    like he doesn't hear me-is it me? He only
    cares about the pussy but then I only care
    about the drugs...we're not so different. I miss
    him, but his eyes are always darting around
    when we're talking, or he says he has to go.

    I miss music, new music, and I miss my friends
    that I started this journey with, but most of all
    I miss my sanity. I can't wait to get off this
    fucking tour. I'm so tired of touring. I wanna
    kill management for not listening to us.
    Something bad is gonna happen, I just know. We
can't be this close to each other and be slipping away
from each other at the same time and expect this to last.

P.S. Supposed to go out for Thanksgiving Dinner...I'd
rather order room service.

353

YOUR EGO IS NOT YOUR AMIGO

NoVEMBER 27TH 1987 DAY OFF
Sheraton Hotel, Fort Myers, Room 538, 2:10 p.m.

Played a show in Jacksonville last night, got
in about 3 a.m. I met a friend of my old dealer
Jason's last night with a gram of Mexican tar but
no rigs. I had to order aluminum foil from room
service when we got in. Man, my mouth was watering.
I smoked a bit and hit the sack...woke up today feeling sick. I know it's not that. Had Slash, Steven
and Duff fly on our jet last night. Izzy wouldn't
come 'cause I threw his girlfriend against a wall.
Hey, Izzy, I fucked her first so fuck off.

Axl never comes. He's a twat.

DOUG THALER: I joined the tour in Jacksonville
and Nikki was pretty fucked up on Jack Daniel's. He
showed me some gummy black substance he had
that he claimed was some kind of exotic cocaine
that he was going to snort. I thought, Good luck
snorting a gummy substance! Then the next morning
he said he had lost that weird shit, and he asked me
what had happened to it. I told him I had absolutely
no idea.

TOMMY LEE: We hung out with Slash every day on
tour but Axl was a lot more reserved. There were times
he would be really cool, but then at other times he just
had that fucking singer thing that they all get–LSD:
Lead Singer Disease.

I gotta find myself some love
I gotta find myself some drugs
I gotta find some liquid sunshine
I gotta find myself, I gotta find myself
I'm a sick motherfucker
I'm a sweet sucka mutha
Ain't no one tougher
I'm a wreck, I'm a sleaze
I'm a rock 'n' roll disease
I'm a pusher, I'm a shover
Ain't no motherfucker tougher
I gotta find myself some glue
I gotta find some suction
Now my aim is destruction
I gotta find myself, I gotta find myself
I got to deal with my neurosis
I got to deal with my neurosis
I gotta sniff myself some glue
I got to find myself

NOVEMBER 28TH 1987
LEE COUNTY CIVIC CENTER, FORT MYERS, FL
On the jet, 2:05 a.m.

Had a show tonight in Fort Myers. Right now we're
on the jet on our way to Fort Lauderdale. I just got
done fucking with Emi. Everyone except Mick was laughing
their asses off. She's always talking about God and
she was on one of her rants. It makes me sick so I
stood in the middle of our jet with my pants down with
two middle fingers pointed towards her God, yelling,
"Fuck you, God! If you're so real, strike me down!"

over and over. Emi kept crossing her heart and started crying and the more she cried, the more I got into it. Needless to say I'm sitting here in my seat, still alive and well. She's just like my mom and Vanity, full of shit, and in the end she'll take Mick for everything, 'cause one thing I can smell is a fucking gold digger.

P.S. Tommy got the pilot to do a barrel roll-I bet Emi pissed her saggy little panties after all I said...

CHICKS = TROUBLE.

MICK MARS: Nikki was pretty horrible to me and Emi through the whole *Girls* tour. He was nasty when he was on smack, Jack Daniel's, Halcion, sober, whatever. He used to pour food on us, pour drinks over us, hassle me a lot, make a lot of threats-he just could not bear the idea of Emi and me being together. He made that tour a nightmare.

TOMMY LEE: You know what? Maybe we went a bit too far. It pissed us off because we had this protocol about not fucking the hired help and then suddenly there were Mick and Emi sneaking down staircases and into each other's rooms together. But Mick is a pretty sensitive guy and, let's face it, he just fell in love with Emi–I mean, he ended up marrying her!

But once Emi got involved with Mick her attitude changed and she got all fucking diva with us so we wanted to teach her a lesson. I remember we were always accidentally-on-purpose spilling Jack on her on the plane, pushing her buttons, seeing just how far we could piss her off...we were just fucking around and being really retarded, stupid kids.

BABY KILLS
She carries Mother's Bible
Mixes Valium with her beliefs

NOVEMBER 29TH 1987
HOLLYWOOD SPORTATORIUM
PEMBROKE PINES, FL
Hotel, 3 p.m.

Just woke up. Tonight is the last show of the US tour...thank God. Gonna order some breakfast...but it's scary 'cause I'm going home...

Backstage 6 p.m.

At the gig. We're gonna have our pyro guys shoot off a ton of shit during Guns' show in a little bit. They have never used pyro so I'm sure it's gonna freak them out...should be fun.

357

8:20 p.m.

Now that, my friend, was insane. We loaded up about 25 pyro blasts and when Guns kicked into Welcome to the Jungle they all went off at once. The band looked like they were gonna shit their pants and then got the biggest smiles I've ever seen. Axl was wearing a Mötley T-shirt...THAT was unexpected. Gotta get ready... last show...

NOVEMBER 30th 1987
END OF U.S. TOUR
Airport, noon

Sitting on the plane waiting for it to take off for home. I still haven't been to bed...last night topped all nights of debauchery. We got a huge conference room again, about two ounces of blow, but this time we had the goods to base with...tons of pills, booze. We lined these chicks up, six or seven of them, snorted coke off one's back then stuck our dicks in her, then go on to the next one, do a line, on and on...talk about farm animals! We were outta our minds.

Lots of hugs and gonna miss yous and thank yous. We smashed the whole room up pretty good and then when it was about time for the airport, T-Bone took some sleeping pills and passed out. We had to push him in a wheelchair to get him on the plane. They sat him next to a little girl and she started crying.

Oh God, we need a break...I'm so tired, my eyes are sunk into the back of my head. I see it on everybody's faces. I love these guys and I know we're a great band but it's all spinning outta control and nobody is taking the wheel. As long as we make money we're the darlings of the world...

Goodnight...I'm on my way Home Sweet Home...

TOMMY LEE: Fuck, dude, the Sportatorium show! We called it the Snortatorium, because all these fucking coke dealers turned up at the show. One even had a license plate that said D-E-A-L-E-R. There were just endless amounts of free cocaine. The second that the last show was over, Nikki and I both stuck our faces in these huge piles of coke and didn't come up. I remember them wheeling me in a wheelchair through the airport, because I was fucking *done*–I couldn't walk, talk, think, nothing. Maybe there was a little drool.

DOUG THALER: After the last U.S. date everybody was just fucked up on blow and alcohol. Tommy took a bunch of downers at about eight or nine in the morning and Rich Fisher had to wheel him on to the noon flight back to LA in a wheelchair. Some horrified guy in first class nearly shit his pants when they started to plop Tommy, semiconscious, into the seat next to him. The stewardess wisely positioned Tommy in a lone first-class seat by himself. It was about the only time on that tour that Tommy was more of a mess than Nikki.

SAVE OUR SOULS

It's been the hard road; edge of an overdose
No matter how high you're still too low
I've been the dancer, the wicked romancer
It's a never-ending nightmare, edge of disaster

DECEMBER 1ST 1987

Van Nuys, 1:50 p.m.

Abdul is coming over while Karen is at work. I feel so burned out, ripped and torn from the tour right now and I need a break from reality…hence Abdul. I'm so tired of being tired. I feel like I'm vanishing into a ghost right before the world's eyes.

I really don't think the office knows how brittle we've become. Karen doesn't know that I know she's a spy. I must be careful to have Abdul come at the right times. His appearance is a dead giveaway—he looks like a decaying rat, even more so than me. Karen could see him coming a mile off 'cause he looks like junk. Karen is a girl who's blind as a bat to dealers but even a bat could see he's bad news.

I wonder how the guys are doing. I know whenever a tour ends I feel like a stranger in my own home. Without room service it's hard to even figure out how to eat. Gate just buzzed…gotta go…

DECEMBER 2ND, 1987

Van Nuys, 3:45 p.m.

Just laid around yesterday feeling nothing, no remorse and no celebration. Actually I'm lying, I feel hatred, but for whom I've forgotten…does it really matter anymore? Maybe not.

The sky is gray outside today and it makes me feel safe, like I'm under a huge down comforter and I'm drifting off to sleep. I bought $5k worth of dope yesterday 'cause I don't wanna see Abdul every day for a few reasons. I don't think I can face seeing anybody right now 'cause I'm on the verge of having a human contact breakdown. The tour has left me completely

without personality. Also Karen is keeping an eye on
me and visitors will set off red flags.

I will venture from my bedroom soon but for now I'm
praying the clouds don't lift.

Van Nuys, 4:20 p.m.

Been shooting dope 4 or 5 times a day. The good
news is I won't have bad tracks if I stay on track
(there's a cool lyric)…it feels so good to not feel.
My nerves have been like live wires for months and
months. People, they just wear you down, they get in
close, look in your eyes and say stupid shit. You have
to restrain yourself or you come off as a heartbreak
to them, especially if you're their hero.

Mostly Vince has the most impact on my sanity. I may
be an asshole, Tommy may be self-centered, Mick may be a
recluse and insane but Vince is a drama queen and that
wears you down…little episode-by-episode temper tantrums.
When you're brittle it doesn't take an earthquake to wear
you down. Repeated tremors do the job just fine.

Karen is coming home from Doc's office in a few
hours. I guess I need to use the old junkie fave excuse
that I think I'm coming down with something…maybe the
flu…I just can't get out of bed…

Van Nuys, 2:30 a.m.

It's official, I feel strung out again.

I guess I knew it all along.

DECEMBER 6, 1987

Van Nuys, 2:05 p.m.

Today would have been Nona's birthday. I feel too ashamed to call Tom and ask how he's doing. I'm sure he's sitting somewhere with a broken heart too. So I sit here and shoot dope in my bedroom alone. Watching TV, watching life pass me by—I went from a kid with a dream to a loser, a hero to a zero. I hope she can't see me now 'cause who I turned out to be would break her heart. I was a good kid, she loved me, I guess I just didn't love myself enough and now that I'm unraveling I must be a true disappointment. I'd say I'll see her soon, but I know as you do diary, if there is a heaven, it's not where I'll be going...

NONA

Nona, I'm out of my head without you...

DECEMBER 7, 1987

Van Nuys, midnight

I'm heading down a road I know I shouldn't be going but I can't seem to find the brakes. I'm not sure I want to find them. Abdul told me today he's taken to selling blow to a select few since the junk business isn't doing so good. I told him I was enjoying not having to worry daily about deliveries since I bought quantity from him and I would take 1 oz if he could get some pure pink. He said he has a lead to get it before it gets cut but I'd have to pay extra so he didn't have to step on it and I'm fine with that...I have more money than I can ever spend so what's an extra $500 to me? I don't wanna start cooking and all that hassle plus Karen is still watching me like a hawk. I know the minute she walks into the office it's always the same—How's Nikki? I've even taken to calling the office before I shoot up to throw everybody off my track (wow, another song title). Abdul said he'd bring me 100 fresh rigs when he comes over. I'm running low and you triple your shots with coke. Now, the dilemma—do I shoot so I don't get caught, and when I go into Japan, how do I hide the tracks?

I have to tell you I don't feel like I'll ever be off this shit and I'm settling into being OK with that. If I could just fade away I might be the happiest I've ever been...

Pete stopped by and we shared a shot...he's strung out again too.

KAREN DUMONT: Doc and Doug liked the fact I was staying at Nikki's because they hoped it would be grounding for him, but they never asked me to spy on him. I'd tell them that we'd had a good weekend but that was pretty much it. Nikki wasn't straight, but he hid it well because he knew I can't handle being around anyone drugged out of their mind and I would have just taken off. There was a dealer who would come late at night and ring the gate bell. I would answer and tell him to go away, then Nikki and I would fight about it. If I was there, they wouldn't get in, so I guess Nikki had to plan other visits.

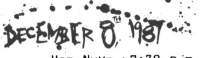

DECEMBER 8ᵀᴴ, 1987

Van Nuys, 7:30 p.m.

Karen asked me why when I go to the store I only buy plastic lemons and ice cream. I told her I use the lemon in my tea after she goes to work and the ice cream—I just have a sweet tooth lately...

I haven't really eaten food in a week...junk is like that. So Karen has to go to the store and buy real food, which I never eat. I tell her I eat when she's at work. I'm getting so thin it's hard to find clothes to fit in my closet. Of course, they say you can never be too rich or too thin.

NIKKI: I'd use the plastic lemons to cook up my Persian heroin with. You can use real lemons but they are such a hassle. I would have garbage bags of used plastic lemons in my bedroom and the maid would ask me if she could throw them away and I'd say no. Nothing is worse for a junkie who's using Persian than running out of lemon for your dope...other than running out of dope. I remember going into the market with a shopping cart and wandering up and down the aisles. I must have spent hours there and only bought lemons and ice cream. What a beautiful picture of decay I must have been to all the mothers doing their weekly family shopping.

DECEMBER 11ᵀᴴ, 1987

Van Nuys, 3:10 p.m.

I just woke up and realized today is my birthday. I ran to the machine to check it...no messages. Nobody has called to wish me a Happy Birthday. No presents, no cards, nothing. Nice. Wake up junk sick with a head full of sorrow.

I have to go to Japan tomorrow and I know I'm gonna
kick on the plane just like I did in '85. Karen knows
something is up but as with all things junkie, I'm good
at hiding it. My arms on the other hand tell a torrid
tale. Thank God it's December because if it was summer
it would be highly suspect wearing a long sleeve shirt
and a leather jacket all the time. I haven't had sex
since the tour…I've lost all drive or interest.

5 p.m.

Abdul came by. He gave me a balloon of high-grade
china for my birthday. He said if I wanted he could
get me a great price if I bought bulk like I did the
Persian. I'm not sure if this is what you'd call a
conventional birthday gift but considering it's my
only one, I'll take it.

I've yet to unpack from the US leg of the
tour so I'm gonna dump my clothes out
and grab some clean clothes so
I'm ready to go tomorrow. I
feel sorry for my maid—
she hasn't been in
my bedroom in al-
most two weeks.
It smells like
death in here. I
gotta dispose of
everything before
I leave, I know
Karen will snoop…

.Happy birthday.

7 p.m.

Just got back from the store. I need a few things for my trip to Japan. Karen said I should take a shower 'cause I smell. I'll try but I'm so strung out and I just don't give a fuck anymore.

This is sad, but it's my destiny.

DECEMBER 12th 1987
On the plane to Tokyo, 5 p.m.

I brought a small amount of dope to snort but I ran out 6 hours or so ago. I'm going into a kick. Everybody keeps saying how much weight I lost. I told them I was dieting and stopped drinking...at least the drinking part is true 'cause junkies hate alcohol. But right about now I need a shot and Jack is all there is. I got a stash of Valium to help but even that can't remove this pain. Fuck, I'm feeling like shit...sweating up a storm. It's amazing what a difference 12 days can make in your life. I went from completely drunk and coked out to strung out again.

This is my second trip to Japan on a kick. It's fucked but good, 'cause one thing I know is you can't get junk in Japan...at least, I haven't ever been able to. Thank God...

DOC McGHEE: While Mötley was in Japan they basically tortured poor Mr. Udo the promoter, who is the nicest man on the planet. When we got to Tokyo they found some pot in Tommy's drum case at the airport so the cops took all our equipment. Tommy didn't have a clue how serious that could be. He just said, "Dude, what's a little pot?" Mötley just didn't understand—or care—that in Japan there is a very low tolerance for any kind of disturbance. When we got to the hotel, Tommy dropped a wine bottle out of a tenth-story window and couldn't figure out why that might have been a big deal.

DECEMBER 13TH, 1987
SOGO TAIKUKAN RAINBOW HALL, NAGOYA, JAPAN
Backstage, 5 p.m.

Getting ready to go onstage. I'm so sick. I keep to my lie that I must have the flu but everybody knows the truth...it's an unspoken truth. I'm gonna go out and sweat some of this poison out. I'm very jet-lagged and feeling depressed. Trying to smile and be up but to be honest this is the worst it's ever been...but I knew what I was getting into.

DECEMBER 14TH 1987
FESTIVAL HALL,
OSAKA, JAPAN
Hotel, Nagoya, 2 a.m.

Still awake, can't sleep. My legs are cramping so bad and the Valium isn't doing much good. Everybody got smashed and fucked lil Japanese girls. I couldn't fuck if I wanted to...

369

NIKKI: You know what's not glam-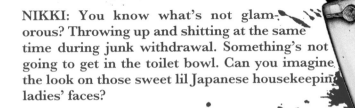
orous? Throwing up and shitting at the same
time during junk withdrawal. Something's not
going to get in the toilet bowl. Can you imagine
the look on those sweet lil Japanese housekeeping
ladies' faces?

On the bullet train to Osaka, 2 p.m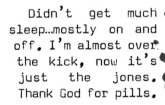

Didn't get much
sleep…mostly on and
off. I'm almost over
the kick, now it's
just the jones.
Thank God for pills.

I'm on the bul-
let train. These
fans are amazing,
it's like we're
the Beatles over
here. It's basi-
cally a riot, all
screaming Nikki!
Tommy! Nikki!
Tommy! They seem
to love me and
T-Bone here for
some strange rea-
son. I would think
it would be Vince,
with his blonde hair
and California cool.
He's perfect to be
idolized here.

  The sick thing is, they keep saying, Oh Nikki-san, we so sorry you have a flu! Fucking lies travel fast...gonna try to sleep.

  3 p.m.

Can't sleep...

  4:30 p.m.

  Just got to Osaka. Last night's show was fucking crazy...I can't believe it—the band seems to be in love again. But fucking Emi is still with Mick like she's his girlfriend or something. Fucking whore!

Sound check time.

DECEMBER 15th 1987. DAY OFF
Hotel, Tokyo, 5 a.m.

Just got out of jail...will write later...

Hotel, 11:45 a.m.

  Well, I feel like shit...not from last night's event, from my head killing me. So let me see if I can piece last night together. We played a show, got on the bullet train to come back to Tokyo, me and Tommy started drinking a lot. We were pouring drinks on Emi and starting trouble and then I sort of blacked out. I guess I threw a Jack Daniel's bottle at some Japs or something. I sorta remember being in jail and Doc and Mr. Udo being there. I guess I'll make some calls and see who's mad and who thinks it's funny.

  First some shitty runny eggs...eating eggs in Japan is like committing hari-kari.

TOMMY LEE: Dude, we were just being an ugly American drunk fucking rock band on that bullet train. We looked like fucking freaks. We were pouring JD on Emi, then Nikki thought somebody was looking at him wrong so he just cocked the Jack bottle and heaved it across the passenger car. It smashed against the wall, and glass and whisky went all over this fucking Japanese businessman who got up and freaked the fuck out. Then we pulled into the station and it was lined up with police officers. The Japanese guy pointed Nikki out and they took him to jail. I think he was even doing blow in the holding pen area. He had it hidden in his sock.

MICK MARS: I still think Nikki threw the bottle down the bullet train because of me and Emi. He had thrown a load of rice and crap all over our seats and down our necks and then suddenly he came at us all pinned. His face had turned about fifteen shades of red with anger. He started yelling at me and was going to hit me with the JD bottle, but at the last second he spun around and threw it down the end of the train, and it smashed all over a bunch of people at the front.

VINCE NEIL: Nikki and Tommy were completely out of control on the bullet train, and I was totally embarrassed by it. They were just being awful to the Japanese people, yelling, "Fuck you–you lost the war!" to these sixty-year-old businessmen who didn't know who Mötley Crüe was; they were just on their way home from work and had these fucking psychos yelling and throwing bottles of JD at them when they probably didn't even understand English. It was totally unacceptable. When Nikki got arrested I just said to Mick, "Fuck these guys, let's not get involved with this." I didn't give a shit if Nikki went to jail and stayed there. I just thought, You know what? You've dug your own grave.

DOC McGHEE: When we arrived in Tokyo there were a hundred police waiting to arrest Nikki. Tommy wanted to fight them and kept yelling for them to arrest him too. I told the police chief, "Look, I'm the manager. Can we talk about this?" and he said, "You the manager? Under arrest!" So they dragged Nikki and me away. We were sitting in the cells and if I could have unhandcuffed my hands I would have beaten the shit out of him. Nikki was so far out of it he was just saying to me, "Dude, shall I show them my tattoos?" Mr. Udo had to come to the police station at four o'clock in the morning and we had to sign an apology note for the guy who had been hit with the bottle.

NIKKI: I remember Fred Saunders telling me that when I was in jail in Tokyo, I asked the police captain, "If my balls were on your chin, where would my dick be?" The police captain asked what I had said and the translator told him that I had said I was very sorry and didn't mean any disrespect. I guess that was the Mötley Crüe way. Somebody was always bailing us out of trouble.

DECEMBER 16ᵀᴴ 1987
NIPPON. BUDOKAN, TOKYO, JAPAN (SHOW1)
Hotel, Tokyo 2 p.m.

Lately I've been slipping deeper into thoughts of... why? I don't know why, I just am slipping deeper. Some days I don't know how much longer I can hold on, or why I would even want to. You'd think I'd be excited about selling out three nights at the Budokan but I'm rotting inside and all I smell is my putrid past...it haunts me. Maybe to you it would seem like a surface burn but the pain is too deep for surgery.

P.S. I'm so lonely I called Vanity. It must have been the cocaine I got from the Yakuza...

P.P.S. Fucking Tommy pisses me off. He says I punched him in the face last night—I fucking should have. Vince almost got shot by a Yakuza. Interesting evening. Nobody in the band is talking to each other. Lovely...fucking lovely...

NIPPON BUDOKAN, TOKYO, JAPAN. (SHOW 2) DECEMBER 17TH 1987
Hotel, Tokyo, noon

Another show last night...like I do anything else! We got offstage early as usual here in Japan. I went straight into a blackout drunk. I can't seem to stay sober 'cause my guts are trying to kill me. I know I'm dying from depression. I feel like a lost soul...like the only person left on Earth. If I died, would anybody cry? It seems to me by putting myself out of my misery I'd be killing two birds with one stone.

Rich Fisher said I called the hotel front desk and complained about the fans banging on my window last night. Fuck—I'm on the 26th floor. I'm losing it... unraveling at the seams. And this is news?

P.S. I have press today but everybody can fuck off. I'm not showing up...

DECEMBER 18TH 1987 NIPPON BUDOKAN, TOKYO, JAPAN (SHOW 3)
Backstage, 10 p.m.

Just got offstage. Last show of the year. I don't wanna be on the road and I don't wanna go home. If I go home I'll get strung out again. I'm going to Bangkok to explore. I got $50k in cash

coming from the accountant and everybody is
telling me, "No." I'm so sick of all these assholes. Let me live or die my way. I know I'm your
meal ticket, but haven't you milked it enough? If
I don't come back you make millions on the dead
rock star merchandise...

I'm done, I'm fried and I don't care. My heart is
broken from my childhood. I'm worn to the bone from
being driven like a slave and I've lost my will to do
anything but fade...please...

DECEMBER 19TH 1997
Hotel, Tokyo, 11 a.m.

Well, today I was shot down in flames.

Doc and everybody demanded that I don't go to
Bangkok and said in exchange Doc and Mr. Udo would
go to Hong Kong with me. I just don't wanna go home
so this is better than nothing-but they only gave
me $15k in cash! I sometimes wonder why I let them
lead me by a ring in my nose like a cow on its way
to slaughter. I have every intention of ditching Doc
and Udo but I'll play like I'm excited to go (for
now...).

I have a plane to catch and I can't find my
clothes so I'd better figure out what happened last
night. I'm so bummed. It's Christmas and I don't
have a reason to go home. Is there anybody out
there? Or am I gonna be a rock 'n' roll casualty?
Is death an option? Or am I a fucking martyr? Why
am I alive? Why do I care? What do I care about?
Am I a...

Fuck me, I hate me...fuck off and die already...

ANYBODY OUT THERE?

I'm gonna die
You're gonna die
We gotta live for tonight
'cause we're runnin'
Out of time
Lookin' for a lover?
Let me ask ya
Is anybody out there?

KAREN DUMONT: Doc McGhee was so depressed and embarrassed about Nikki in Japan because Doc really respected Mr. Udo and saw him as a friend as well as a business partner. Doc offered to take Mr. Udo to Hong Kong to make amends and they were talking about it when Nikki came wandering over and said, "Hong Kong? That sounds great–I'd love to come!" Mr. Udo, being so polite, said, "Please come with us." Doc was just dying of shame.

TOMMY LEE: I actually thought deciding to go to Hong Kong was one of Nikki's more sober moments. He didn't want to go home because that meant the party was over and he told me he wanted to buy some furniture for his home. He seemed really sincere about wanting to go to Hong Kong and get amazing deals on furniture.

VINCE NEIL: When Nikki announced he wasn't coming back to LA but was going to Hong Kong I couldn't have cared less. I didn't give it a second thought, just said, "Fine, have a nice time, 'bye." We weren't close in any way and I wanted to keep my distance from him because he was fucking bad news.

On a plane to Hong Kong, 4 p.m.

Mr. Udo just said to me, Nikki-san, you're gonna
die if you don't stop. He said he told the same thing
to Tommy Bolin and Tommy didn't listen. He died a few
days later. Udo looked like he was gonna cry. It made
me feel loved...more than my father ever did.

Hotel, Hong Kong, 7:20 p.m.

Doc, Mr. Udo and me are going to go to a Chinese restaurant
that Mr. Udo says is one of the best in the world. I
haven't eaten in a few days. I'm too weak to attempt to
go out afterwards. When I told Doc, he breathed a sigh of
relief. Oh Doc, you're not getting off that easy. Tomorrow
is just around the corner and hell only a few feet away.
Sounds poetic, doesn't it? Right. Off to dinner...

P.S. I smell so bad. I haven't showered since LA and
I can see people actually look repulsed when they get a
whiff of me. Sometimes I stand next to people just to
fuck with them. I didn't
bring any clothes
with me, just cash.
Fuck, what else
do I need?

December 20TH 1987

Hotel, Hong Kong, 11 a.m.

I have an interpreter Li meeting me in an hour and
I'm gonna buy some antiques for the house. Doc said
he will join me. I'm feeling good since I slept
but I still don't have any interest in a shower
or food.

I have a feeling of
relief at being away from
everybody. If I could
just disappear into
some place like this,
maybe I could find
myself. My life is
loud. Everywhere I go,
people are talking to
me, but nothing is as
loud as the screams in my
head. They are far off,
distant, and I can't make
out the words...I have come
to realize it's most likely
the drugs. They are always
calling me. Right now I have
given up. I really don't care anymore...they win! To be honest my life
has been an abortion. Or at least it should have been.

If being a rock star is an accomplishment I've
failed miserably and I feel miserable. Be careful what
you wish for as they say (whoever they are). I commend
them. They were right...rotting is painful. Isn't there
an easier way? To go shopping for antique snot wondering if you will be alive at Christmas is about as
empty as you can feel. It's like trying to enjoy the
last cigarette before your execution.

Hotel, 5 p.m.

Just got back...Li (a girl) looked horrified when she saw me. I think the tangles in my hair and the days of growth on my face add to my homeless look. Anyway I bought a beautiful Chinese table for my dining room...cherry wood, pearl cherry blossom...quite the cliché to be honest but I like it. I ordered some food and I'm getting ready to go out tonight...

9 p.m.

Just woke up passed out facedown on the bed with a bottle of Jack and a steak next to me. I guess they just brought my room service in. I wonder what they thought.

DECEMBER 21 1981
Hotel, Hong Kong, 1 p.m.

Well last night was an interesting evening...an exercise in excess...

Mr. Udo, Doc and myself had a few drinks in the bar and went off to a club that's actually a brothel. There were two ballrooms, two bands playing-I can't believe I'm in Hong Kong and I heard a band play a Mötley song in a whorehouse. We were escorted (no pun intended) to a private booth where we had 4 bottles of Cristal, 2 bottles of Jack, 1 bottle of vodka and huge plates of food...this is one of those things I have to write down...

So this is how it worked...there were beautiful girls walking around with number tags on them. You tell the madam what number you want and any special requests (a white dress, black boots or anything else that takes your fancy)...in other words they are there to please on every level. At one point I noticed Number 800...fucking

800 girls to pick from! I picked about 8 numbers and the evening began. They will take you in the back but for a few extra American dollars they will meet you at your hotel so I remember asking the madam if I could have a girl in a nun's habit with army boots and seeing Doc wince...he probably knew this was just the tip of the iceberg. Well, I got the nun outfit organized but they had no army or more importantly Nazi boots to add to the mix...the other girls were run-of-the-mill whores...perfect as imperfection could be...

My real intention was to find drugs and lo and behold (after all isn't that what strippers and whores are really for?) a gram of junk is 100 bucks...beats the 500 I pay at home...so I got a gram of coke and a quarter of china white (easy to sniff)...as the evening wore on I decided to grab the girls and go back to the hotel...but not before I sent a bunch of girls to Mr. Udo's room. Funny how when I do nice things I always seem to step in shit...Doc called this morning saying that Mr. Udo was insulted...fucking hell...just when I thought things were going good...

Well the kicker to the story is I woke up with all my clothes on and all my money and drugs gone...I have no idea what happened and I guess I don't care. Doc nervously asked me to go back to LA...this is my chance to ditch the fucking No Fun Police, so I agreed. Good news, we're on different flights, so I ain't gonna make my flight...once Doc and Mr. Udo are in the air I'm grabbing Li and heading out...

DOC McGHEE: Nikki sent prostitutes to my door and to Mr. Udo's door. They turned up in the middle of the night. As a parting joke when I left the club I'd said to Nikki, "Don't send us any girls in Nazi helmets and Gestapo boots," and he must have thought

I meant it because they turned up in helmets but not the boots. As I opened my door to them, Mr. Udo called me and said, "Nikki has sent three girls to my room!" Poor Udo was out of his mind. I had to do a buyout and give the women some money just to go away.

2:30 p.m.

I have a 9 p.m. flight tonight—not that I'll be catching it, ha ha! Doc has a 6 p.m. and Mr. Udo is leaving now. I need to find a bank, I don't have any cash but at least those fucking whores didn't steal my credit cards...

.I guess I should call home. I haven't called in weeks...

7 p.m.

I'm alone. It's not nice...

Waves of depression come over me, then anger, then disinterest. I'm already drunk, I guess, if half a bottle of Jack is drunk. I .actually don't feel anything, but maybe that's just me. I'm going out tonight to walk around. I don't have any plans. I leave tomorrow and I'm sure Doc will have a fucking coronary when he finds out I didn't make my flight.

I told Li not to tell anybody or I'd have to kill her. Then I smiled...she didn't...

I put a call in to Abdul...he's gonna meet me at LAX tomorrow. I'm having a limo pick him up and I told him to bring a precooked Persian shot with him. I can't wait... my mouth is watering...at least it shuts up the screams.

DECEMBER 22ND, 1987
Hotel, Hong Kong, 4 a.m.

I've been back a few hours. I'm bored...nothing happened. I think Li was steering me away from anything that would put her job on the line. The only thing of interest was I was walking down a street and I looked down an alley and saw an old guy sitting with one single light on next to steam rising out of the gutter. I asked Li what it was and she said it's a fortune-teller. So I said, Cool, let's go talk to him. We walked down the street and up to the old man who looked at me and then at Li and then back at me. He sorta looked freaked out. That's OK, I'm used to it...but I didn't expect what came next.

They started chattering in Chinese, back and forth, and then Li announced he didn't want to do my fortune. I said, Look, isn't that his job? She said that I wouldn't like what he had to tell me. I said I would and he slowly reached for my dirty hand and looked in my eyes then spoke to Li. She said, "He says if you don't change your ways you won't live until the end of the year." I said to tell him, "Thank You...that gives me a week longer than I expected."

He looked at me, old and tired, and said 3 or 4 words softly to Li. She said he was serious. I said "Thank You" and asked Li if those guys were just part of the tourist traps in Hong Kong. She looked sad and said, Nikki, they are never wrong. Then she said, Maybe we can go back to the hotel, you have an early flight. I agreed, if only out of boredom...

Goodnight...

On the plane to LA, noon

I'm on the plane...we just took off. I feel good. Slept well and took a shower but didn't have a comb to get the knots in my hair out so I think I probably look even worse. These leather pants really feel slimy. It's worse to be clean in dirty clothes, it's like I'm wearing a homeless person's clothes. I have a blanket on my legs to cover up the odor. I had breakfast and coffee, almost like a normal person. I have a couple Halcions in my jacket somewhere...think I'll sleep all the way to LA.

5 p.m.

I'm not sure what day it is...is it the 23rd or still the 22nd? But I just got asked to raise my tray up—we're landing in LA. I hope Abdul is here. I left messages for Robbin and Slash asking them if they want to go out...I forgot to call Karen.

In Hong Kong I noticed my ribs are sticking out but also my face is puffy and yellow. I have some weird scabs on my legs and a rash on my chest and arms. I'm sure it's just from not showering...I've seen it before. OK, buckle up...we're descending into Hell. Satan is home (ha ha)!

Van Nuys, 7 p.m.

Home sweet home. Wow, is it nice to get outta those leather pants. I took another shower and got the rat's nest outta my hair. I feel great—Abdul gave me a 10cc shot as soon as I got in the limo. I feel great. This is what I've been missing.

I got a message from Robbin and Slash. We're all going to the Cathouse tonight. King's got some Persian but no needles so I'm going up to his house in the hills to chase the dragon and then off to the Franklin Plaza Hotel to pick up Slash. I kept the limo.

9 p.m.

Karen won't go out—she said she has to work! I asked her if Doc knew that I didn't come home from Hong Kong when I was supposed to and she didn't think so. I guess threatening the interpreter's life worked. It always does, ha ha. I just realized that it's Christmas and I haven't got anything for anybody. Karen got a Christmas tree though, and finally got rid of last year's one. I could always give people the presents that I got last year that I haven't opened yet...

This is just a courtesy call
This is just a matter of policy
This is just an act of kindness
To let you know that your time is up

COURTESY CALL

DECEMBER 23rd, 1987
Van Nuys, 9:30 a.m.

Unraveling, unsure, undetermined, unnecessary...this is what my life has boiled down to. I either have to stop or die...I can't straddle this fence any longer. I have taken into my lungs the longest breath of hell and I'm still here.

Maybe there is a God...maybe, just maybe, there is such a lifeline. Something happened last night...good, I died. Sounds insane, doesn't it? I feel different today. I think for the first time in my life I feel hopeful. I can't remember ever feeling happy but I feel something has snapped. I feel, I don't know...

Last night was not unlike many nights for me, driving towards hell, hoping to be welcomed into death's arms or simply to kill the pain and fill the hole of emptiness inside. I'm too weak and sick to write the whole evening down, I'll try later...so here is the short version...

Picked up Slash, his girlfriend Sally, Steven Adler and Robbin and went to the Cathouse. Lots of coke, alcohol, pills...I really don't remember much. At some point the usual blackouts. Then we went back to Slash's hotel to get some junk. I was too wasted and let this cat shoot me up. I turned blue on the spot. This is what they tell me.

Steven and Sally came in and tried to revive me. I'm sure all the usual drama behind a junkie dying in your place happened at that point. But then something that's never happened before—I couldn't come back. The ambulance was called and I was well on my way to getting out of my skin.

I saw something...fuck...OK here we go. I was on the gurney, the sheet over my head. I saw something... there was my limo. There were people crying. There was an ambulance...there was a body with a sheet over it being loaded into the ambulance. It was me. I saw it all.

I was up, above it all. I couldn't know this if I was dead. I don't understand. But something feels different to me. I'm just gonna have to write later. I need to collect my thoughts.

SALLY McLAUGHLIN: I'm originally from Scotland but moved to America in 1987 because I was dating Slash. When I arrived I went straight out on the road with Guns N' Roses supporting Mötley Crüe, then Guns went straight on to Alice Cooper's tour. So December 22, 1987, was my first day in Los Angeles.

Slash and I were staying in the Franklin Plaza, and Nikki called up Slash and came over. Nikki, Slash, Robbin Crosby and I went to the Cathouse in Nikki's limo and we were there for hours. The boys kept running off to the limo to do coke and then coming back to the club. The last time they did it, they never came back for me, so I had to walk back to Franklin Plaza on my own. I was steaming.

SLASH: I can't remember too much about it. Nikki had asked me at the Cathouse if I knew where he could get dope. A friend of mine had just become a junkie so we called him and all went back to Franklin Plaza. I was so screaming drunk that I couldn't even find the floor to fall on. My friend turned Nikki on, but I didn't even notice.

SALLY McLAUGHLIN: Guns had two suites at the Franklin. Slash was in one and Steven Adler was in the other. I came storming into our suite, furious, and Nikki said, "Uh-oh, we'd better leave them alone for a while." Nikki and Steven went to Steven's room with their dealer, and I started yelling at Slash, but he was too drunk to even argue back.

A few minutes later, there was a knock at the door. It was Nikki, looking dreadful, and he came in and just fell on the floor. I was thinking, Great, now I've got *two* drunks to deal with here, but then the dealer came in, took one look at Nikki, yelled, "Nikki's dead!" and ran off. He literally jumped out the window and over the balcony and ran off down the street.

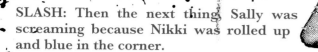

SLASH: Then the next thing, Sally was screaming because Nikki was rolled up and blue in the corner.

SALLY McLAUGHLIN: Slash was paralytic and Nikki was turning blue. Steven helped me drag Nikki into the bathroom, then he ran off, so I was left on my own with him. I tried to get Nikki into the shower to pour water on him, but then Slash came in, saw Nikki and started freaking out. Slash had a friend named Todd who had died of a heroin overdose a few months earlier, so he started yelling, "Todd!" and smashing up the bathroom.

By now I was giving Nikki mouth-to-mouth resuscitation over the bath while trying to hold Slash back with one hand. Slash smashed the shower screen, and the glass showered over me and Nikki, so I got up and punched Slash and laid him out. I was screaming for somebody to call 911, which they did, and said, "Nikki Sixx is dead!" I later found out that Nikki's limo driver heard that and phoned Vince Neil.

VINCE NEIL: I got two phone calls saying Nikki was dead, one from the limo driver and one from our tour manager, Rich Fisher. Maybe deep down I knew it was going to happen one day, but it still tore me to pieces because I loved Nikki–even though he was an arrogant selfish shit. I cried. And I never used to cry then.

SLASH: Then paramedics were there, but I was so drunk I'd passed out. When I came around, the first thing I noticed was that for some reason I'd destroyed the fucking bathroom. Sally was freaking out at the influx of people in white uniforms taking Nikki away.

SALLY McLAUGHLIN: The paramedics came pretty quickly and took over from there. I was still giving Nikki mouth-to-mouth, and the weird thing I remember is that when my breath came back out of his mouth, it sounded like he was snoring. I thought, Fuck, what if he's just asleep, wakes up and thinks I'm snogging him?

The paramedics ripped off Nikki's T-shirt to give him adrenaline, then whisked him off. I hadn't managed to bring him around but the paramedics later said that I'd kept him going. After they had taken him away, the police moved us into Steven's room. We had to carry Slash in. He was still passed out. The police questioned us all and checked the other room. Then later, when I went back in, I found a bag of dope on the floor and a vial of coke on the table. They had just missed it.

TOMMY LEE: I got a phone call in the middle of the night from Slash. He said, "Dude, don't freak out, but Nikki's in an ambulance on the way to the hospital." Slash said that they had done everything they could to make him wake up—put him in the bathtub, splashed his face, pounded on his heart—but nothing they had done had worked. I thought, Oh fuck!

KAREN DUMONT: Doug Thaler called me at 3 A.M. to ask if Nikki was home. He said a limo driver had called Vince and said that paramedics had pronounced Nikki dead at Franklin Plaza and taken him away in an ambulance. I began frantically calling hospitals but couldn't find him anywhere.

SLASH: He was in and out of operating rooms all night. His management came down later and yelled at me as a horrible influence, but the truth was that I was seventy-five percent oblivious to what was going on. To me, it wasn't a big deal. I used to do it all the time.

NIKKI: I came to in a hospital bed. There was a cop asking me questions, so I told him to go fuck himself. I ripped out my tubes and staggered in just my leather pants into the parking lot, where two teenage girls were sitting crying around a candle. They had heard on the radio that I was dead and looked kind of surprised to see me.

The girls had this pissy little Mazda and gave me a lift home as we listened to my obituary on the radio. One of them gave me her jacket and they made me promise to never do drugs again. Karen opened the door to me. I went straight to my answering machine and changed my message so it said, "Hey, it's Nikki, I'm not here because I'm dead." As soon as Karen had left for work I went straight to my bedroom, shot up and passed out.

KAREN DUMONT: At 5:45 A.M. there was a knock at the door and I opened it to see Nikki standing there, shivering like crazy. He was missing his boots and shirt plus he was wearing what looked like a little girl's jacket that was so tight across his back that his shoulders were heaved up. He just said that he couldn't find his key.

The next day I went to get his boots and give Slash and the Guns a piece of my mind. Sally told me that the ambulance guys had been going to give up on Nikki but a couple of girls had hysterically begged them to try again, and that was when they had managed to bring him back.

12 noon

I just woke up. My body hurts like it has never hurt before. I'm hungry, I'm dirty and I want to take a shower. I need to return some of these messages. When I came in last night I changed my message to HI, I'M NOT HERE BECAUSE I'M DEAD. I need to change that...

All my messages from everybody are saying things like, "You're an asshole" or "That's not funny" or "What's wrong with you Nikki, are you OK in the head, dude? That's fucked." For the first time I agree with all of them and I don't think it's funny either. (Well, maybe a little.)

One last thing...I might as well admit now. I'm done with drugs. I'm done with being unhappy and I'm done trying to kill myself. I woke this morning with a needle still in my arm and blood in my hand. How sick am I that I came home and shot after I died? But more important, I threw all my rigs away. I'm sick of being a selfish, egotistical, self-hating, alcoholic junkie.

TO USE A CLICHÉ: I'M SICK AND TIRED OF BEING SICK AND TIRED.

KAREN DUMONT: Only later did I find out that Nikki had shot up again when he went to bed. We had a very proper relationship, or otherwise I would have gone into his bedroom to make sure he was sleeping before I left for work. He was clearly shaken and should not have been left alone, but I just didn't really know any better.

5 p.m.

I told Karen I'm done with drugs. She said she hopes so but looked like she didn't believe me. I think it will take a while till people believe me. Shit, I don't know if I believe me.

6:25 p.m.

I'm so tired. I need sleep. I feel like I haven't slept in years. It's the only way to explain how tired I am. You know, I feel like maybe coming undone isn't such a bad thing after all. I found my AA book under my bed when I was clearing away all my drugs. I read this. It makes sense to me...for the first time...

STEP 1

WE ADMITTED THAT WE WERE POWERLESS AND THAT OUR LIVES HAD BECOME UNMANAGEABLE

DEANA RICHARDS: When I heard Nikki had nearly died it was not unexpected because it was what I had always feared but prayed would never happen. I was so terrified that he was going to die without anything being resolved–without him finally realizing just how much I loved him.

MICK MARS: When I heard Nikki was dead, my first reaction was, "I knew that fucking prick was going to do something like that!"

VINCE NEIL: I have to say, there have always been rumors about people in Mötley Crüe dying. We used to get loads of crank calls. I even got a call a couple of weeks ago saying that Tommy had died–and that was from my own mother.

DECEMBER 25, 1987
Christmas morning, Van Nuys, 9:30 a.m.

Good morning and Merry Christmas. I've decided to put this diary away and start a new one...with a new day upon us I feel hopeful. Life, I think, has somehow taken a turn for the better.

I don't know how I survived the last year but I know there has to be a reason. Today for the first time ever I don't care about the outcome or the whys and whens. I just wanna live. I woke up happy. I can't believe it. I didn't wake up with my head screaming and my instincts telling me to run and hide inside a needle or inside a coffin, whichever came first...as long as I became numb or better yet dead...I want to live and I don't know why.

Hey...why ask why...I'm going to go wake Karen up and tell her "Merry Christmas." I think I'll even call the guys in the band.

Merry Christmas.

NIKKI: I'll never forget waking up after sleeping almost forty-eight hours and feeling so different. I knew something had happened to me but I wasn't ready to look into it. What I had experienced was, I believe, something spiritual. Drugs had brought me to my knees and I knew it. Even though it would take a few attempts I was gonna get off drugs. I had been given another chance to live and I was gonna grab life by the back of its neck and shake the hell out of it.

I've lived my life to the max ever since. Yes I've fallen a few times but I always get back up. I always say I wouldn't have wanted to know that guy back then— and neither would you.

KAREN DUMONT: After he'd died, Nikki didn't want to do anything at Christmas but I invited a couple of my friends over. I said, "I don't want to sit here miserable, even if you do." I went out on Christmas Eve and bought food and a tree, which one of the guys from Ratt helped me decorate. Then Nikki decided it was a good idea after all and invited Slash over.

SALLY McLAUGHLIN: On Christmas Day, Slash and I went to Nikki's in a limo with all the presents we'd bought. I remember Nikki gave Slash a moleskin hat. Slash and I spent the night in Karen's room. Slash wet the bed again: he always used to after taking coke and drinking. He didn't want to tell Nikki, so he begged me to do it. When I did, Nikki just said, "Ah well, at least he isn't shitting himself like I used to."

I actually ended up buying Slash adult nappies, but he never wore them.

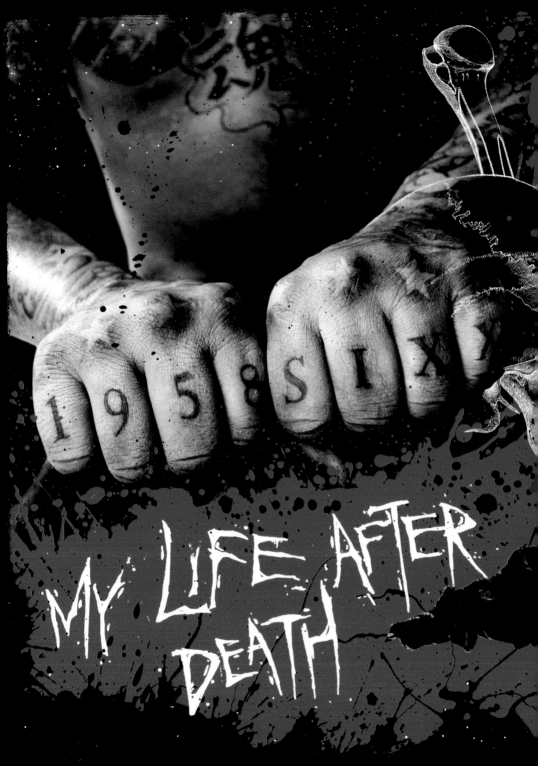

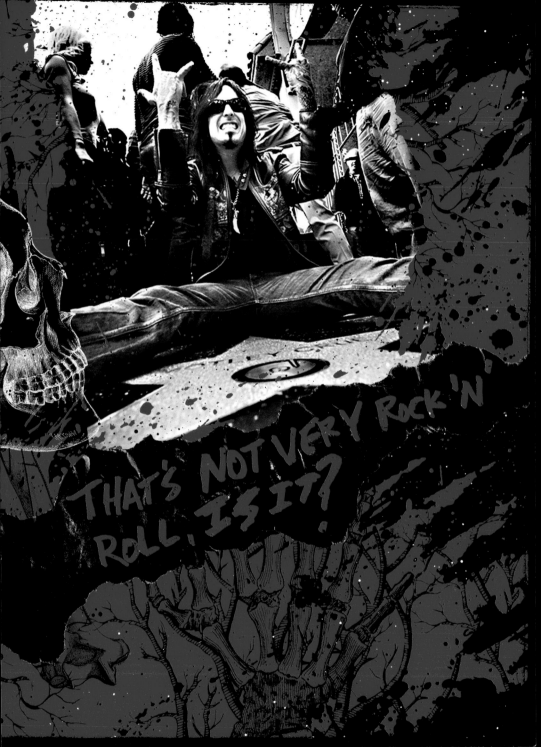

Not too long ago I said to a friend, "I died once but I'm better now." He reminds me of the humor in this from time to time. Nobody knows why we do the things we do until we're willing to peel the onion to get to the core of all our bullshit. I found out a lot about myself when I was finally ready to do so—not all bad, by the way. One of the gifts I've been given in sobriety is the ability to see through other people's bullshit. (Nobody knows a bullshitter like another bullshitter—but I'm better now.)

I said to Lemmy from Motorhead recently that I should have been on one of those T-shirts alongside Sid Vicious and Johnny Thunders, and he said, "Nah, you're better than that, mate." I guess someone else should have written my biography but instead I'm still alive and kicking so I sit here, typing away. I was gonna write the end of my story here but I realized,

I'M NOT AT THE END YET.
HELL, I MIGHT ONLY BE HALFWAY THERE.

There's plenty of time for grave markers and eulogies later…there I go, laughing at death again. I'm like a man on a bed of nails. I may grimace in pain but I somehow find it in me to laugh at the irony of where I lay my head, yet there is frustration. It comes not from the puncture wounds, but from the fact that I haven't made the *Guinness Book of World Records* for my life yet. Like I say, I'm only halfway there.

The first half was one enormous roller-coaster ride through hell. I can only imagine what the second half of my life is gonna be like. OK, enuff of me and my rambling. Let me bring you up to speed so far. I will try and give a sorta recap of the insanity and beauty that came after December 25, 1987:

- Canceled the European tour.

- Skipped rehab and went cold turkey.

- Moved from the Heroin House in Van Nuys to a well-concealed home in a place called Hidden Hills.

- Became reclusive for months at a time. I didn't even go to the grocery store, and lost complete contact with reality.

- Wrote most of the *Dr. Feelgood* album.

- Went to a psychiatrist and told him that life on drugs was better than this.

- Got diagnosed as clinically depressed and chemically imbalanced (or should that be embalmed?).

- Went on a new drug at the time, called Prozac.

- For the first time, felt comfortable in my own skin without being high.

- Hired a band therapist to improve communication with the guys in the band.

- Met my future ex-wife.

- Moved to Canada to record *Dr. Feelgood* with Bob Rock.

- Stayed sober in Canada.

- Finished the album and moved back to LA.

- Went over to Tommy and Heather's house and did a couple of 8-balls. Doug Thaler came over and flushed the drugs.

- *Dr. Feelgood* went Number 1.

- Went to Russia and I played my first show sober.

- Fired Doc McGhee.

- Sold out the *Dr. Feelgood* tour.

- Got married in Hawaii to my now-ex.

- Gunner Sixx, my first child, was born.

- Received an American Music Award.

- Storm Sixx, my second child, was born.
- My marriage hit the rocks.
- I hit the drugs.

BOB ROCK: I met Nikki when I produced *Dr. Feelgood.* He had just gotten sober for the first time. I've always known him as not normal but sober and straight, and in that state he's one of my best friends.

I've seen him slip twice. After we finished recording *Dr. Feelgood,* I was in a studio with Nikki and Tommy. It was a Sunday night in Hollywood, and he and Tommy decided to have a glass of wine with dinner. I was telling them, "Guys, you can't do that," but Nikki said, "Rockhead, one glass with dinner will be fine." Of course after the glass came another one, then suddenly the bottle was gone and Nikki was on the phone to his dealer. I asked him, "Nikki, what are you doing?" And he said, "Why wait? I know where I'm going tonight, so why wait?"

He went to the total extreme in ten minutes. Then the whole night just became pure pandemonium. Nikki and Tommy went to a club–there was probably only one club open on a Sunday night, but they found it. All the old dealers came out of the woodwork; there were girls, drugs, debauchery. We ended up back at the studio because I figured that was the best way to keep them out of jail. They ended up carving swastikas in the wall of A&M's studio. We had to blow out the first week of recording while Nikki went home to try to mend his marriage.

The second time, we were in Vancouver doing the Corabi album. We found out that Tommy's first wife, Candice, who was a stripper, was dancing at a club, so Nikki and Tommy decided to dress as Canadian lumberjacks, to not be recognized, and go to see her. They put on lumberjack shirts and false mustaches, and I fell down laughing, saying, "Guys, there's no way you look like anything but Nikki and Tommy!" They went anyway and the next thing I knew, Nikki called me from the club saying, "Come on down, Rockhead, we're doing shooters!" When I got there Nikki had gotten some blow as well. The next morning he woke up next to somebody he didn't know and the biggest pile of blow he'd seen outside of *Scarface* on a table. He flew home that morning and never went back to Vancouver. All I could do when he was in that state was try to make sure he didn't go to jail...or crazy.

- Wrote some new songs for the *Decade of Decadence* compilation.
- Went to Europe with AC/DC and Metallica.
- Slipped on drugs.
- Vince quit or was fired (depending on who you ask).
- Mötley got a new singer—John Corabi.
- Back to Canada to record the *Mötley Crüe* album.
- Can't stay sober.
- Marriage crashed on the rocks but I held on so I wasn't replicating the actions of my dad. Being unhappy seemed a better alternative to leaving my children fatherless—or so I thought.
- The *Mötley Crüe* album was released and flopped.
- The *Mötley Crüe* tour flopped.
- My soon-to-be ex-wife got pregnant the one time in the year that we actually had sex.
- Decker Sixx, my third child, was born.
- Marriage was finally over. She sued me for $10 million, saying she "deserved" it.
- The court said I could keep my mansion.
- We agreed to joint custody and she lost the $10 million suit in court.

- I met then-*Baywatch* star and *Playboy* playmate Donna D'Errico and fell head over heels in love in 1.2 dates.
- Sold the mansion and moved into a small rental in Malibu with all my kids, Donna and her son Rhyan.
- Married Donna on December 23, 1997.
- John Corabi quit under pressure and Vince returned to Mötley Crüe.
- *Generation Swine* was released to moderate success.
- Toured with Cheap Trick to mostly empty arenas.
- Tommy recorded two tracks for our *Greatest Hits* album before he went to jail. While I was visiting him in jail, he told me he didn't know if he wants to be in Mötley Crüe anymore.

- Toured the *Greatest Hits* album to almost sold-out houses. Tommy quit in the middle of the tour after a drunken Vince punched him. A security guard punched a fan and I called him a nigger from the stage. I had to go to court later for this stupid remark and received death threats. On the tour, I got arrested for assault. I called Elektra Records CEO Sylvia Rhone a cunt in *Spin* magazine and called her from my cell phone every night onstage having the audience tell her to fuck off…plus plenty of other insane shit.

- We got Randy Castillo from Ozzy's band and played sheds with the Scorpions, selling 25,000 to 35,000 tickets every night.

- Released a side project called 58. It didn't sell but rave reviews reignite my creativity.

- Started a record company called Americoma. It doesn't work but it also reignited my creativity (and hatred for major labels).

- We released all the Mötley Crüe albums on our own label and sold 500 percent more albums than on the major label.

- Still sober and happily married.

- Donna and I bought a fifty-acre ranch in the Malibu Hills.

- My ex moved to Orange County with some guy and lost custody of the children.

- Mick Mars would not return calls to help me write the next album so I enlisted James Michael. We wrote the *New Tattoo* album. (Later I find out Mick was lost in his own addiction.)

JAMES MICHAEL: Nikki and I used to be signed to the same label, and we'd say hello when we met in the corridor. I released a solo album and he called me to say there were some amazing things on there and he'd like us to work together. We started writing and it worked amazingly well right away. We wrote two songs on the first day.

Nikki is a very creative and talented guy, and he thinks in a very dark and twisted way. Energy just pours out of him. He's always thinking, always creating. Nikki is one of the most inspiring songwriters and exceptional people I have ever met.

- James and I wrote hits for Meat Loaf and Saliva.
- New Tattoo came out and the tour did pretty well until Randy Castillo got cancer.

NIKKI: Randy was too ill to tour. He used to call me his brother and another mother. I used to call him from the road and always check up on him. He wanted to be on the road so bad but he just wasn't strong enuff. Everybody was worried the touring would wear him down and he needed all the strength he could get to fight this horrible disease. When he passed away and we went to the funeral I put my skull ring in his casket. We both had the same ring but his was missing from his finger. Randy was one of the greatest rock 'n' roll drummers alive and now Heaven's house band is just that much better.

- Continued tour with a female drummer.
- Donna got pregnant with our first child.
- Started doing prescription pills to deal with stress.
- Resumed drinking.
- Resumed cocaine use.
- Had an affair with the drummer.
- Mötley Crüe agreed to take a five-year break.
- Frankie-Jean, my fourth child, was born.
- Moved out of family home after Frankie was born. To this day it's hard to even think about what I did.
- Started heading down the highway to hell. Again.

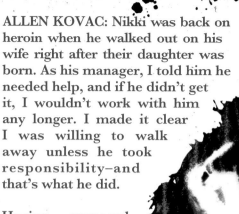

ALLEN KOVAC: Nikki was back on heroin when he walked out on his wife right after their daughter was born. As his manager, I told him he needed help, and if he didn't get it, I wouldn't work with him any longer. I made it clear I was willing to walk away unless he took responsibility–and that's what he did.

Having managed some great artists who have a keen sense of lyrics, melody and structure, I put Nikki right up there with the all-time greats. Barry Gibb, Debbie Harry, John Mellencamp and Luther Vandross all understood it also took passion and a great eye for image. Nikki has it all–the complete artist in every form of his art. He will be revered for his talent and his place in rock 'n' roll history. Moreover, he is a crown jewel of rock 'n' roll. He may never win a Grammy because the industry does not always judge on talent, but he deserves many.

Went to rehab and finally "found myself" in the desert in Tucson, Arizona. My life was at the lowest point it had ever been and I wanted to change it forever. Vowed that, no matter what, I will never use again.

- Donna, through much work on my part, learned to forgive and I learned to be forgiven, and I moved back in to our family home.

- Finally sober—*really* sober—but the wounds were slow to heal in our family.

- Started a band called Brides of Destruction.

- Recorded an album called *Here Come the Brides* to a lot of excitement but not a lot of sales.

- It was time for the Crüe again.

- Toured with the Brides, which confirmed the above.

- Loving being sober...closer to Donna and the kids than ever before.

- Put the Mötley Crüe train back on the tracks. It wasn't easy...but this band never has been. At the same time I sued Vans shoe company and got $1 million for using my image in their ads without my permission.

- Mick got his hip replaced and was weaned off prescription drugs.

MICK MARS: Nikki is like a completely different person today. He has made a total turnaround and is more about the music and his children. Like I said, he and I have always had a love-hate relationship, but today he is a much more loving and caring person and has his shiznit together. Our relationship is a lot healthier. It's great to be able to talk openly about anything and everything.

- Vince did a reality show, got a face-lift on TV and got in shape.

- Tommy did a reality show called *Tommy Lee Goes to College* and a solo album.

- Still clean, sober and emotionally and physically ready to take on the world.

- Mötley Crüe recorded four new songs with Bob Rock. Released the *Red White and Crüe* album and it sold more than a million copies.

- Decided to risk it all and go on tour without promoters or support acts. Sold out the first leg of the tour.

- Took the monster around the world and found out we had a new audience so we enlisted young bands Sum 41, the Exies and Silvertide for our summer tour.

RICK NIELSEN: I saw Mötley Crüe recently and rather than just being chaotic, as it used to be, it was the tightest I've ever seen them. I'd always told Nikki that as a bassist he was like Gene Simmons–it sounded better when he wasn't playing. But that's not true anymore.

Nikki has taken on a lot more responsibility now and he puts more energy into positivity rather than into positively tearing himself to bits. He's still crazy, but that is never going to change. I think he might have finally figured out that lawyers don't know it all, wives don't know it all, kids don't know it all–and guess what? Not even Nikki Sixx knows it all either!

- Donna, myself. and our friend Paul Brown (who designed this book) went to Cambodia and Thailand to do photography. What we found was heartbreaking.

- Started the Running Wild in the Night charity with Covenant House to help runaway kids nationwide. Those kids-like the one writing this book-could do so much in life. They just need a second chance.

- Mötley Crüe released first live DVD with all four of us.

- Released a live album not using the industry's standard formula.

- Not to sound all warm and fuzzy, but at this point in my life, I was so happy every morning when I woke up that I was pissing smiley faces. I could go on and on and on...but I think you get the point. Let's face it, I can't believe some of this myself. Oh hell, let me brag, it's my fucking book after all.

TOM ZUTAUT: Nikki lives and breathes for creativity. He has a great visual eye and now that he is into photography he creates some amazing visual images through his camera lens. If he set his mind to it, he could help many a new rock band develop and write better songs–maybe he will produce *this* generation's *Appetite for Destruction*. And I'm proud of the fact that he is a good father to his kids and has given them the childhood he never had.

VINCE NEIL: Nikki and I are closer now than we have ever been. From being a complete fuck-up he is now totally rational and the stuff he says always makes sense. He will advise me on how to handle things, or how to stay on an even keel like he's our band counselor. You know what? He could get a job as a counselor now, and that's pretty scary. He's still a control freak, but he's even working at that. Nowadays Nikki and I are real close friends, and I *never* thought I would say that.

I recently got off a world tour with Mötley Crüe, nearly all sold-out. Now the band members come to me with their problems, their good news and their dreams, and they tell me they love me. I flew from Australia on my birthday and they all sang "Happy Birthday" to me and gave me the usual ribbing about getting old. I caught my plane and checked my messages on a stopover in Hong Kong. They had each called me separately and wished me a happy birthday again. Wow—from guys I used to be a dictator and a downright dirty bastard to. Amazing. Then after twenty-two hours in the air I arrived home to handmade birthday cards from my kids. Amazing again...

TOMMY LEE: I totally commend Nikki for how he is today. He's great to deal with now that he can actually go out sober with people and whoop it up and have a good time and not be all freaked out. We still hang out a lot.

On a personal level he has gotten great at thinking things through. People with addictive personalities make really quick decisions and don't think them through, be they musical or business or whatever. Nikki and I were always real spontaneous gut guys who would just go with it, but now he gets all the information so he can make the right decision.

407

We're as close as ever but Nikki is a dark, funny individual who has realized that he has got one very dark street in his fucking head that isn't lit up by too many streetlights. You don't want to throw heroin and cocaine in there as well, dude! The point is that Sixx is already a sick fuck and always will be. He doesn't need that fucking stuff.

My life after death obviously has not been without bumps and I don't think it's supposed to be. When I returned from tour Donna filed for divorce, and I'm able to stay clean even in this disastrous situation. To move on with my life, separately from the girl I thought I'd be with for the rest of my life, was the hardest thing I've had to deal with in many years.

As I write this, I'm sitting in a hotel room in India, missing what we had. I'm single and I don't wanna be but sometimes we don't get what we want, we get what we're supposed to have. I don't know what's in store for me, but I'm sure somehow it will be a higher path. Listening to the monkeys and birds outside my hotel window all night long, it's the hardest thing in the world not to pick up the phone and say, "Let's give it one more try." But I am supposed to be alone at this time in my life, and to be at one with my loneliness. It hurts deep inside.

I have to be honest, this has been painful, but I have to be strong for the kids. You know, for a man who has just bared his soul in this book, it might seem ironic that I'd rather keep this mostly private, but I feel it's the right thing to do...again, for the kids. This curve in the road is not unlike drugs. Some things take a while to get out of your system.

What I've learned in this life so far is to let the little things go as much as possible and try to swerve to miss the big things. Life is like a long ride to nowhere in particular. We're bound to get a flat tire somewhere along the journey and it's never a good time for it to happen...in fact, it's usually pouring rain or a blizzard when you feel the car jolt from the tire that just blew out underneath you and ripped away at your safety and support.

But we don't have a choice really. We have to get out, fix the flat, get back in the car and head back out on the highway of life.

There are a few sayings I used to loathe that I now cherish:

1. You gotta give it away to keep what you got.
2. Let go and let God.

What the hell does this gibberish mean, anyway? Let me explain:

1. To keep my happiness I've got to give away as much as I can. It works. Amazing. A guy who mostly consumed, took and would go out of his way to bust people's balls using this as a mantra. Amazing.

409

2. I never thought there was a God (well, maybe I thought I was him), but I know now there is a power greater than myself and that has been a huge part of my sobriety. So I let shit go, and let the man upstairs deal with it. A guy who was a complete control freak letting go as a way of life...amazing...

EVANGELIST DENISE MATTHEWS: I hear Nikki is now sober and seeking. That is beautiful. Praise God!

Addiction was my downfall and yet it's been the very thing that has given me a spiritual connection and awareness that I never thought existed. Quitting drugs and alcohol was the hardest thing I've ever done and has given me the most satisfaction. I'm actually glad I'm an addict, 'cause through recovery I have the ability to give back.

I feel like I've led two lives (maybe more) and again I could go on and on...but I think that really is another book, another time. Right now I have a full tank of gas and a deep desire to know what's around the next corner.

Oh yeah...

You know, it's pretty easy reading this book to see why I was angry and confused for all those years. I lived my life being told different stories: some true, some lies, some I still don't know which is which. Children are born innocent. At birth we are very much like a new hard drive—no viruses, no bad information, no crap that's been downloaded into it yet. It's what we feed into that hard drive, or in my case my "head drive," that starts the corruption of files.

It got so convoluted, polluted and distorted that I ran with the only info I was given. I turned it into my armor, my defense mechanism, my weapon of self-destruction. I did have a fucked-up childhood and I was a troubled teen-these are facts. How I got there is a story told by many voices, but it's not my job to blame anymore. I need to accept the path I was given and turn lemons into lemonade.

I know one thing-a lot of people were hurt besides myself due to the fact that my family is full of lies and secrets.

I have forgiven my mother, because she did have a part in this. Maybe not the same info I was given, maybe some of her story is convoluted too. It doesn't matter anymore. Family comes first, and I love her-she's my mom. She really did do the best she could with the cards that she was dealt in her life too. She's a nice lady, a very creative lady, and loves me very much. I don't want her to live out the rest of her life feeling guilty. I think, unfortunately for her, I tortured her long enuff. I love you, Mom.

DEANA RICHARDS: Nikki has said a few times that he wants us to have a better relationship, and I want it more than anything in the world. There's not a day gone by when I haven't hurt and prayed for Nikki. We were separated for all those years and it wasn't my choice, but I never got the opportunity to explain that to him. He is my son. I love him.

My dad? Well, I couldn't make peace to his face, so Donna found out where he was buried and took me there in 1999. At first I was gonna piss on his grave, but I decided it was time to let it all go. I had been carrying a vendetta since I was a young kid that was killing me, and to carry it any further (especially since he was dead) was just two steps back. It was finally time to step forward and let go of the anger and pain. Dad, all I have to say is, you missed out on one hell of a son.

My grandfather and grandmother? Well, Nona loved me, I know that for sure, and that feels good. I think right about now she's breathing a sigh of relief and I'm sure when we hook up again I'm gonna get a good talking-to...ha ha...

Tom has been there for me thru thick and thin. He raised me and did the best he could, and you know what? It wasn't even his job. He took on my father's role and for that he deserves the Medal of Honor, 'cause it was a fucking war zone.

ALMOST LAST. BUT DEFINITELY NOT LEAST

What is my part in all this?

Well, my part is somewhat simple (if anything about me can be said to be simple).

1. I injected everything I could get my fucking hands on, and then some (and then some more). We really don't need to go over the list again...besides, we're running out of paper and quickly outta time here.
2. I *was* a drug addict, alcoholic, depressed control freak and egomaniac.
3. To be honest with myself, I was really just running, running away from the shit 'cause I couldn't take the smell. Whether *I* was chicken shit or *it* was chicken salad it fucking reeked and I just didn't deal with it...so I let it deal with me.

We're at the end and at the same time the beginning of this misadventure. Why I had to go down a dead-end street at 200 mph screaming for vengeance and embracing death is something I'm coming to terms with every day in my life after death. But like they say, life's a journey, not a destination.

Part of me (Nikki? or Sikki?) thinks this was all part of a master plan to expose the raw nerve endings of dysfunction so I could heal. But alcoholics always think everything's about them, so chances are this is just another character defect I have to work on. I always said, "Anything worth doing is worth overdoing"...well, actually I still say it, and live it too. But now I'm gonna be an overachiever with a different, healthier agenda.

DEFINITELY LAST, BUT STILL NOT LEAST

Someone asked me why I was writing this book and I said, "Maybe one person will read it and it will help them." They said, "That's not very rock 'n' roll, is it?" I said, "Fuck off" and smirked, because I know it's the most rock 'n' roll thing about me—doing what I wanna do in life.

I guess Lemmy was right—I *am* better than that.

NIKKI SIXX

DECEMBER 2006